China's
& Soft Power
in Africa

# AFRICAN ISSUES

●

AFRICAN ISSUES

# China's Aid & Soft Power in Africa

## The Case of Education & Training

KENNETH KING
Professor Emeritus
University of Edinburgh

**JC** JAMES CURREY

James Currey
is an imprint of
Boydell & Brewer Ltd
PO Box 9, Woodbridge
Suffolk IP12 3DF (GB)
www.jamescurrey.com
and of
Boydell & Brewer Inc.
668 Mt Hope Avenue
Rochester, NY 14620-2731 (US)
www.boydellandbrewer.com

© Kenneth King 2013

First published 2013

1 2 3 4 5 16 15 14 13

**British Library Cataloguing in Publication Data**
A catalogue record for this book is available on request from the British Library

ISBN 978-1-84701-065-0 (James Currey paper)

The publisher has no responsibility for the continued existence or accuracy of URLs for
external or third-party internet websites referred to in this book, and does not guarantee
that any content on such websites is, or will remain, accurate or appropriate.

Papers used by Boydell & Brewer are natural, recycled products
made from wood grown from sustainable forests.

MIX
Paper from
responsible sources
FSC
www.fsc.org    FSC® C013604

Typeset in 9/11 Melior with Optima display
by Avocet Typeset, Somerton, Somerset
Printed and bound in Great Britain
by CPI Group (UK) Ltd, Croydon, CR0 4YY

# DEDICATION

Pravina

# CONTENTS

This book is an account of China's support to education and training in Africa. Not just an account but a discussion about How and Why it is doing this. But it is not an account of schools or training institutions run by China in Africa, as it might be of American international schools, French Lycées, German schools or British schools. China, like Japan, has built schools in Africa, but it doesn't run them. It hands them over to local ministries of education. The same is true of the few institutions of tertiary education that China has built in Africa. Even the Confucius Institutes in Africa are not run by China; they are directed jointly by Chinese and national deans as parts of their host universities.

Nor is it an account of China's involvement in education sector support, or in what other development agencies have termed sector-wide approaches (SWAPs) in education (co-ordinated external support to the education sector). China does not follow other agencies in this aid modality or in aid coordination. Nor does it pursue large-scale project approaches in the manner of the United States or of Germany.

Rather, this is an account of how China perceives and implements educational cooperation or human resource development for Africa. So the book uses the same lens that China uses to define this cooperation, and like China, it pays attention to the history of this cooperation over the last sixty years. This means that it is concerned with China's training of thousands of students and professionals from Africa on the Chinese mainland. Students are in China for the long-term, and professionals just for a few weeks. It also covers China's version of university cooperation between China and Africa, as well as Chinese language teachers and volunteers going to Africa. China's lens on cooperation also covers capacity-building of some of its own people in China through Centres and Institutes of African Studies. Effective cooperation between China and Africa requires expertise and understanding of Africa (and by Africa of China).

This account goes beyond these formal training modalities and exchanges of students, volunteers and professionals, however, and it explores the training implications for Africans of the tens of thousands of Chinese business people in Africa, both at micro-enterprise level and in medium and large-scale enterprises.

The analysis comes out of a comparative framework. Hence it is concerned with the difference and similarities of China's cooperation with that of traditional donors. It pays a good deal of attention to how the discourse of China's aid differs from that of OECD donors. But it also seeks to capture something of what it feels like, in practice, to be on a China scholarship, training award or training seminar as a recipient from Africa. China has changed the core concepts of its official development discourse much less than Western donors over the last sixty years. Contemporary Chinese analysts, whether in policy or academic positions, are aware of this long record of consistency in the development discourse, and frequently refer to it.

But how does the robustness of the discourse affect the realities of being a student in China, or a short-term trainee on a specialist course? Perhaps the official discourse doesn't affect at all the business of being a trainee in China or an employee in a Chinese enterprise in Africa. These are the issues we investigate through the experiences of African students and trainees in China, and African engagement with Chinese business in Africa.

Soft power was not part of China's development discourse before 2006, and it is not yet fully accepted by China's development assistance community. Indeed, it might appear to come out of a different world than the framework of mutual benefit, common development and win-win cooperation that characterises China's preferred development discourse. However, even if there are dangers of soft power becoming a catchall phrase, it can be used effectively to disaggregate types of aid and it can also usefully connect the impact on others of China's foreign and domestic policies.

Since my doctorate in 1968 which was an account of the West's first major international, educational missions to Africa in 1920 and 1924, and of their respective reports, I have been regarded as a critical analyst of aid to education, particularly in Africa. And for the last more than twenty-five years, I have edited *NORRAG News*, whose first objective is the 'Collection, critical analysis, and synthesis of research on education and training policies and on strategies, and on international cooperation'.[1]

A great deal of this critique has been attached to the recommendations of these 'missions' whether of the Phelps-Stokes Fund in the 1920s, just mentioned, or those of the World Bank in the 1980s, or many other agencies, bilateral or multi-lateral, which have prescribed for Africa. These priorities for Africa may have been 'the four simples' of the Phelps-Stokes'

---

[1] The website for NORRAG and *NORRAG News* was inaccessible in Mainland China from early 2010 until late 2012. It is now (as of April 2013) readily accessible once more (See: www.great-firewallofchina.org/index.php?siteurl=)

Reports, 'minimum essential learning needs' and non-formal education in the 1970s, education for all in the 1990s and most recently the preoccupation with 'Education and Skills Post-2015'. But what these reports, missions and commissions all have in common is that they offer very particular prescriptions for Africa's education and training by external agencies. Much of this was and still is deeply resented in Africa.

China, and perhaps also Japan, has done very little of this 'telling Africa'. Of course, there are really no education policy papers for Africa, elaborated by China, as we shall see shortly. But the absence of reports on education in Africa is not the issue. Japan has many such reports, including specifically on Africa, but they are not prescriptive. The two Asian nations would both claim that their aid to Africa is in the 'response mode', and that their mechanisms for commitments to Africa reflect such a response. So would South Korea.

In addition, the relative modesty or humility of China's and Japan's aid workers in the field, as well as of their 'experts', is doubtless appreciated in Africa. If soft power is 'getting others to want what you want', then China and Japan don't spend a lot of time on lobbying or on advocacy, at least in the fields we are covering in this book.

The jigsaw of China's cooperation in education and training in Africa still has a number of pieces missing, and not least in understanding some more of the impact on Africa of the modalities of their support. We have highlighted some of these missing pieces, and pointed to many of the gaps. But hopefully, we have filled in enough of the jigsaw that the main shape of the history, rationale, ethics and modalities of China's human resource development with Africa can be more clearly seen.

Finally, why is an understanding of China's approach and support to education and training in and for Africa important? China's aid to Africa is organised around a whole series of apparently separate silos of cooperation, in Agriculture, Investment and Business, Medicine, Trade, Finance, Infrastructure, Science and Technology and many more, including Human Resources Development (HRD), Education, Culture, and People-to-People Exchanges (FOCAC, 2006b). At one level, this book is concerned with these last four items. But at another level, China's lens on HRD is critical to understanding the modalities and capacity-building dimensions of many of the other aspects of its cooperation such as medicine, agriculture, or science and technology. Shinn and Eisenman acknowledge this centrality: 'Although it often receives less attention than economics, foreign aid, and strategic topics, Chinese scholars and policymakers consistently emphasise education cooperation in publications and public statements' (2012: 210).

Beyond this cross-cutting relevance to understanding the delivery of China's development cooperation in general, the issues around HRD also turn out to be one of the hottest topics in relation to the rapidly increasing number of China's small, medium and large-scale enterprises in Africa. The very common claim that China brings in planeloads of its 'Hordes of experts' and seldom employs or trains Africans is simply wrong (Brautigam, 2009: 154). But because it is such a frequent assertion, it is crucial to tease out what we know about HRD in Chinese projects as well as Chinese investments in Africa.

We have a great deal still to learn, however, about how the Chinese themselves regard their sojourn or settlement in Africa. We currently lack detailed personal, written accounts of how the Chinese 'settlers' of the last ten, twenty or more years have adapted to Africa.[2] It would be a very high priority to capture and synthesise what has been written or, if not written, thought, about living and working in Africa.[3] The sheer power and impact of David Livingstone's 700 and more pages of *Missionary Travels and Researches in South Africa Including a Sketch of Sixteen Years' Residence in the Interior of Africa* (1858) cannot be exaggerated, including its influence on many thousands of Scots following his example and residing in Africa.[4] The attitudes towards Africa and Africans were powerfully captured in these and many other early accounts of the continent.[5]

In this age of the internet and social networking, there is, arguably, no longer perhaps a need for written, published accounts of Chinese travel and residence in Africa. The individual summaries through social networking and blogs can potentially reach huge audiences of those who are linked in or connected to those commenting on their experiences in Africa. But they do not constitute an accessible research resource.

Without such detailed accounts, it will be a challenge to determine whether the official Chinese discourse of friendship with Africa is in fact mirrored in the realities of residence and adaptation to the local environment.

[2] There are insightful documentaries such as Francis and Francis (2011) *When China Met Africa*. Even though not made by Chinese, this offers a compelling account of Chinese farming in Zambia.

[3] 'There are now so many Chinese who've lived in Africa and returned to China that a well-organized effort to find and interview them would likely result in a rich ethnography' (Sautman to KK, 16.12.12).

[4] It is not widely known that Livingstone, like many others at the time, had set his heart on being a medical missionary in China, but was deterred by the opium wars. What the impact might have been of a volume on *Missionary travels and researchers in China* can only be imagined (Livingstone, 1858).

[5] Livingstone comments on the Southern African people he first met: 'They might be called stupid in matters which had not come within the sphere of their observation, but in other things they showed more intelligence than is to be met within our own uneducated peasantry' (Ibid.: 22).

# ACKNOWLEDGEMENTS

This research and this volume would not have taken place had not Professor Mark Bray invited me to come to China as a Distinguished Visiting Professor in the University of Hong Kong's (HKU) Faculties of Arts and of Education in 2006–7. Several years later, after the Chinese and African fieldwork had been completed, it was hugely important to be invited back to China, by Zhejiang Normal University (ZNU) for August 2010, and by Hong Kong Institute of Education (HKIEd) for five months in that same year. For these two spells of time, which allowed me to update my work, I am grateful to Professor Wan Xiulan of the Institute of International and Comparative Education of ZNU and Professor Lou Shizhou, and to Professors Mark Mason and Bob Adamson of HKIEd.

The research funding which made the initial desk research on Africa and China possible was provided by the British Academy, the Carnegie Trust for the Universities of Scotland, and the Leverhulme Trust. After I had been in Hong Kong for almost a year, it was possible to apply to the Hong Kong Research Grants Council for funding to allow longer field exposure to Africa. This was done successfully with a younger HKU colleague, Bjorn Nordtveit, and we were able separately to visit Africa, as well as visit the Chinese Mainland.[6]

There are a number of people who made a great difference to the research at different points over the years since 2006. These would include Gu Jianxin, Chen Xiaoxi, Hu Ziyuan, He Wenping, Philip Snow, Barry Sautman, Yan Hairong, Okitsu Keichi, Yu Bai, Li Wei, Zhang Zhongwen, Ma Yue, Marius Vermaak, Zhang Weiyuan, Ying Danjun, Zhao Qiong, Trey Menefee, Zhou Zhifa, Asfaw Yimeru, Ma Xin, Niu Changsong, Kunle Osidipe, Steven Sabey, Liu Gaoqiong, Lydia Larbi, Jonathan Jansen, Zheng Song, Adrian Davis, Liu Haifang, Obame Romuald, Li Zhibiao, Bjorn Nordtveit, Zacchaeus Ojekunle Olusheyi, Li Anshan, Penny Davies, Mahamat Adam, Mark George, Deborah Brautigam, Matsunaga Masaei,

[6] Research Grants Council of Hong Kong (Project No. HKU 750008H).

Ignace Pollet, Tang Changan, Merriden Varrall, Zhou Nanzhao, Dan Large, Ben Kipkorir, Jesse Mugambi, Sandra Gillespie, Soyeun Kim, Emma Mawdsley, Tang Qian, Yuan Tingting, Yoon Park, Murray Macrae, Richard Carey, Bob Wekesa, Yokozeki Yumiko, Peter Wakaba, Wei Yanggen, Li Jun, Adams Bodomo, Philip Barber, Mogens Jensen and Maeda Mitsuko. With many of these, contact was retained from the time of the original meetings right up to the completion of the writing in late 2012.

Beyond these, there were well over two hundred others who were interviewed in Africa and over seventy in China, many of them more than once. In several cases it was possible to continue to interact through email contact several years after the initial interviews. Others invited me to make presentations of the work in all three fieldwork countries of Africa, as well as in Mainland China, Hong Kong, Germany, Belgium, Denmark, South Korea, and the UK.

I am of course deeply grateful to James Currey, Douglas Johnson, Lynn Taylor and Jaqueline Mitchell for taking on this manuscript and bringing it to fruition. I am in debt to Piet Marais for crucial assistance in Xinhua allowing the photograph on the front cover to be used.

In Ethiopia, Kenya and South Africa as well as in China, all the interviews were carried out jointly with my wife, Pravina. She also tolerated my timings and anti-social 'imprisonment' during the period of final write-up, through November 2011 and from January to April 2012, taking in her stride the care of my hip replacement in February 2012, and the reading of the near-to-final drafts of all chapters. I owe her more than I can possibly say. Though I have written these chapters, they have hugely benefited from her joint interviews with me, and from all her insights. Generally therefore I use 'we' in preference to 'I'.

Kenneth King, Saltoun Hall, Pencaitland
1 April 2013

# ABBREVIATIONS

AAA      Accra Agenda for Action
ADB      Asian Development Bank
AERC      African Economic Research Consortium
ALRN      African Labour Research Network
ASU      African Students Union
AU      African Union
BA      Bachelor of Arts
CASS      Chinese Academy of Social Sciences
CCS      Centre for Chinese Studies
CERC      Comparative Education Research Centre
CICC      China Information and Culture Communications
CMU      Chongqing Medical University
CRBC      China Road and Bridge Corporation
CRI      China Radio International
CSAC      Cameroon Students Association in China
CSCUK      Commonwealth Scholarship Commission (of the UK)
CSR      Corporate social responsibility
CC      Confucius Classroom
CI      Confucius Institute
CSFP      Commonwealth Scholarship and Fellowship Plan
DAC      Development Assistance Committee (of the OECD)
DAAD      German Academic Exchange Service
DFID      Department for International Development
DRC      Development Research Centre
DSA      Development Studies Association
EADI      European Association of Development Research and Training Institutes
ECNU      East China Normal University
EFA      Education for All
ECPC      Ethio-China Polytechnic College

| ERASMUS | European Community Action Scheme for the Mobility of University Students |
| ETC | Ethiopia Telecom Corporation |
| FAO | Food and Agriculture Organisation |
| FCO | Foreign and Commonwealth Office |
| FDI | Foreign direct investment |
| FOCAC | Forum on China-Africa Cooperation |
| GDP | Gross Domestic Product |
| GIZ | German Agency for Development Cooperation |
| GOI | Government of India |
| GMR | Global Monitoring Report |
| GUASC | General Union of African Students in China |
| GUAST | General Union of African Students in Tianjin |
| HEI | Higher Education Institution |
| HKIEd | Hong Kong Institute of Education |
| HLF4 | Fourth High Level Forum |
| HR | Human resources |
| HRD | Human resources development |
| HRW | Human Rights Watch |
| HSK | Chinese language equivalent of TOEFL |
| IAS | Institute of African Studies |
| IDS | Institute for Development Studies |
| ILO | International Labour Organisation |
| IPRCC | International Poverty Reduction Centre in China |
| ITEC | Indian Technical and Economic Cooperation |
| IWAAS | Institute of West Asian and African Studies |
| JICA | Japan International Cooperation Agency |
| JOCV | Japan Overseas Cooperation Volunteers |
| KOICA | Korea Overseas International Cooperation Agency |
| MPA | Masters in Public Administration |
| MDG | Millennium Development Goal |
| MOE | Ministry of Education |
| MOFA | Ministry of Foreign Affairs |
| MOFCOM | Ministry of Commerce |
| ND | No date |
| NDD | Non-DAC donor |
| NGO | Non-government organisation |
| NORRAG | Network for Research Review and Advice on Education and Training |
| NUGS | National Union of Ghanaian Students |
| ODA | Official Development Assistance |
| ODA | Overseas Development Administration |
| OECD | Organisation for Economic Cooperation and Development |
| OSSREA | Organisation for Social Science Research in Eastern and Southern Africa |
| PRC | People's Republic of China |

| Sida | Swedish International Development Cooperation Agency |
|------|------|
| SSC | South-South Cooperation |
| SSA | Sub-Saharan Africa |
| SWAP | Sector-wide approach |
| TAZARA | Tanzania Zambia Railway Authority |
| TC | Technical Cooperation |
| TICAD | Tokyo International Conferences on African Development |
| TUTE | Tianjin University of Technology and Education |
| TVET | Technical and Vocational Education and Training |
| UNESCO | United Nations Educational, Scientific and Cultural Organisation |
| UNDP | United Nations Development Programme |
| UNICEF | United Nations Children's Fund |
| USAID | United States Agency for International Development |
| VSO | Voluntary Service Overseas |
| WHO | World Health Organisation |
| ZNU | Zhejiang Normal University |
| ZTE | Zhongxing Telecommunication Equipment Corporation |

# 1

**China & Africa** Origins, documents & discourses in relation to human resource development

Just over forty years ago, in 1971, I published my first book about educational aid to Africa (King, 1971). It was a critical account of the two famous educational aid missions to Eastern, Western and Southern Africa undertaken by the Phelps-Stokes Fund of New York, and it looked particularly at the Commission's recommendations for Kenya as well as at the institutional developments in that country following *Education in Africa* and *Education in East Africa* (Jones, 1922; 1924). The choice of the topic was partly coincidental, derived from stumbling by chance upon the two extraordinary volumes of the Phelps-Stokes Commissions of 1922 and 1924, with their very strong message that the education of Africans should draw inspiration from institutions such as Tuskegee and Hampton for Black Americans in the Southern States. Needless to say, the word China did not appear in the indices of my book or of the two Phelps-Stokes Fund reports.

Twenty years later, I wrote a second book about aid and education (King, 1991). It was about the role of donor agencies in carrying out and promoting research and analysis on education in the developing world. Surprisingly, neither Japan nor China were mentioned in the index as donors, and China only appeared as a place where there had been research carried out by other agencies such as the World Bank on skills development, literacy and non-formal education.

A further twenty years later, in 2011 when I started writing this book, I realised that there had been something of a parallel with 1971 for its origins. I had just arrived in China in early 2006 to spend a year in the University of Hong Kong, and I was asked in the first few days if I could do a seminar in two weeks' time. What would be the title? Should it be on the issues I had been working on in 1995–2005 in Edinburgh University's Centre of African Studies, such as skills and poverty reduction, education and the knowledge economy, the critique of targets in education, or the politics of higher education? I thought, why not look instead at something different? As an Africanist, I had stumbled across the fact that China had

1

just declared 2006 to be 'The year of Africa'. Moreover, it had also just published *China's African Policy* on 12 January (China, 2006). So why not talk about China's aid to Africa if that was something it pursued in its African policy (King, 2006a)?

Unlike the two Phelps-Stokes Reports (317 and 417 pages respectively), *China's African Policy* was only eleven pages long. Of course, it was not just about education and training like the Phelps-Stokes volumes, but about every form of China's cooperation with Africa. This is the key word, 'cooperation'; it occurs no less than 78 times in eleven pages and it covers every conceivable form of cooperation: agricultural, political, economic, media, tourism, health, cultural, environmental, science and technology, military, South-South, and of course human resources and education. By contrast, the word 'aid' does not occur at all except once in the context of emergency 'humanitarian aid'.

In other words, China had an *African Policy*; but it did not have a separate education policy. Or rather, as part of its policies on education, science, culture, health and social aspects, it had just a few lines of education policy. Here they are from *China's African Policy*:

COOPERATION IN HUMAN RESOURCES DEVELOPMENT AND EDUCATION

The Chinese Government will give full play to the role of its "African Human Resources Development Foundation" in training African personnel. It will identify priority areas, expand areas of cooperation and provide more input according to the needs of African countries so as to achieve greater results. Exchange of students between China and Africa will continue. China will increase the number of government scholarships as it sees fit, continue to send teachers to help African countries in Chinese language teaching and carry out educational assistance projects to help develop Africa's weak disciplines. It intends to strengthen cooperation in such fields as vocational education and distance learning while encouraging exchanges and cooperation between educational and academic institutions of both sides. (China, 2006: 7)

These twelve lines are largely what this book is about: China's commitment to assist Africa in human resource development (HRD). Most of the elements that we shall look at in much more detail are captured in these few lines: training of personnel, scholarships, exchange of students, despatch of teachers, Chinese language teaching, vocational education, educational projects and institutional cooperation between China and Africa.

Importantly, China also pledges here to examine what are Africa's own priority needs. This is another way of saying that China's education support will to some extent be demand-driven, a response to Africa's own priorities. This parallels the long-standing approach of the Japan International Cooperation Agency (JICA) emphasising the importance of the response mode in its own interaction with partners in the developing world (King and McGrath, 2004).

Throughout this book, we shall examine also to what extent China's approach to Africa is different from that of traditional OECD donors who are mostly members of its Development Assistance Committee (DAC). This will be challenging, as there is no such thing as a Western donor; they differ hugely from each other, even within their support to education. Thus some, such as Germany and France, allocate a considerable amount of their educational aid (over 70%) to higher education, whilst others such as USA, UK, Netherlands, Canada and Sweden allocate to basic education over 69% of their total aid to education (UNESCO, 2011b: 110; 2012b: 219–20).

Again, many Western donors, but by no means all, claim that their aid is aimed at poverty reduction. Thus the UK's Department for International Development (DFID) has produced several White Papers since 1997 emphasising that aid is essentially about eliminating world poverty (e.g. DFID, 1997; 2000a; 2006; 2009). The words 'poor' and 'poverty' appear literally hundreds of times in these four reports. By contrast, in *China's African Policy* these words do not appear at all.[1] How do we explain this?

Interestingly, in China's White Paper on *China's Foreign Aid* (China, 2011a), the words, 'poor' and 'poverty', also appear very few times, and several of these refer to China itself. Even though the document refers to Asia and Africa as being 'home to the largest poor population' (ibid.: 11), and to these regions receiving 80% of China's aid, it is clear that China continues to see this activity, in Zhou Enlai's words about China's mission in Africa in the early 1960s, as 'the poor were helping the poor' (Snow, 1988: 145).[2] Fifty years later, the White Paper still presents China as a developing country, with a low per capita income and 'a large poverty-stricken population' (China, 2011a: 1).

What is intriguing about these relatively recent Chinese documents (2006 and 2011) on China's African policy and foreign aid, is that they maintain some of the same discourse as had been used by China in the 1950s and 1960s. Thus the language of the Five Principles of Peaceful Coexistence, first developed between India and China in 1954, is restated in the Bandung Conference of April 1955. Amongst these are the key terms 'equality and mutual benefit' and 'mutual non-interference in each other's internal affairs'. These turn up eight years later in Zhou Enlai's famous Eight Principles of China's aid to foreign countries, laid out in his tour of

---

[1] It is interesting to compare the way in which different African countries are represented by China's Foreign Ministry and by DFID. The latter's Operational Plan, while acknowledging that Ethiopia has come a long way, emphasises that 'Ethiopia remains one of the world's poorest countries' DFID, 2011: 2). By contrast, China's Foreign Ministry has the following in the first two sentences about Ethiopia: 'The two sides had frequent high-level exchanges and their political mutual trust continued to deepen. On 24 November, President Hu Jintao and President Girma Wolde Giorgis exchanged letters of congratulations in warm celebration of the 40 years of diplomatic ties.'Accessed at http://www.fmprc.gov.cn/eng/wjb/zzjg/fzs/gjlb/2984/
[2] A brilliant chapter, 'The poor help the poor', on Chinese assistance to Africa from the late 1950s sees this aid as 'a heroic endeavour' (Snow, ibid.: 144–85).

Africa;[3] and the very first of these reinforces the emphasis on equality and mutuality: 'The Chinese Government always bases itself on the principle of equality and mutual benefit in providing aid to other countries. It never regards such aid as a kind of unilateral alms but as something mutual' (China, 2000a: 1). The second underlines China's strict respect for the sovereignty of other countries.[4]

One cautionary note is in order, however. It is important not to take Premier Zhou Enlai's 1964 influential statements about China's foreign aid out of context, and look at them as if they were an extract from some early Chinese policy paper on aid. Snow has argued that these Chinese principles were a direct reflection of their own experience of foreign intervention in China over the previous 60 years (Snow, 1988: 145). They were in fact enunciated on the same journey in which the Premier had declared Africa was 'ripe for revolution'.[5] This message, from China's first foray into Africa was heard by the West 'with foreboding' (ibid.: 76), resonating with what would be heard from the West 50 years later about China's dramatic presence in Africa.

It will be important, therefore, despite the apparent continuities, to recognise some of the differences between the Chinese teachers who went to Africa in the early 1960s, those few who were there during the dark days of the Cultural Revolution, and then those teachers and volunteers who came in the years of reform and opening up from the early 1980s.[6]

More than 40 years later these same phrases, such as 'equality and mutual benefit', appear several times in *China's African Policy*, as well as in the White Paper on *China's Foreign Aid*. But there are many other dimensions of this continuity apart from the notions of the poor helping the poor, China as a developing country helping other developing countries, and the strong emphasis on mutuality. Connected with these, of course, are China's attitudes towards 'aid' and 'cooperation' which we have already mentioned above.

Central to the cluster of ideas surrounding China's view of aid and cooperation is the notion of avoiding a donor relationship, in which the rich help the poor, as a charity. There is, rather, the focus on how China can avoid making countries dependent, but 'help them embark step by step on the road of self-reliance and independent economic development'

[3] From 13 December 1963 to 5 February 1964, Premier Zhou and Vice-premier Chen Yi visited ten African countries: Egypt, Algeria, Tunisia, Morocco, Ghana, Mali, Guinea, Sudan, Ethiopia and Somalia. See Appendix for the Eight Principles.

[4] It is an interesting affirmation of China's concerns with continuity, and with history, that the first Appendix of *China's Foreign Aid* (2011) contains Zhou Enlai's Eight Principles, now termed 'China's eight principles for economic aid and technical assistance to other countries' (January 1964).

[5] It should not be thought that Premier Zhou's trip was all revolutionary talk and no play. There was a splendid photograph available in the Ghana Pavilion of the Shanghai Expo of 2010 showing Zhou playing table tennis with Kwame Nkrumah, many years before the West's ping-pong diplomacy. The photograph is also in Snow (1988).

[6] For a compelling account of China-Africa relations during the 1960s and 1970s, see the chapter 'The Chinese as Missionary' in Snow 1988, 69ff.

(China, 2000a: 1). Apart from the well-known avoidance of conditionalities in providing aid, there is the positive assertion that cooperation is about solidarity and friendship.

Thus, when China does pronounce about development cooperation, it avoids the language of donor and recipient. Instead, the discourse has a strong emphasis on solidarity, deriving from a claim about China and Africa's shared 'developing country' status, and it is weathered by several decades of working together. The following, taken from the Beijing Declaration of 2000, produced by the first ministerial meeting of the Forum on China-Africa Cooperation (FOCAC),[7] typically affirms China's preference for the language of South-South cooperation and symmetry, to which we shall shortly return. The July 2012 Fifth FOCAC (V) retains the same emphasis:

> We also emphasise that China and African countries are developing countries with common fundamental interests; and believe that close consultation between the two sides on international affairs is of great importance to consolidating the solidarity among developing countries and facilitating the establishment of a new international order. (China, 2000b: 2)

> The two sides applauded the active contribution FOCAC had made over the past twelve years since its inception in consolidating China-Africa traditional friendship, strengthening political mutual trust, deepening practical cooperation, enhancing exchanges and mutual learning and advancing the comprehensive development of the new type of China-Africa strategic partnership. (China, 2012: 1)

This term 'friendship' turns out to be an important marker of China's claim about the nature of the aid relationship, which distinguishes it, for example, from DFID's White Papers on international development. In these latter four substantial volumes, the words 'friendship', 'friendly' and 'friend' do not occur at all in describing bilateral relations between the UK and its partner countries in Asia, Africa and elsewhere. By contrast, in the mere eleven pages of *China's African Policy* there are no less than thirteen instances of 'profound friendship', the long history of 'China-Africa friendship', 'friendly relations', 'friendly cooperation' and much else. Similarly in *China's Foreign Aid* there is much talk of friendly relations and friendly cooperation with Africa and developing countries more generally.

'Equality' and 'mutuality' are repeatedly used to capture the nature of the friendship and the partnership between China and Africa. In this respect, Wen Jiabao's discourse is no different from former President Hu Jintao's declaration three years earlier at the opening of the Beijing Summit of FOCAC (Hu, 2006). Sometimes it is political equality; sometimes it is

---

[7] FOCAC has convened four times at three year intervals; we shall call these meetings FOCAC I, II, III, and IV. The latest FOCAC meeting, FOCAC V, was in July 2012.

'treating each other as equals'. Mutuality is sometimes expressed in terms of 'mutual benefit', but also in terms of 'mutual respect', 'mutual support' and 'mutual trust'. The term 'mutual' occurs no less than seventeen times in the eleven pages of *China's African Policy*. The same is true of the frequent use of 'mutual trust', 'understanding', 'accommodation' and 'learning' in the latest FOCAC V Action Plan (China, 2012). Mutuality does not, of course, imply equal endowments; it could refer to African resources and Chinese finance.

'Mutuality' is much more frequently deployed to describe the China-Africa relationship than would be commonplace in much North-South expression. Thus the term does not appear at all in the Paris Declaration on aid effectiveness (OECD, 2005), nor in the Accra Agenda for Action (AAA, 2008). And the word 'mutual' is significantly only used in these two documents for the key phrase 'mutual accountability'! Interestingly, however, in the final draft of the Busan Partnership for Effective Development Cooperation, which has been much more open to South-South and triangular cooperation, the terms 'mutual learning' and 'mutual respect' have crept into the discourse about aid effectiveness (OECD, 2011).

'Common development' is another marker of China's cooperation discourse. Development is not something China is helping Africa to achieve; rather it their shared goal. Common development therefore is the other side of the frequent assertion that China is the 'largest developing country', helping 'the continent which encompasses the largest number of developing countries' (China, 2006: 1). Thus, in the Action Plan of the 2012 FOCAC V, China does not promise to act upon the poverty of its partners, but to 'share its experience in poverty reduction with African countries through seminars and training sessions' (China, 2012: 30). The new strategic partnership is clearly both part of an ethical universe [8] but also, through its use of 'win-win economic cooperation', it promotes the vision of a world where there are no losers, only winners. Although the emergence of the phrase 'win-win economic cooperation' is linked to the introduction of the market economy in China, even in Zhou Enlai's very different era, there had been an emphasis on aid contributing to 'self-reliance and independent economic development' (China, 2000a; Jin, 2010).

It will be important in the course of the following pages to tease out what these ethical claims about friendship, solidarity, and mutuality amount to. A crucial dimension of the claim is that China sees itself as engaged in what it frequently now terms 'economic win-win cooperation', or in other words the search for 'common development' and 'common prosperity' (China, 2006: 3). The notion that aid and cooperation are reciprocal, bringing advantage to both parties, goes right back to Premier Zhou's repeated affirmation 'that mutual economic assistance among the African and Asian countries was the kind of assistance between poor friends who were in the same boat pulling oars together' (China, 2000a: 1), and right up

[8] It is interesting to note that Alden and Large (2011: 27) also refer to the 'moral basis of China's engagement'.

to the present, where the claim is more ambitious: 'Through foreign aid, China has consolidated friendly relations and economic and trade cooperation with other developing countries, promoted South-South cooperation and contributed to the common development of mankind' (China, 2011a: 1). Arguably, the same could be said of China's approach to the developed world.

Our earlier comment that China wanted to avoid being seen as a 'donor', and hence seemed very strongly to prefer the word 'cooperation' to 'aid', as in *China's African Policy*, is apparently challenged in *China's Foreign Aid*. Here, surprisingly, the word 'aid' appears no less than 133 times in eighteen pages, whilst 'cooperation' only turns up 38 times. Whether this more frequent use of the term 'aid' reflects some wider interest by China in establishing an aid agency rather than having a department for foreign aid within the larger Ministry of Commerce is not known, but it would be surprising, in the light of its growing aid volumes, if China were not thinking about a stand-alone aid agency. Indeed, in the White Paper of 2011 there is an acknowledgement that there has been the establishment by the Ministries of Commerce, Finance and Foreign Affairs, of a foreign aid inter-agency coordination mechanism in February 2011 (China, 2011a: 16). Whether this will eventually transform into a body such as the China International Cooperation Agency (CICA), like Korea's KOICA, and Japan's JICA, will need to be seen.

In this connection it may be noted that in the years following Zhou's announcement of the Eight Principles, in the 1960s and 1970s, a special aid ministry was set up: the Ministry of Foreign Economic Relations, and there were provincial aid bureaux for the dispatch of experts. Interestingly, these early provincial commitments were on the basis of twinning, between a province like Hebei and an African state like Zaire (Snow, 1988: 147; Li, A., 2011).

It could also be that the shift from 'cooperation' to 'aid' reflects a sense of moving from being 'first among equals' in the non-aligned states and in the earlier period of opening up, to being now an emergent superpower. In other words, there is perhaps an acknowledgement that in addition to the discourse of South-South cooperation which China maintains, it is also operating as a major aid agency, even if it has by no means joined the donor club of the Development Assistance Committee of the OECD.[9]

## China's development discourse in the landscape of South-South cooperation (SSC)

The terms which we have picked out in these few sources (and they could be endlessly replicated in speeches from China's ambassadors in Africa on anniversaries of diplomatic relations being established and many other

---

[9] I am indebted to Bob Adamson of HKIEd, Hong Kong for this suggestion.

occasions), lay claim to an ethical landscape in which Sino-African development is pursued. The terminology of mutual benefit, common good, friendship, political equality, solidarity, and learning from each other are very much the red threads of South-South cooperation (SSC). They can be found not just in Beijing Declarations about Africa, but also in Delhi Declarations, and doubtless also in Brasilia. Thus, in the Delhi Declaration derived from the India-Africa Forum Summit of April 2008, the affirmation of age-old civilisational links between India and Africa is made and the same ethical principles asserted on the first and last page of the Declaration as we have been discussing:

> This partnership will be based on the fundamental principles of equality, mutual respect, and understanding between our peoples for our mutual benefit.

> This Forum summit has further cemented the age old relationships between Africa and India, a relationship that has been of mutual benefit and is based on mutual trust, equality and solidarity. (GOI, 2008: 5;10)

These 'symbolic claims' of Southern development partners have been valuably synthesised by Mawdsley as follows: rejection of hierarchical 'donor-recipient' relations; expertise based on recent direct experience of successful development; empathy derived from shared identity; mutual benefit and reciprocity; solidarity with other developing countries; (Mawdsley, 2011: 1, 9; 2012: 152). Arguably, these claims could be extended to South Korea, which has only just crossed the threshold from non-DAC into the DAC club (Kim, 2011). While these different dimensions of SSC resonate very strongly with the discourse surrounding the fundamental principles of *China's African Policy* and *China's Foreign Aid*, as well as the earlier statements of aid principles, right the way back to Zhou Enlai, it will be important to tease them out in terms of HRD Sino-African *practice*. This will be followed up in some detail in the three following chapters on HRD modalities, African students in China, and training through Chinese business in Africa. But some indications of how the principles of SSC may translate into actual practice may be given briefly here.

First, in respect of avoidance of the hierarchical donor-recipient relationship, this is clearly evident in the language of declarations, action plans, and speeches about China-African relations. The preference wherever possible is to state that 'The two sides agreed...' Thus in the Beijing Action Plan from the FOCAC III Summit in 2006, the commonest phrase is 'The two sides noted' (or 'agreed', 'welcomed', 'reaffirmed', 'recognised', 'decided' etc). This underlines of course that, unlike the G8 at Gleneagles, this is not a donor document, but a joint commitment to act by both China and African countries.[10] On the other hand, when it came to the specific pledges, the language changed significantly:

---

[10] In the FOCAC V of 2012, 'the two sides' appears no less than 139 times in a document of 42 pages; and 'the Chinese Government' just eight times (China, 2012).

The Chinese Government decided to:

Increase the number of Chinese government scholarships to African students from the current 2000 per year to 4,000 per year by 2009. (FOCAC 2006b. 5.4.4.)

At the level of development in practice, of course, it is commonplace to note that distinguishing the Chinese engineers from Chinese technicians or Chinese skilled workers on a construction site is extremely difficult. Equally, for Chinese 'experts' on projects, they do still seem to exemplify something of the standard set out by Zhou Enlai:[11]

The experts dispatched by China to help in construction in the recipient countries will have the same standard of living as the experts of the recipient country. The Chinese experts are not allowed to make any special demands or enjoy any special amenities. (China, 2000a)

When it comes to expertise based on recent successful development, again it seems clear that the message going to the thousands of Africans coming on short-term training courses in China is simple: this is what we have learnt; and what we do.[12] There is no attempt to judge or analyse what is done poorly in Africa, as might happen with short-term training in the UK. The other overpowering message coming to African students and African professionals in China is that this success is inseparable from effort; the ethic of hard work is conspicuous both to the thousands of Africans visiting China, and to the thousands of Africans working with Chinese entrepreneurs in Africa.

In the case of empathy or solidarity based on a shared developing country identity, the story is more complicated when it comes to practice. As will be seen when we come to the experience of African students in China, and Chinese student attitudes to African students, there has been a long history of critical racial attitudes in both directions, and the jury is out on whether there has been a dramatic change even today.[13] We examine this in depth in Chapter 3 on African students in China.

In the sphere of mutual benefit and reciprocity, the fundamental principles are clear, going all the way back to the spirit and the language of Bandung: 'The Chinese Government always bases itself on the principle of equality and mutual benefit in providing aid to other countries. It never regards such aid as a kind of unilateral alms but as something mutual.' (China, 2000a). It is important to be clear about this mutuality. What it patently cannot mean is that there is necessarily an exact financial symmetry in China-Africa relations. Just three years after this statement by

[11] The same is the case even today with many Japanese experts: the preferred image is that they should be found working or demonstrating in the paddy field, and not in an office next to the minister.
[12] In the words of one Chinese embassy official explaining the purpose of the training courses in China: 'To see is to believe' (official to KK, 12 October 2012).
[13] See for example the discussion in Barr (2011: 110) about the Chinese-Black American singer, Lou Jing in 2009.

Zhou about foreign aid, China was signing the agreement with Tanzania and Zambia to build an astonishing 2000 kms of railway line between the two countries. Unlike the reciprocity of the resources-for-technology agreements with Japan that would start in 1973 (Brautigam, 2009), there was no direct material benefit to China from the Tanzania-Zambia Railway Authority (TAZARA) project (Dowden, 2008: 490) or on some of its other early cooperation projects in Africa. But by contrast with Western or Russian aid to Africa at the time, it was a dramatic representation of what we noted Zhou Enlai had termed 'The poor help the poor' (Snow, 1988: 144 ff.). In other words, it was solidarity, and not charity (alms). But this is not to say that the mutuality was without any sense of reciprocity at all. Within one year of construction starting on the railway in 1970, China had regained its seat in the UN, thanks particularly to the votes of African member states.

Another illustration of how the reciprocity may actually work out in practice in the case of China-Africa relations is that an Action Plan, as in the case of FOCAC III of 2006 can contain the pledge about the China-Africa Development Fund which primarily supports Chinese enterprise in Africa, along with the pledge which covers all the dimensions of China's support to human resources in education, health and agriculture, which primarily benefits Africa. There is therefore no direct symmetry within the human resources silo, as almost all the awards, scholarships, volunteers and experts are one way, with China providing them to Africa.[14] But across the pledges as a whole, there is certainly reciprocity and mutual benefit. This is very different from what Mawdsley calls the 'unreciprocated giving from the generous rich to the needy poor' in Western grant aid (Mawdsley, 2011: 9).

Reviewing all these dimensions of South-South cooperation, however briefly, we can see that they do help to flesh out the general principles of cooperation and what they may mean when faced with the challenge of practice. We shall in due course illustrate this in detail in the following chapters. But there is one further lens on China's cooperation that we should examine before taking up the education storyline again.

## Soft power versus the spirit of South-South cooperation

It is perhaps not coincidental that the term 'soft power' came into use in 1990 just after the hard structure of the Berlin Wall was dismantled and the Cold War era came to an end (Nye, 1990). So it has been in existence for twenty years; but it has only begun to be picked up by Chinese policy makers and academics about fifteen years later, not least influenced by the

---

[14] There are a small number of scholarships provided by Egypt for their students to go to China and Chinese students to come to Egypt. See Chapter 3.

then Chinese President's using the term for the first time in connection with the role of culture in January 2006.[15] Even though this was just a week before *China's African Policy* was released, there is a sense in which Hu's reference to soft power and the *African Policy* come out of somewhat different worlds and different discourses.[16]

Former President Hu's address later that same year to the Beijing Summit of African leaders, FOCAC III, in November 2006, would relate to the discourse of South-South cooperation which we have just been analysing: 'the principle of friendship', 'treating each other as equals', 'mutual support', 'common development', 'mutually beneficial cooperation' (Hu, 2006). In that speech, the role of culture was perceived as a landscape of common endeavour, learning and exchange between China and Africa:

> Third, expand exchange for cultural enrichment. We will strengthen cultural and people-to-people exchanges to increase mutual understanding and friendship between our two peoples and particularly between the younger generation [sic]. We will enhance exchanges and cooperation in education, science and technology, culture, public health, sports and tourism to provide intellectual motivation and cultural support for China-Africa cooperation (ibid.).

By contrast, in the soft power discourse, culture and media are key instruments in the armoury of a single nation. They are not so much seen as win-win elements in a new strategic partnership between China and Africa as a competitive arena in which there are winners and losers. In other words, at one level soft power suggests a deliberate attempt by a nation to reach out and win the hearts and minds of others. There is a sense, therefore, in which China's shifting to use the term 'aid' rather than 'cooperation' in its 2011 White Paper is part of the same universe as 'soft power'. Aid and soft power are both part of the 'donor-recipient' discourse; soft power is certainly about recipients rather than friends, brothers or partners. Thus, it is not surprising that Mawdsley does not refer to soft power at all in her critical analysis of the nature of South-South cooperation (2011), and there are only two short references to it in her book on emerging powers (2012); nor does Kim in her review of the 'ethical case for South Korean aid' (2011).

Even Brautigam only refers to China and soft power three times in her

---

[15] Hu Jintao first used the term in 2006: 'Party chief and President Hu Jintao made this clear at the Central Foreign Affairs Leadership Group meeting on January 4, 2006: "The increase in our nation's international status and influence will have to be demonstrated in hard power such as the economy, science and technology, and defence, as well as in soft power such as culture" (Li, 2008: 289): The term soft power appeared in the titles of articles in the China National Knowledge Infrastructure just eleven times between 1994 and 2000, and 58 between 2001 to 2004; then 416 between 2005 and 2007 (Li, 2008: 291–2).

[16] See Sheng (2010:264): 'Hu Jintao calls for enhancing "soft power" of Chinese culture', XinhuaNet, (15 October 2007), available at: http://news.xinhuanet.com/english/2007–10/15/content_6883748.htm (accessed 30 November 2008).

whole book, so suggestively entitled *The Dragon's Gift* (2009). Once it is to emphasise that Beijing needed to persuade others that China's rise would not be a threat but 'peaceful'; a more visible aid programme could play a role in that (ibid.: 86–7). This might suggest that Beijing saw soft power as being as much part of its discourse about a harmonious world as about global competition. Her second reference to soft power was in relation to Beijing's provision of FOCAC aid, including scholarships to study in China (ibid.: 121). A last reference is quite explicitly to the human resources side of soft power, as it refers to the young volunteers serving Africa, as the 'face of China's newest "soft power" aid programme' (ibid.: 123).

Of course, scholarships have been conceived of as soft power long before that term was first used in 1990. In fact, part of the paradox of scholarships-as-soft-power is that certain countries like Russia, USA and the UK dramatically cut back their provision of scholarships with the end of the Cold War, which is another way of saying that soft power cannot so easily be separated from hard power.

Scholarships were perceived as 'cultural diplomacy' on both sides of the Cold War, and it was even argued that the work of the great foundations, Rockefeller, Carnegie and Ford, in their targeted staff development programmes for Africa and other parts of the developing world, became part of this process (Berman, 1983). The attempt to create through careful scholarship programmes what was once called 'the good African', someone who could come to the USA and not be radicalized by racial discrimination against blacks, goes right back to the 1920s and 1930s (King, 1971).

We have argued above, however, that China's scholarships and training awards can also be located within the discourse of reciprocity and South-South cooperation, provided that is seen as a meta-narrative covering much more than the HRD commitments of China.

We shall suggest in Chapter 2 that the same is true of the Confucius Institutes (CIs), even though they have been seized upon as one of the most dramatic examples of China's soft power offensive. Indeed it has been argued that the CIs 'are China's 'most systematically planned soft power policy' (Yang, 2010: 235). The reality is more complex, not least because in general CI expansion is not supply-led by the Chinese state but demand-driven by overseas academic institutions.[17] Hence the largest number of CIs turns out to be in the United States, and the demand for CIs shows no signs of abating.

In summary, we can see that soft power does provide an alternative lens for conceptualising some of what China is attempting in HRD, but it is a lens that stresses China's role as agency and strategist rather than as the partner that we saw in the discourse of South-South cooperation.

---

[17] It is not therefore accurate to state that: 'With a shortage of qualified Chinese teachers abroad, through its Office of Chinese Language Council International (Hanban), China establishes CIs to spread the teaching of Mandarin and Chinese culture worldwide' (Yang, 2010: 240).

Equally, it is not inevitable to portray the spread of Chinese culture as inimical to the West; if the link of soft power to the concept of peaceful rise and harmonious world is maintained, then the spread of cultural influence can be viewed mainly as an attempt 'to share fundamental values and principles of cultural diversity' (Jiang, 2009). Interestingly, it has also been argued that China's utilisation of soft power abroad is partly the result of its using soft power at home to promote harmony and conditions for sustained growth (Barr, 2011).

We shall revisit soft power in much more detail in Chapter 6, and will explore a way of using the concept of soft power that perhaps does not conflict with principles of South-South cooperation or with the ethical discourse used by China in discussing its engagement with Africa.

## Continuities and change in China's educational storyline

We have already alluded to some of the items in *China's African Policy* that make up the storyline in China's aid to education in Africa. These same things are confirmed in *China's Foreign Aid* for both Asian and African countries:

> Most [of] China's foreign aid for education is spent in building schools, providing teaching equipment and materials, dispatching teachers, training teachers and interns from other developing countries and offering government scholarships to students from other developing countries to study in China. (China, 2011a: 14)

*China's Foreign Aid* develops the education story just a little further than the *African Policy*. In particular, it makes the point that historically much of the formal training of technicians and managers was related to ongoing Chinese aid projects, including the famous Tanzania-Zambia Railway Authority (TAZARA). This underlines the fact that 'technical cooperation' goes far beyond China's support to formal education. The great numbers of individuals coming to China each year, and the Chinese experts going to the African continent are very much larger than those covered by educational cooperation alone. For instance by the early 1980s, Snow reports that China had sent no less than 150,000 technicians to Africa (Snow, 1988: 149–50). Indeed, in its current policy on foreign aid, technical cooperation certainly seems to include education. Under the section, technical cooperation, China embraces a whole array of different fields: industrial production, farming, handicrafts, culture and education, sports, medical and health care, clean energy, geological survey and economic planning (China, 2011a: 8).

In contrast to formal education and technical cooperation which, on the whole, both deal with long-term training, China uses the term 'human resource development cooperation' to refer to the short-term training of personnel from developing countries. Like many of China's initiatives, this goes back to the early 1950s, but it really began to expand rapidly from 1998. Now, in 2012, there are roughly 10,000 short-term trainees coming on Chinese funding to China each year, covering many of the same fields just mentioned under technical cooperation and long-term training. We shall note in Chapter 2 that the range of courses offered has continued rapidly to expand in the period from 2009.

Apart from these modalities, China has also had a small but expanding 'Overseas Volunteer Programme' since 2002. This has almost certainly included the 'Young Volunteers Serving Africa', which was announced in 2006. There was no reference to volunteers in FOCAC IV in Egypt, but they are back in the agreements of FOCAC V of 2012. Numbers remain small compared to other volunteer schemes, reaching only 364 in total as of September 2012, but volunteers also need to include the Chinese language volunteers, which is a much larger operation. These language volunteers had their origins in earlier traditions, but only small numbers had been despatched up till 2003. But from then until 2009, it is claimed that some 7,500 Chinese language volunteers had been sent to over 70 countries round the world.

Interestingly, neither *China's African Policy* nor *China's Foreign Aid* White Paper mentions the words Confucius Institute (CI) or Confucius Classroom (CC). Yet by the time of the *African Policy* in 2006, the first Confucius Institute had been launched in Seoul, in November 2004, and by the time of the White Paper on *Foreign Aid*, there were well over 700 hundred CIs and CCs world-wide. These too were responsible for large numbers of both short and long-term language trainees coming to China, as well as substantial numbers of full-time language staff going from universities and schools in China to Africa, Asia, Latin America, and to most OECD countries. Perhaps because Confucius Institutes and Classrooms are not exclusively an aid project, they were not referred to in *China's Foreign Aid*. We shall discuss this further in Chapter 2.

## China's education and human resource development in the wider China-Africa context

A long shelf-full of books on China-Africa behind my desk confirms the widespread interest, especially in the West, in what China is doing in Africa. We are anxious therefore to ensure that the human resources story pays some attention to this wider critical context. How much recognition should be given to China's offers of scholarships, traineeships, academic partnerships, volunteers, language teachers, experts, or, in a word, to China's offer of capacity-building, both in China and in Africa, as opposed to the widespread view that China floods Africa with its own Chinese labour? What can be said about China's education and training aid, compared to the educational aid modalities of many of the traditional OECD donors, including Japan? In that regard, how different are the education and training pledges at the China-Africa summits compared to the longer-standing Tokyo International Conferences on African Development (TICAD)? Alternatively, how different is the HRD face of China in Africa, compared to, say, India, Brazil or the other so-called emerging donors?[18] It would, for instance, still be difficult to assemble even a small shelf of recent books on India-Africa, even though India has held two India-Africa Summits in April 2008 and May 2011. India-Africa interest is, however, certainly growing. From a different angle, again, how significant for our theme is the physical presence in many parts of Africa, from Egypt to South Africa of tens of thousands of Chinese migrants, many of whom are not Chinese employees on labour contracts, which numbered 114,000 in 2007 (Brautigam, 2009: 154), but are micro-entrepreneurs, traders, even farmers and settlers? What may be the impact, in terms of training and technology transfer of these hundreds of thousands of Chinese workers in Africa? How vital to the role of China's cultural influence in Africa, including the widespread interest in learning Mandarin, are the training and job opportunities associated with Chinese companies? We shall analyse this further in Chapter 4.

## The challenge of studying China's HRD for Africa

Before concluding this first chapter, some comments are in order on the challenge of studying China's support to HRD in Africa, the methods which we have adopted to do so since March 2006 and our first exploratory seminar in the University of Hong Kong on 'China and Africa: new approaches to aid, trade and international cooperation'.

The first of these we have already alluded to; it is the apparent paucity of official written material on aid from China as compared with traditional DAC donors such as UK and Japan, or even much more recent DAC donors such as South Korea. We have already mentioned that DFID, for example, in the period since May 1997 has produced a series of four major White Papers on international development (DFID, 1997; 2000a; 2006; 2009); it has also produced a series of target strategy papers, linked to the international development goals[19] of the OECD, including on *Education for All* (2000). In addition, in 2010, it published *Learning for All: DFID's Education Strategy 2010–2015* (DFID, 2000b).[20] Beyond these, there has been a

---

[18] For a rapid review of the activities of these many Non-DAC (Development Assistance Committee) donors, see NORRAG News No 44. See also Mawdsley (2012).
[19] DFID has called these the International Development Targets though their correct name is International Development Goals.
[20] With the change in government, shortly after its publication, this is no longer official policy. It is still of academic interest.

DFID briefing paper on *The importance of secondary, vocational and higher education in development* (2006) and a DFID practice paper on *Technical and Vocational Skills Development* (2007). In other words, in DFID's publications, it is possible to find sections on education in the White Papers as well as separate policy studies on different aspects of education. Furthermore, at the country level, there are a series of country assistance plans, many of which will refer to education amongst other sectors. Finally, there has been a whole run of some 70 research monographs, funded by DFID, on the education and training sector alone, entitled *Researching the Issues.*[21] No less than 50 of these were published in the decade between 1997–2007.

By contrast in China, educational aid or cooperation are handled in a very different way. As we have seen, there have been the two policy papers, on Africa and on foreign aid, and these do have short sections of one to three paragraphs on education, as well as on human resources, but there are also the action plans and declarations following the five different summits and conferences of the Forum on China-Africa Cooperation (FOCAC) which we shall examine in some detail later on. The eight pledges of the major FOCAC Summit of November 2006 (FOCAC III) are also one of the appendices of *China's Foreign Aid.*[22] Within this, education and human resources more generally for health and agriculture are covered typically as follows:

> Train 15,000 professionals for African countries in the next three years; send 100 senior agro-technology experts to Africa; set up in Africa 10 agro-technology demonstration centers with special features; assist African countries in building 30 hospitals and provide African countries with a grant of 300 million yuan that is used to supply anti-malaria drugs like artemisinin and build 30 centers for prevention and treatment of malaria; dispatch 300 youth volunteers to African countries; help African countries set up 100 rural schools; increase the number of Chinese government scholarships for African students from the current 2,000 per year to 4,000 per year by the end of 2008. (China, 2011a: Appendix III)

If we compare this paragraph with the single paragraph on education from *China's African Policy*, quoted on p. 2 above, the general statements about strengthening and increasing cooperation have been turned into fixed targets between the publication of the *African Policy* in January 2006, and the China-Africa Beijing Summit of November 2006. There is a similar quantitative feel to the education section of *China's Foreign Aid.*

---

[21] For the detailed titles of these, see: http://www.dfid.gov.uk/r4d/PDF/Outputs/PolicyStrategy/ResearchingtheIssuesNo70.pdf

[22] Another iconic example of China's brevity in describing its aid can be seen in *Brief Introduction of China's Aid to Foreign Countries*, Ministry of Commerce, 2009. Just 14 pages long, half in Chinese and half English, it still covers in detail the eight principles, and even has black and white photos of Zhou Enlai and Chairman Mao from the 1960s.

We shall look more closely at the philosophy of China's aid to education later on, but for now it can be said that the pledges, targets and goals relating to education and training are not linked to the education dimensions of the international development goals or their successors, the Millennium Development Goals (MDGs), or the Education for All (EFA) Goals. Rather, they consist of triennial targets, set between China and Africa, and especially so since FOCAC III of 2006.

However, there is no education policy statement beyond the short sections in these more general reports. Possibly there are good reasons for this. One explanation is that there is no major education portfolio of support to developing countries from China, on the scale of USAID, DFID, the World Bank or the Asian Development Bank (ADB). Another may be that the kind of discourse that is to be found in the EFA Global Monitoring Reports and other global reports about support to basic versus post-basic education is not something that the Chinese policy people engage with in the education field. Perhaps as important as any, there are simply not the personnel available in the small international sections of the Ministry of Education, or more generally in the Department of Foreign Aid, in the Ministry of Commerce, to undertake such a policy analysis task. A final challenge may be that the various components of China's human resources cooperation are dispersed across many different departments and institutions.

Meanwhile at the field level in Africa, there are just two Education Councillors, one in the Chinese embassy in Pretoria, South Africa and one in the embassy in Cairo. It is worth noting that the presence of an Education Councillor was historically much more to do with there being Chinese students studying in that country than about a role in respect of development assistance. Thus Councillors can be found in London, Washington, Tokyo etc. But there is no parallel to DFID, for instance, which has more than 40 staff whose professional or policy responsibilities include education.

The responsibility for building schools, colleges or vocational centres is firmly located in the Ministry of Commerce. The body responsible for long-term scholarships is the China Scholarship Council (CSC) in Beijing, operating ultimately under the Ministry of Education. However, the thousands of short-term awards offered to Africa and Asia are administered through the Ministry of Commerce and its overseas offices. The key education resource centres in China which take responsibility for the actual short-term intensive training of participants from Africa and Asia are largely based in universities and thus come under the Ministry of Education. The increasing number of Chinese language scholarships are largely offered through the Chinese Language Council, Hanban. But it seems that the Young Volunteers' Programme is handled by the Ministry of Commerce, and by the Commercial Councillor's Offices at the field level in Africa. There is an annual meeting that draws together most of this dispersed constituency of support to education and training overseas; this would include the main resource centres for support to international education at the university level, as well as senior representatives from the Ministry of Education, Hanban, the China Scholarship Council and also the Ministry of Commerce.

In this somewhat constrained and fragmented HRD cooperation environment, the external appetite to know what China is supporting where, why and at what cost greatly exceeds the capacity of the small number of professionals in the relevant ministries to respond to inquiries, or to meet to discuss with outsiders. There is however an awareness in China more generally of the importance of improving access for research and press inquiries; and hence departments are being asked to appoint focal points and or spokespersons who can deal professionally with the growing interest in different dimensions of China's aid and cooperation.

Beyond this, it would clearly be valuable if there were a centralised facility where the different dimensions of China's HRD aid were easily accessible. For years, of course, the China Scholarship Council has had its own website (www.csc.edu.cn) and all the participating higher education institutions (HEIs) are readily noted there. Candidates interested in applying to the Chinese Government Scholarship Programme to study on the Mainland of China can rapidly review eligible institutions by province, but excluding Hong Kong and Macao.[23] The same is true of Hanban on whose website can be found detailed information on most of the 390 Confucius Institutes and 500 Confucius Classrooms, in 108 countries, which had been developed by the end of 2012.[24] It would be useful if a similar website were available related to the hundreds of training courses offered by the Ministry of Commerce through resource bases in the Chinese universities and other institutions. This is something that Indian Technical and Economic Cooperation (ITEC) has done for years. We shall return to consider this in more detail in Chapter 5.

## Methods adopted for researching China's HRD cooperation with Africa, 2006–2012

In a first phase of our analysis, from March 2006 to May 2007, the research focus was primarily on understanding China's discourse about cooperation in general and its approach to education and HRD in particular. Why was China supporting what appeared to be a series of ever-increasing pledges of scholarship and training awards to Africa, every three years from 2000? How did it view the role of its own experts, technicians, volunteers and teachers who were going to Africa? Did China have an explicit

[23] Currently, Chinese Government Scholarships cannot be held in Hong Kong or Macao. Under the agreement of One Country: Two Systems, Hong Kong, for instance, maintains its own international scholarship programme (see Pong, 2011; and more generally King (2007a).
[24] 568 of the total were fully operational at the end of 2010 according to the Director General of Hanban (Xu, 2010a).

strategy of capacity-building in Africa, into which these elements fitted? Why is it that 'The Chinese government always attaches great importance to aid in education for developing countries' (China, 2011: 14)? Even Moyo's account of China's 'race for resources' (the subtitle of her latest study) pays attention to the labour and human resource dimensions (Moyo, 2012: 158ff.).

Even if, as we have said, China does not have an education sector policy paper in the manner of the World Bank, DFID or USAID, it would be possible to construct a policy-in-practice from its pledges and its actions. In this regard, it is worth underlining that so far there appears to have been a very close connection between human resource pledges and their implementation within the respective triennia. Hence the construction of policy is a possibility, but explaining its rationale and its relationship to other policies is one of the challenges of this book.

Returning now to the first phase of the research, it took place at the University of Hong Kong to whose Faculties of Education and of Arts I was attached for a year. This entailed examining the website of the Ministry of Foreign Affairs, and the sections dedicated to the Forum on China-Africa Cooperation, as well as other relevant sites and literature.

What was invaluable in 2006, the Year of Africa, and the year of preparation for the Beijing Summit of the Forum on China-Africa Cooperation (FOCAC III) in November 2006, was that the website of the Ministry of Foreign had been updated, and there was detailed information available on all the African countries with which China had diplomatic relations.[25] Also, the FOCAC site had brought together all the information on the earlier conferences of FOCAC, including the declarations, action plans and relevant speeches. In the FOCAC archives (also on the website) there were some relevant earlier documents relating to China-Africa such as an account of Zhou Enlai's three tours to Africa and Asia in the early 1960s.

In that special year for China-Africa (2006), there were many academic conferences and policy seminars on different dimensions of the topic. These were held in many different locations over the first nine months that we were based in Hong Kong. There were even cultural celebrations in that city with the Museum of History putting on an exhibition of Admiral Zheng He, who is said to have reached Lamu in present-day Kenya 600 years ago. The academic occasions included meetings organised by the African Studies Group in the University of Hong Kong (May 2006); by the Royal African Society, New Partnership for Africa's Development and the South African Institute for International Affairs in Johannesburg (October 2006); by the Centre on China's Transnational Relations in Hong Kong University of Science and Technology (November 2006); and by the Chinese Academy of Social Sciences (CASS) and the Depart-

---

[25] The information on each of the African countries with which China has diplomatic relations was updated again in 2011, but from 2006 there were data on all levels of cooperation for each African country, however small.

ment for International Development (DFID) in Beijing (December 2006).[26] These were only four of many that were held in different locations in the year when we were based in China; others were held in Tokyo, Cambridge, Bonn and London, to mention just a few.

I was also able to visit Mainland China on several occasions and give seminars or hold discussions on my growing interest in China's educational cooperation at different academic and policy institutions, including the Institute of West Asian and African Studies (IWAAS) of CASS, the China Institute of Contemporary International Relations, as well as at Peking University, and East China Normal, and Shanghai Normal Universities. Of great importance were visits to agencies with offices in Beijing such as DFID, the World Bank and the UNDP, all of which had been engaging with China in relation to Africa in many different ways for several years. In the spring of 2007, it was possible to visit Zhejiang Normal University (ZNU) where there was a growing interest in the study of Africa. Later that year, this interest was formalised with the establishment and launch of the Institute of African Studies (King, 2007).[27]

Finally, it was very important to visit the Division of Asian & African Affairs of the Department of International Cooperation & Exchanges of the Ministry of Education, and to meet with its then Director, Xue Yanqing. It was on this occasion that I was given a copy of the commemorative volume entitled *China-Africa Education Cooperation* (2003) which is just one of a tiny handful of official publications related to this research (see Chapter 2).[28]

It was also possible to discuss our research with a senior member of the Department of Foreign Aid in the Ministry of Commerce; later it would prove very useful to visit that Ministry's Commercial Councillors' offices in different African countries.

The next stage in the research process was to apply to the Hong Kong Research Grants Council for funding to carry the investigation to Africa. This was successfully achieved, also providing for the addition of a colleague, Bjorn Nordtveit, already mentioned, and the grant was made available from the Autumn of 2008 to carry out further fieldwork in Africa as well as on the Mainland.[29] The three African countries on which I intended to focus were to reflect a variety of different regions and colonial and non-colonial histories.[30] Unlike most traditional donors, China does not have a set of 'programme countries' in Africa, but has diplomatic rela-

---

[26] The papers presented by the author at these four meetings are available on the website of the Comparative Education Research Centre (CERC) of the University of Hong Kong: http://www.hku.hk/cerc/KK-Article.htm

[27] The author was invited to be an international advisor to the Institute from that time.

[28] A parallel slim volume (72 pages) with the same title was published in Chinese by Peking University Press for the Ministry of Education in 2005.

[29] Valuable preliminary research on China-Africa was made possible through grants to the author from the British Academy, the Carnegie Trust and the Leverhulme Trust.

[30] Nordtveit chose to focus his fieldwork on Egypt and Cameroon. For the latest development in Egypt-China relations with Mohamed Morsi's visit to China of August 2012, see He (2012b).

tions with all but four of the 54 states on the continent. Equally, the three countries for my fieldwork were deliberately not to be those where China had already made major investments in natural resources such as oil; aid-for-trade might be different in such countries. Finally, and after some discussion with Chinese Africanists, I selected Ethiopia, Kenya and South Africa.

Fieldwork started in China in October 2008, and was followed by research in Ethiopia in February 2009 and in Kenya during July 2009. South Africa was visited in March 2010 and in September/October 2012, and Ethiopia again in April 2010. The total number of interviews in Kenya over five weeks was seventy; in Ethiopia sixty; and in South Africa ninety. Apart from interviews in the Chinese embassies of all three countries, and in the Commercial Counsellors offices, there were discussions with Confucius Institutes in Kenya (2), Ethiopia (1), and South Africa (3).[31] Meetings were also held with those involved with the so-called Confucius Classrooms, which are mostly at the school level, in Kenya and South Africa.

Interviews were purposively selected in relation to the main themes of the six chapters of this present volume. Because of the author's long-standing institutional and research connections with Kenya,[32] it was possible, for example, to talk to a range of Kenyan students who had been in China at very different periods, and to discuss their experience with senior members of the policy and academic communities in Kenya. Equally, through the author's long involvement with research on aid or development cooperation in Africa, we were in a position to discuss China as a development partner with many bilateral and multi-lateral agencies in all three countries. In the case of all the main themes in the book, certain key repondents emerged, whether among former African students in China, staff in Confucius Institutes, Chinese embassy staff responsible for professional training, or Chinese or foreign academics working on China-Africa. Thus it has been possible, from the time of the original interviews, to maintain conversations with our collaborators face to face or by email right up to December 2012. This may have provided as many as fifty exchanges with a single individual.

African students who had studied in China at different periods were identified through a snowballing process, particularly in Kenya. A detailed discussion of the students is to be found in Chapter 3. Equally, during the four weeks' research in ZNU, a further set of individual African students from many different countries was interviewed. Academics working on dimensions of China's presence in Africa were met in all three countries visited by the author, as were many of the other development agencies

---

[31] There are three operational Confucius Institutes in South Africa; a fourth has been agreed with the Durban University of Technology in early 2013; and we held discussions with those who were hoping to develop a fifth. There are two operational in Kenya but a third has been agreed between Egerton University and Nanjing Agricultural University.
[32] The author taught in the University of Nairobi from 1968–1972, and carried out research on Kenyan informal enterprises over the following twenty years.

involved in giving support for education and training in these countries. The Indian embassies were interviewed in three capitals, Addis, Nairobi and Pretoria. Attention was also given to discussions with Chinese businesses because of our interests in their training policies. This was particularly the case in Kenya and in Ethiopia. Finally, it was important to hold discussions with the ministries of education; this duly took place in all three settings.

In each of the countries visited by the author, a seminar was held to discuss the preliminary findings, including some of our respondents in the process. These were located in the Organisation for Social Science Research in Eastern and Southern Africa (OSSREA) in Addis Ababa University, in the Institute for Development Studies (IDS) in the University of Nairobi, and in the Faculty of Education in the University of Cape Town, as well as in the Centre for Chinese Studies in the University of Stellenbosch, in the Centre for African Studies of the University of the Free State, in the Education Policy Unit of the University of Witwatersrand, and in the University Teaching and Learning Office of the University of KwaZulu Natal (UKZN). Summary papers were made available in both the OSSREA and IDS seminars, as well as in UKZN.[33]

Similarly in China, feedback seminars for researchers and policy makers were arranged in Hong Kong throughout the life of the project, and on the Mainland seminars were held in Beijing at the IWAAS and the International Poverty Reduction Centre in China (IPRCC) in July 2010, as well as in the Institute of African Studies in ZNU in the same month, and in the Education Faculty of East China Normal University in December 2010. It was possible to continue the research while based in ZNU for four weeks in August 2010, and in the Hong Kong Institute of Education (HKIEd) for the five remaining months from late June 2010.

## Different China-Africa research environments

Researching our theme was very different in the three case study countries for which the author was responsible. First, the visible presence of China is fundamentally different. At least physically, China's impact on the infrastructure and on the road system of Addis Ababa is massive. The Chinese Embassy, for instance, could well be reached by using the dramatic interchange at Gotera and taking the ring road round to near where it currently ends.[34] Both these features were constructed by the Chinese. For the first time in January 2012 the African Union summit took place in its new headquarters in Addis Ababa, built by the Chinese, along

---

[33] A keynote paper on 'South-South Cooperation in the internationalisation of African higher education' was delivered at the University Teaching and Learning Office annual conference in September 2012 (King, 2012c).

[34] There is bridge just nearby constructed by the Ethiopian Highways Authority which was nick-named 'China wept', as it took so long for it to be completed.

with the African Union Commission Office Complex. In the view of one senior Ethiopian analyst, the physical impact of China on Ethiopia has been quite unparalleled in the country's history.

In South Africa, directly visible impact on the infrastructure is not as evident, though the new Chinese Embassy is the largest of any embassy or high commission in Pretoria. There are Chinese shopping malls in many of the main cities including Cape Town, Johannesburg, Bloemfontein and Durban; and in the rural areas, a large number of the small villages now have a Chinese store. Of course the purchase by the Industrial and Commercial Bank of China of 20 per cent of the Standard Bank of South Africa, for more than 5 billion US dollars, is significant if not particularly visible to ordinary South Africans. Academic interest, however, in China by South Africa is strong; there are now no less than four Confucius Institutes and one Confucius Classroom in the country; Africa's only Centre for Chinese Studies is there; and there is of course the historical link back to Chinese indentured labour, as well as the period of strong Taiwanese links and investment. Confusingly, as the Chinese were discriminated against along with other non-Whites in the apartheid era, those who were in South Africa prior to majority rule in 1994 can claim the privileges of the black population today, while those Chinese coming after 1994 cannot.

The visible impact of China in Kenya is more scattered than in Ethiopia, but the Chinese have been responsible for renewing a large part of the most important trunk road from Mombasa on the coast to Uganda, and for whole sections of roads around Nairobi. Chinese traders and importers have become much more evident in the capital, even leading to anti-Chinese protests in August 2012, to which we shall return. There is also a new hospital just on the outskirts of Nairobi, and extensive plans for linkages from the Kenya coast to Ethiopia and for new port facilities. Kenya receives large numbers of Chinese tourists; hence the interest in learning Chinese is strong among tour operators and interpreters.

Many Chinese enterprises operate in both Kenya and Ethiopia, which has a very direct impact on the interests of young people in learning Chinese. It is not by chance that 50 well-known Chinese universities held a China Education Exhibition in the University of Nairobi, in the very centre of town, in July 2011. There are already some 350 Kenyans now going annually to China on various Chinese scholarships and awards, both long- and short-term, without taking account of the substantial numbers of privately-funded students.

## Openness, access and transparency

We have already referred to the sheer amounts of information about the education sector that can be picked up from the websites of Western donors such as DFID. Similarly, within a few seconds on the web, the Korea Overseas International Cooperation Agency (KOICA) can be checked out for its support of education. There are tables illustrating sub-sectoral breakdowns of expenditure, as well as a very useful listing of education projects for the current year, their duration and the amount allocated in US dollars. Equally there is a listing of projects for skilled workers and for fostering advanced human resources. Compared to this, there are thin pickings on the web for China's support for international education in any detail, as we shall discuss in depth later in this volume.

Various attempts via Google to reach the Department of Aid to Foreign Countries, located in the Ministry of Commerce, fail immediately to bring up the Department but rather bring up the papers of those who have worked on foreign aid such as Brautigam. Under the home page in English of the Ministry of Commerce, it is possible to find the Department of Aid to Foreign Countries, but there are just five lines about the functions of the Department:

> To formulate and implement plans and policies of foreign aid, to boost the reform on China's foreign aid methods, to organize negotiations on foreign aid and sign related agreements, to tackle inter-governmental aid affairs; to formulate and implement foreign aid plans; to supervise and inspect the implementation of foreign aid projects.[35]

It seemed possible that the Chinese version of the Department's website would be much richer, but this revealed,in March 2012, exactly the same eight functions of the Department as were available in March 2006.[36] These eight functional responsibilities are a world away from the eight principles of foreign aid enunciated in 1964 by Premier Zhou Enlai. They do not address mission or vision, but just the terms of reference for the Department:

> The major 8 functions of the Department of Foreign Aid, Ministry of Commerce of China:
>
> (1) To make and implement foreign aid policy, and to draft out laws, rules, and regulations regarding foreign aid; to study and advance reform approaches of foreign aid.
> (2) To make foreign aid plan and then implement, to draw out aid schemes for individual countries, and to confirm aid programmes;
> (3) To take charge of inter-government aid negotiations, to underwrite aid agreements, to deal with affairs of inter-government aid; and to take charge of the repayment of foreign aid loans and debt restructuring.
> (4) To approve the bid qualification of enterprises to participate in all kinds of foreign aid programmes, to decide the results of programme bids, to deliver foreign aid programmes and tasks, and to supervise and inspect the implementation of all kinds of foreign aid programmes.
> (5) To draft out the budget of foreign aid funds, in particular annual funds, and to take charge of the statistical work related to foreign aid.

[35] http://yws2.mofcom.gov.cn/, accessed 8 March 2012.
[36] I am grateful to doctoral candidate, Li Wei, of Zhejiang University for this information.

(6) To make use of the foreign aid expenditure (funds), to supervise and administer the concessional foreign aid loans and foreign aid joint-venture & cooperation funding programmes, and to deal with major issues in inter-government aid.

(7) To guide the relevant foreign aid activities of the Bureau of Foreign Economic Cooperation (the predecessor of the Department of Foreign Economic Cooperation).

(8) To undertake other activities entrusted by ministers of MOC (Ministry of Commerce [MOFCOM] 2006)[37]

However, in a separate attempt via the search function of the Ministry site for the 'Department of Aid to Foreign Countries', no less than 684 pages come up, covering over 13,000 records, the first detailing a Vice-Minister of Commerce meeting with the Director General of the Department of Trade and Industry (DTI) of South Africa on 25 November 2011, then going right back, astonishingly, to items from as early as 1951 on regulations governing foreign trade. Not many Western donors have such an historical facility on line. Many of the items are about meetings between high-level officials from China and the developing world. Apart from this, there is a regular 4–5 page Annual Report of the Department of Aid to Foreign Countries in the huge *China Commerce Yearbook*. That would normally have just a brief note on training programmes for capacity-building.

By contrast, there is a good deal of China-Africa information about individual countries available on the Ministry of Foreign Affairs website (www.fmprc.gov.cn/eng/gjhdq/). For each African country, however small, substantial and detailed information is provided about high level meetings and exchanges, the progress and completion of Chinese-supported projects, and the signing of bilateral agreements, including in the area of culture and human resources training. Thus, in the case of Malawi, the most recent African country to develop diplomatic relations with China, it is possible to learn how many officials went for training to China in 2010 (140); how many volunteers from China came to Malawi (20); and how many medical workers to the latter (12). The site was last updated on 22 August 2011.

For most African countries, there is a full page or two of very detailed information on who has met whom between China and Africa. This information relates particularly to ministers on both sides, but includes senior provincial level meetings and even some major non-government organisations (NGOs) and development agencies. In almost all cases, the actual names and dates are provided of who met with whom for what reason. There are also copious data, with financial information, on the various ongoing projects. Thus in Kenya, one of our case study countries, there is a good deal of information on cultural and historical activities, including the signing of an agreement on archaeology in the Lamu archipelago

---

[37] I am grateful to Dr Jiang Kai of Peking University for a translation of these responsibilities.

between the National Museum in Kenya and its counterpart in China, as well as with Peking University. The subject is not mentioned in this resource but is in connection with exploring the 600-year-old history of Admiral Zheng He's having reached the Kenya coast.

One of our other case study countries, Ethiopia, also has a good deal of information about who came to China and vice versa. This includes information about a workshop in China for leadership capacity-building for Ethiopian officials, as well as a delegation to attend the opening of the Confucius Institute in the Ethio-China Polytechnic. Not least, there are the multiple visits to China of the late Ethiopian President, Meles Zenawi.[38]

By far the greatest amount of information is reserved for our third case study country, South Africa. There are over two very detailed web-pages of information. These cover military cooperation, arts and culture, book publishing, as well as detail on economic and trade cooperation. As for the other two countries, this information was updated on 22 August 2011. The feel of the material can be gained from the few lines, below. It is worth noting that there are bilateral agreements made in some 30 fields, outside the FOCAC framework:

> President Zuma paid a state visit to China from 23 to 26 August. President Hu Jintao held talks with President Zuma. NPC Chairman Wu Bangguo, Premier Wen Jiabao and Vice President Xi Jinping met with President Zuma separately. The two heads of state signed the Beijing *Declaration on the Establishment of a Comprehensive Strategic Partnership Between the People's Republic of China and the Republic of South Africa*, taking the relations between the two countries to a new level, and making overall plans for the practical cooperation between China and South Africa in nearly 30 fields. (www.fmprc.gov.cn/eng/wjb/zzjg/fzs/gjlb/3094/)

We already mentioned that the last time this information was updated for all African countries was just before the FOCAC III summit in Beijing in 2006. This time, it is not clear why the update should have been made in August but it was just a few months before the large aid effectiveness High Level Meeting in Busan. It would of course be a pity if it was not updated again for five years, because although there is not consistency on the kind of information provided across different kinds of cooperation, this is a layer of rich information.

The same is even more true of the FOCAC site (www.focac.org/eng ). This provides direct access to the whole twelve years of FOCAC meetings back to October 2000, along with relevant speeches, communiqués, declarations and action plans. It also provides access to relevant African websites and links to institutions in China.

These sites, linked to the Ministry of Foreign Affairs with which FOCAC is connected, are a marked contrast with what can be found in the

[38] We were told by the Indian ambassador in 2009 that the late President had gone more frequently to India than China in the previous year.

international side of the Chinese Ministry of Education. A good deal of the training in China with which we are concerned in the following chapters is mediated through resource bases set up by the Ministry of Education. The Department of International Cooperation and Exchanges is the key player here, but if the relevant section of their site is checked out: 'Cooperation & Exchanges with Asian and African countries', only two paragraphs appear: (202.205.177.9/english/international_7.htm). In one of these it is mentioned that the major ongoing cooperative projects between China and Africa include 'the cooperative project with African countries'. That is it. There is no way of learning more about this project.

It must be remembered that the Chinese websites of the ministries have much more detail and more frequent updates than the English medium. This must be borne in mind in any criticism of access to information. It is not however the case with the Chinese version of the Department of Foreign Aid; it would appear not to have much more information than is available on the English language site. We shall look at this in more detail in Chapter 5.

Reflecting on the transparency of China's aid more generally, even an attempt rapidly to access information on education and HRD from these four sources, Department of Foreign Aid; Ministry of Foreign Affairs; FOCAC; and the Department of International Cooperation & Exchanges, underlines great differences within government on making relevant information available. The situation of accessible data is well captured by Grimm of the Centre for Chinese Studies in Stellenbosch University: 'The Chinese government, overall, publishes less data than "traditional donors", but provides more than usually believed' (Grimm et al., 2011: 22).

In concluding this section on access and transparency, we should confirm Grimm's view that working on China's aid is a bit like doing a jigsaw puzzle but the missing pieces are larger than would be the case with other donors (ibid.). However, we should also note that bits of the jigsaw are coming together, for example in the *Preliminary Mapping of China-Africa Knowledge Networks* (Carayannis & Olin, 2012).

It may also be useful to acknowledge Nordtveit's view that there is a rather different culture of research operating in the Mainland, and that an understanding of that and of its forms and norms is critically important, including the role of *guanxi* – connections (Nordtveit, 2011b). Be that as it may, it has been particularly challenging to pursue this research topic, but also very rewarding. It would have made a huge difference, given my interest in discourse, text and in language, if I could have read Chinese. On the other hand, all those Chinese working in different roles in embassies, aid projects and major enterprises in our three Anglophone case study countries spoke English, as did all the African students, whether interviewed in China or in Africa.

We have looked briefly in this first chapter at China's support for education and training in Africa using three lenses: their own favoured view of long-standing historical connections; the approach through South-South cooperation; and lastly the perspective of soft power. All are helpful in constructing a rationale for this important relationship.

Now we need to look in much more detail at what these claims and this rhetoric amount to in practice, in five specific fields (and chapters): the delivery of higher education partnerships, short-term training, and Confucius Institutes; the experience of African students in China over a 50 year period; what Chinese enterprise in Africa brings to our understanding of capacity development; the difference between Chinese and OECD education aid; and finally, and very importantly, the relations amongst Chinese aid, education and soft power.

# 2

## China's Higher Education Partnerships with Africa

## Modalities for mutual cooperation?

## Background

Most of China's support for education and training in Africa is at the higher education level. The same is probably true of many of the middle-income countries which are not part of the OECD's Development Assistance Committee (DAC). These non-DAC donors (NDDs) such as Brazil, India, South Africa, and Turkey are not in this way making a statement about the importance of basic education which has been central to the educational aid of many OECD donors since the World Conference on Education for All (WCEFA) of March 1990 put it so powerfully on the world's agenda. Indeed, the NDDs do not generally engage with the long-standing debates amongst the mainly Western agencies about trade-offs between higher and basic education, or about rates of return for different sub-sectors of education. These sub-sectoral allocations have become a regular feature of the influential Education for All Global Monitoring Report (GMR),[1] and in recent years countries have been ranked by the GMR on the proportion of their educational aid going to basic education. Such issues of allocation within the education sector are not debated by China for its educational cooperation. Or rather, China and India, and perhaps the others also, have not developed education policy or strategy papers in which it might be appropriate for such allocations to be discussed.[2] The same is true of some of the major debates about education-and-development which are pre-eminent internationally in 2013, such as the interest in the place of education in any new global development agenda post-2015. This appears scarcely to be on China's agenda, at least at the beginning of 2013 (King & Palmer, 2012).[3]

[1] http://www.unesco.org/new/en/education/themes/leading-the-international-agenda/efareport/reports/
[2] For a discussion of these allocation issues, see Fredriksen (2010).
[3] There was a national consultation around post-2015 but this was catalysed by the UN Association of China and UN system in China in March 2013.

In any event, China's support for education in Africa does seem to focus on higher education and professional training, but not just tertiary education in the formal sense. This lens covers its support for the long-term degree training of Africans in China (covered in the next chapter), the very large programme of short-term professional development courses in China, including for teachers and principals, and the increasing numbers of Confucius Institutes in the continent, from Egypt to South Africa, and from Ethiopia to Ghana. It would also include its support of science laboratories in some 25 African universities, going back to the 1990s. More recently, as a result of the Fourth FOCAC Conference in Sharm el Shaikh in 2009 (hereafter FOCAC IV), there was the new 20+20 scheme of partnering twenty universities or higher technology institutes in Africa with their counterparts in China.[4] There were also agreements at FOCAC IV to develop a China–Africa science and technology partnership, and support the travel to China of 100 African post-doctoral students. In addition it was agreed that there should be a 'China-Africa joint research and exchange plan to strengthen cooperation and exchanges between scholars and think tanks'. The FOCAC V ministerial conference of July 2012 reinforced this emphasis on higher education through the proposed training in China of almost 50,000 Africans in the next triennium, as well as the continuation of several higher education partnership schemes (China, 2012).

Still, on the software side, it should be noted that one of the largest pieces of on-going research on African education supported by the Chinese Ministry of Education through Zhejiang Normal University (ZNU) is a series of no less than sixteen separate case studies of higher education in different African countries. Half of these are already available in Chinese. We return to ZNU a little later on.

Finally, but on the higher education hardware side, it can be added that China has been entirely responsible for the construction of the Ethio-China Polytechnic College just outside Addis Ababa, as well as for the new Fendell Campus of the University of Liberia, and has supplied Malawi with a Science and Technology University, opening to its first students in 2013. There is also talk of support by China for higher education in South Sudan.

This is not to say that China has not supported some elements of basic education. The best known of these, at least since the Third FOCAC Summit in 2006 in Beijing (hereafter FOCAC III), is the pledge to build 100 rural schools by 2009. This pledge was renewed in FOCAC IV in Egypt but the total number for the triennium to 2012 was just 50 'China-Africa friendship schools'. Compared to the Japan International Cooperation Agency's (JICA's) 2,600 schools constructed in Africa between 1985 and 2008 (130 annually), 150 schools in six years is not a very substantial number. But this is just the point we are making – that support for basic

[4] In fact all of the 20 were universities apart from the Ethio-China Polytechnic College in Addis Ababa.

education is almost notional, just about one primary school per African country with diplomatic relations to China in the triennium from 2010–2012 (King, 2010c).

There is a good deal of interest internationally in determining what makes China's cooperation in education different from DAC donors. We have already discussed in Chapter 1 the differences from the West in China's aid discourse in general. Here our concern is what, if anything, makes China's discussion of higher educational aid and its implementation at all special. This is not just a Western preoccupation. A doctoral thesis by a Chinese scholar in 2011 for Bristol University carried the suggestive title: 'Chinese educational "aid" to Africa: A different "donor logic"?' (Yuan, 2011a).[5]

In itself, there is nothing particularly unusual about China's emphasis on higher education in its educational aid. Despite what we said earlier about the impact of WCEFA, there are several key donors such as Germany and France that allocate some 70 per cent of their educational assistance to higher education, and a great deal of that goes towards the imputed costs of scholarship support in Europe. So any difference has to do with more than merely a quantitative focus on higher education.

In Chapter 1, we discussed the various characteristics attributed to these new development actors or NDDs, such as solidarity, mutual benefit, reciprocity and direct experience of appropriate development (Mawdsley, 2011; 2012). Many of these modalities are loosely referred to as South–South cooperation (SSC), or horizontal cooperation, to distinguish them from North-South, vertical cooperation between traditional 'donors' and 'recipients' (Zimmermann and Smith, 2011; Kim, 2011). However, it will prove important to analyse whether the current examples of China-Africa higher education partnership illustrate any of these SSC characteristics which might differentiate them from DAC donors. The challenge here, however, is that reciprocity should not be equated with exact symmetry. It is not a question, for example, of comparing the number of scholarships provided by China to Kenya, and vice versa, and then reaching a judgement about reciprocity.[6]

Rather, in terms of the eight pledges of FOCAC III of 2006, for example, reciprocity could involve looking across these commitments as a whole and making a judgement about win-win economic and social cooperation. Thus within the eight pledges there is, on the one hand, number three which is: "Set up a China-Africa development fund which will reach $5 billion to encourage Chinese companies to invest in Africa and provide

---

[5] Alden and Large (2011) also pursue the wider theoretical challenge of China 'delivering difference' as well as engaging in a moral discourse to engage with Africa.

[6] We hope that in a small way, this chapter takes forward the challenge in Mawdsley's valuable account of 'giving' in South-South cooperation (2011: 13): 'The arguments here are highly generalised. In attempting to construct the wider case, the paper has not been able to delve into the different profiles of the diverse array of Southern development partners in any detail, or to differentiate between different forms of "aid" (for example, towards humanitarian or 'developmental' purposes, whether in the form of technical assistance, loans, grants and so on).'

support to them"; this would be seen to be principally in the interests of the Chinese enterprises, though undoubtedly much of this investment might be very welcome in Africa. On the other hand, there is number eight which covers all of the HRD provision pledged by China to Africa, in professional development, agriculture demonstration centres, hospitals, youth volunteers, schools and scholarships. This would certainly be judged in DAC terms as mostly official development assistance (FOCAC, 2006). If taken together, these two pledges could perhaps be considered reciprocal.[7]

At the country level in Africa itself there could well be other examples of such wider reciprocity derived from bilateral agreements between China and a particular state. For one country, Kenya, some of these non-FOCAC agreements are discussed elsewhere (King, 2010d). But here it may be important to review briefly whether there are any indications of China's taking an approach to higher education which itself might suggest specific differences with DAC donors.

As mentioned in Chapter 1, China does not yet produce an education sector policy paper which might explain or justify its overseas educational cooperation in Africa, including to higher education. The nearest we can get to such policy declarations are the education segments of its *African Policy* (2006), its *Foreign Aid* white paper (2011), and the Beijing Declaration of the Sino-African Education Ministers' Forum of 27 November 2005.

What is intriguing in the earliest of these three is that although the Ministers' Forum was piggy-backed on the Fifth Meeting of the High Level Group on Education for All (EFA) which was located in Beijing,[8] the Ministers from seventeen African countries and China did not just reconfirm the EFA priorities on basic education. Rather, they went beyond these and emphasised the need to pursue prudent policies for vocational and technical education, as well as encouraging higher education, and cultural diversity. Higher education was particularly underlined for its development impact: 'Developing higher education, enlarging enrollment and improving educational quality and training high-quality talents to meet economic development demands, are the important means for developing countries to accomplish sustainable development of society' (China, 2005).

In *China's African Policy* there were only two paragraphs on education, but, perhaps again significantly, there was no mention of basic or primary education, just training in China through the African Human Resources Development Foundation, as well as increasing the number of

[7] An illustration of a very different kind of reciprocity can be taken from the negotiations about the initially seven Millennium Development Goals (MDGs) after the world leaders had departed from New York in September 2000. One senior bureaucrat reported to a visiting minister of development cooperation from Europe: 'We've managed to get six for them (the South) and one for us (the North).'

[8] This annual meeting, convened by UNESCO, has reviewed the EFA commitments made in Dakar in 2000, usually in advance of the publication of the Global Monitoring Report for that year.

scholarships for Africans to come to China and expanding the dispatch of Chinese language teachers to Africa. Vocational education and distance learning were also mentioned (China, 2006: 7). All of these are of course linked to higher education. Finally, in the 2011 White Paper, *China's Foreign Aid*, (not just to Africa but worldwide) the term 'education' comes up under all three headings of Technical Cooperation (TC), Human Resource Development (HRD) Cooperation, and Education. All in all, in a document of just eighteen pages, 'education' is mentioned no less than 15 times, but 'basic education' just once. All the other references to education are clearly to TC, HRD and education that involve higher levels of educa-tion. The summary of the short section on 'Education' says it all, even if in skeletally quantitative terms:

> By the end of 2009, China had helped other developing countries build more than 130 schools, and funded 70,627 students from 119 devel-oping countries to study in China. In 2009 alone, it extended scholar-ships to 11,185 foreign students who study in China. Furthermore, China has dispatched nearly 10,000 Chinese teachers to other devel-oping countries, and trained more than 10,000 principals and teachers for them. (China, 2011a: 14)

While these sources emphasise more generally that 'China's foreign aid falls into the category of South-South cooperation and is mutual help between developing countries' (China, 2011a: 3), they do not suggest any particular way of conceptualizing mutuality when it comes to higher education. None of these official sources seeks to explain whether China's support of higher education has any 'Chinese characteristics' or special features. So when we turn now to review the main modalities of China's higher education coop-eration with Africa, we shall bear this challenge in mind.

In doing so, we shall follow the main categories of educational collab-oration in higher education with Africa laid out in the only two official sources on China-Africa educational cooperation. One of these was a large commemorative volume, already mentioned, and produced by the Ministry of Education (MOE), in English, French and Chinese, entitled *China-Africa Education Cooperation* (China, 2003). The second, also produced by the Ministry, was a much more detailed but still short docu-ment (79 pages) with the same title but it is available only in Chinese (China, MOE, 2005).[9]

The seven categories include: high-level educational exchanges; student exchanges; cooperative educational programmes; Chinese teachers in Africa; Chinese language training in Africa; seminars and workshops in China for African professionals; and African Studies in China. The second of these is dealt with in Chapter 3 under the heading African students in China. The others, which all relate to higher education, will be discussed in this chapter, but as the Confucius Institutes had not been started at the

[9] This volume is drawn upon in English extensively by He (2006). I am grateful to Zhang Zhongwen for translating it.

time of this first volume in 2003, we shall also comment on their development and rationale. We return to the Confucius Institutes in our discussion of soft power in Chapter 6.

While dealing with these separately we shall also be concerned with how these various components fit together. Are they all part of a coherent package of HRD commitments? Do they perhaps draw on China's own experiences of delivering educational development, e.g. in its own poorer Western provinces? What are the dynamics, the logic and the core principles behind these particular modalities? And do they illustrate the five main principles of the Paris Declaration on Aid Effectiveness (ownership, harmonisation, alignment, results, and mutual accountability) or do they more reflect the characteristics of the new development actors, just alluded to?

## Influences and origins

There has been a long history of China-Africa education cooperation, and it will be important to acknowledge this historical context in analysing the several different modalities of educational aid, as well as the subsequent FOCAC pledges to HRD in Africa from October 2000.

China is often classified as an 'emerging' or more accurately re-emerging, 'non-DAC' donor in the recent fascination with these new development actors, whether with Brazil, India, Russia or South Africa.[10] The well-known truth is that China's educational cooperation with Africa stretches back to the 1950s when the first educational exchanges took place (between Egypt and China). Even in the early days much of the emphasis was on higher education through student exchanges, but there was also despatch of teachers to Africa.

There is a tendency in thinking about China-Africa cooperation in general, and education and human resource cooperation in particular, to focus mainly on the triennial cycle of ministerial conferences of FOCAC of which there have been five, between October 2000 and July 2012. These may be considered to be the formalisation of China-Africa cooperation, but in reality many elements of HRD cooperation were already in place well before FOCAC was inaugurated. He Wenping's account of the periodisation of educational exchange and cooperation between China and Africa captures the range and intensity of educational interaction in each of these periods before the FOCAC process took the headlines, with its time-bound targets for each triennium being set from the time of the second meeting in 2003 (He, 2006; China, MOE, 2005: 1–7). The FOCAC

---

[10] For an analysis of the range of these new actors, see Zimmermann and Smith (2011), also *NORRAG News* 44 (September 2010). Most OECD donors are represented in the Development Assistance Committee (DAC) of the OECD. See also the EADI Working Group sessions on Development Aid of Non-DAC Donors, at EADI/DSA 2011 Conference. Kragelund (2011) talks of the 'rejuvenation of non-traditional donors'.

process actually narrowed the number of HRD modalities to an emphasis on short- and long-term training and scholarships, school building, expansion of Confucius Institutes and the launch of young volunteers for Africa (these latter two from the FOCAC III Beijing Conference). The range of inter-university projects between China and Africa, some of them based on the development of science and technology, do not become part of the FOCAC process until after the 2009 Ministerial Conference, FOCAC IV, even though university partnerships in support of science laboratories had been operating in 25 African universities in some 20 African countries since the early 1990s (He, 2006).

What then of the source of these cooperation modalities for Africa? It is clear that for many new development actors, from China, Brazil, and India, to Turkey, South Korea and Thailand, the offer of long- and short-term training, and the despatch of experts is a natural first step in any capacity-building strategy.[11] If under-development is in part about the absence of indigenous capacity, then seeking to source that expertise through training abroad and the sending of technical expertise from the more developed to the less developed country is an obvious strategy. These modalities could be seen from the earliest days of India's entry to technical cooperation, in the mid-1960s, and they were also present in the first initiatives of South Korea's international cooperation, also in the 1960s. Interestingly, the training of middle and high-level technicians and managers in the 1970s and 1980s is quite explicitly recalled in the White Paper on *China's Foreign Aid*, with examples from Tanzania, Mauritania and Guyana. This training modality does not need, therefore, to be explained in terms of policy borrowing from older, so-called traditional donors. But is it any different from the technical cooperation training programmes of many DAC donors?

Equally when it comes to ideas of twinning and university partnership, there are many different models available, but the particular circumstances that encouraged Chinese universities to go out and seek partnerships may be peculiar to their own needs for internationalisation. Not enough is currently known about the range of reasons why 25 different universities in China made their first connections with universities in Africa, but the Ministry of Education in China played a central role in their initiation; and, above and beyond that, there were a whole series of high-level visits by the president, premier and three vice-premiers to some thirty countries in Africa between 1995 and 1997 concerned with aid and investment (Brautigam, 2009: 83). We shall note later in this chapter that the first Chinese professor arrived in Kenya at Egerton University from Nanjing Agricultural University (NAU) in 1994 (King, 2010d), and the first in Cameroon in 1993 (Nordtveit, 2010).

---

[11] See *NORRAG News* 45, April 2011, on the Geopolitics of Scholarships and Awards: new and old providers, East and West, North and South. Technical cooperation was also the very initial focus of development aid when Truman famously declared that the benefits of USA's 'technical knowledge' should be made available to peace-loving peoples (Rist, 1997: 21).

This raises a more general question of the degree to which China's provision of external cooperation in HRD found its roots in its own national experience of educational provision. Arguably, bilateral education cooperation, especially at an initial stage of development, tends to focus on those elements in a national education system in which it perceives it has a so-called comparative advantage. This is precisely the rationale behind the large number of science and maths projects, as well as other lessons from Japanese experience, which have been supported by Japan's JICA;[12] and similar perceptions of comparative advantage underpinned the large number of English or French language projects which were supported by British and French development agencies in earlier decades (ODA,1990: 12), and even now.

More generally than in borrowings from curriculum development, it was commonplace with several Asian donors to stress the relevance of their own recent, successful development experience in other developing countries. This is particularly evident in the case of South Korea's 'Knowledge Sharing Programme' (Kim, 2011: 12), but has also been long evident in Japan's own rationale for sharing its experience of educational development with the developing world, just mentioned.

It would, further, be valuable to know more about whether China's own experience of educational development, including as a recipient itself of innovative ideas from external development partners, then, in turn, becomes part of its own education cooperation programme.[13] Intriguingly, the new White Paper on *China's Foreign Aid* pays no attention at all to China's role as a recipient of external aid or of the possibility of others learning from China's aid experience,[14] and *China's African Policy* emphasises Africa and China 'sharing similar historical experience' and learning from each other, rather than Africa learning from China's own successful development (China, 2006: 2). However, as we turn now to discuss in more detail the different modalities of China's higher education cooperation, we shall note that the massive short-term training programme is surely predicated directly on the idea of Africa learning from China's development experience.

## Partners in China-Africa education cooperation

Given what we have said in Chapter 1 about China's commitment to a 'strategic partnership' with Africa, it should not be surprising to find that partnership is one of the principal modalities for the delivery of education cooperation. Partnership is not the exclusive mechanism for cooperation and training, but it has been very salient. Thus in the seven modalities of

---

[12] See the fascinating account of *The History of Japan's Educational Development: What implications can be drawn for developing countries today?* (JICA, 2004).
[13] See Begum (2010) for the transfer of donor innovations in China to Africa.
[14] See He (2011) for an account of China's experience as a recipient.

education cooperation which were celebrated in *China-Africa Education Cooperation* immediately after the 2nd Ministerial conference on China-African Educational Cooperation, the majority can be delivered in the partnership mode.

Here again are the seven modalities that were mentioned earlier: high-level educational exchanges; exchanges of students; cooperative educational programmes; professional seminars and workshops in China; Chinese teachers' active involvement in teaching in African countries; Chinese language teaching and research in Africa; African studies and the training of professionals in China (China, 2003). We shall look at them selectively for their reliance on partnerships as the key modality for implementation, and also, if relevant, for where they illustrate an ethical development policy or a policy that is suggestive of difference from traditional Western partnership support, North-South.

More attention will be dedicated to the Cooperative Educational Programmes (with examples from Ethiopia and Kenya), the short-term training of professionals in China, and the language training (including Confucius Institutes). The whole area of African student exchange will be examined in Chapter 3.

*1. Cooperative Educational Programmes*

Naturally, the most likely candidate to illustrate partnership out of the seven modalities would be the Cooperative Educational Programmes. This is indeed the case, though we shall seek to show that several of the other delivery modes also depend very fully on China-African university partnerships. But first, a word on the China-African cooperative educational programmes. These are essentially university partnerships between Chinese and African universities which have been promoted and largely paid for by the Ministry of Education since the mid-1980s.[15] By 2003, nineteen universities in China had established cooperative programmes with 29 higher education institutions in 23 different African countries (China, MOE, 2005: 55). In most cases the partnership involved some of the usual elements in university twinning, but again it is useful to note the discourse of sharing and mutuality in which the cooperation is couched: exchange of students on government scholarships; 'mutual exchange of visiting scholars'; 'information sharing in the form of exchange of research results'; cooperation in areas of common interest; exchange of teachers; co-organising international conferences held in both China and Africa (China, 2003: 59). China also provided some 20 countries with science labs and 6 countries with language laboratories as part of these agreements (He, 2006: 7–9). What is not picked out in the commemorative record of these cooperative education projects in every case is that they are part of a China-African university partnership, for example between Nanjing Agricultural University and Egerton Univer-

[15] One of the earliest of these China-Africa education partnerships was agreed between East China Normal University and the University of Niamey in Niger in 1986 (China, 2003).

sity in Kenya; or between Zhejiang University and Yaounde I University, in Cameroon.

It is interesting to note that some of these university projects appear to be very long-term partnerships. Some are still running today with considerable two-way activity and achievement after more than fifteen years of interaction, notably the Nanjing Agricultural University-Egerton University (Kenya) and the Zhejiang Normal-Yaounde II University (Cameroon) partnerships. This sense of being involved in a partnership over a long period is probably essential to its becoming a two-way sharing and learning, as in the Chinese aid discourse.[16] It would be interesting to know from across the range of China-Africa university partnerships, not only how many there now are, but to what extent they have continued for ten, fifteen or more years.[17] Not all these partnerships will have been trouble-free; but even when there have been difficulties, the African partners, for example in the Cameroon case, judged 'that the Chinese were more practical than experts from other countries' (Nordtveit, 2011a: 105).

We shall turn now to look in more detail at how a few of these partnerships have been constructed over a decade and more. We shall focus on two very different models on the African side (Ethiopia and Kenya) and look also at their partner universities in China. We shall note that multiple layers of interaction from different partnership approaches turn up on both sides of the agreement.

*From vocational and agricultural teachers to the Ethio-China Polytechnic College.*  This partnership derives initially from an Ethiopian Government request for teachers for their expanded agricultural and vocational colleges at the beginning of the 2000s. In combination these brought no fewer than 400 separately contracted staff from China to Ethiopia from 2000 (King, 2011a); it seems likely that some of them were coming from the Tianjin University of Technology and Education (TUTE). The next development was the setting up in TUTE, in 2003, of the first Centre for African Vocational Educational Studies. Its first short term training seminar that same year was for directors of Ethiopia's Vocational Colleges. Resource centres such as this were being established in order to assist the Ministry of Education cater for the short-term training of hundreds of African professionals coming for different specialisations. This in turn flowed from FOCAC's establishing in 2000 the African Human Resources Development Foundation which would eventually bring no less than 45,000 African professionals for short-term training to China over the period from 2000 to 2012.

It was not long before it was clear that instead of sending hundreds of Chinese teachers of technical and vocational education and training

---

[16] In one case, one of the earliest Chinese professors had stayed for as many as 5 contracts in the African university and had married a local woman. Another outcome of partnership.
[17] This will be covered in further research by the author specifically on the 20+20 university partnerships from May 2013.

(TVET) to Ethiopia, they could be trained in Ethiopia itself. And so from 2003 the idea of China providing a polytechnic college was born. This was not itself one of the FOCAC pledges, though the FOCAC II had been held in Addis Ababa that same year, but derived from the usual rounds of bilateral exchanges between China and Ethiopia. This Ethio-China Polytechnic College (ECPC) was duly built for some 15 US$ million by a Chinese company through the usual Chinese Ministry of Commerce procedures, but was delayed by several years.

Be that as it may, China did find itself having to staff the polytechnic, and not just build and equip it. Again, given the strong partnership basis of Chinese aid to higher education, it was TUTE that provided the eleven key heads of department, and the training of substantial numbers (60) of Ethiopian institute staff for Masters degrees, through the China Scholarship Council, while the Chinese Ministry of Education provided the Dean of the college. Other Chinese staff came through the newly launched Young Volunteers Serving Africa programme. Such a package procedure did not make this very different from Western aid; indeed Canadian CIDA and USAID had followed similar processes in earlier years in building, staffing, and training the new staff for whole colleges and universities.[18] TUTE also found itself directly involved in all of this. When ECPC opened its doors in 2009, it was certainly the highest level polytechnic college in the country, but in terms of influencing overall TVET policy in Ethiopia, this was now in the hands of the Germans through a massive Engineering Capacity-Building Project, and there would be other polytechnics opening through South Korean and Italian aid. Thus, the ECPC would not provide the sort of unique influence for China in Ethiopia that the Indian Government had secured by building and staffing the Ethiopian Military Academy in Harar.

By 2010, the development of ECPC through its mother university had illustrated many different modalities of Chinese HRD aid: the despatch of teachers, the development of a resource base in the Chinese university, the sending of staff to China on short-term professional training courses, the physical construction, and staffing of the college, the acceptance of volunteers, and the sending of Ethiopians on long-term training scholarships.

If this was not enough, it had been decided in late 2009 that a Confucius Institute (CI) should be opened in the Polytechnic College. This happened in early 2010, and, not surprisingly, it was TUTE again that was chosen by the Chinese Language Council (Hanban) as their Chinese partner. Or perhaps it was a little surprising since the usual procedure in starting a CI is that the host country institution's president makes the proposal. But at the time of the CI proposal, arguably the lead role in the Polytechnic was still in the hands of the Chinese Dean, though there was also an Ethiopian Dean in residence and sharing the leadership.

[18] India's agricultural universities, even earlier, had been developed and supported by the US Land Grant colleges, for example.

But the final modality has still to be noted: following the FOCAC IV meeting in Sharm el Shaikh in November 2009 when the 20+20 scheme for partnering 20 universities in China and Africa was one of the agreements in the Action Plan, it was later announced that the ECPC would be one of the 20 institutions on the African side, and its partner would be TUTE.

We have spent a little time on this to illustrate how a single institution in Africa can benefit from several different layers of cooperation, involving different ministries and institutes in China, while the same is true of the Chinese partner. In the latter's case, Africa can be seen as one pathway for the internationalisation of China's universities (King, 2012b). We shall illustrate this from Zhejiang Normal University (ZNU) later in this chapter.

As to our larger question of whether all these overlapping dimensions of Chinese support, mostly linked to a single institution in China, make this polytechnic special and different from traditional aid, we would need to argue that though there have been parallels in total institutional development by Western universities, the addition of culture and Chinese language across the institute through the Confucius Institute (CI) is certainly one distinguishing feature. We shall return to this in reviewing the CIs as partnerships. But one of the other differences in day-to-day partnerships may be identified in the Chinese culture of work but also in the Chinese respect for their Ethiopian colleagues:

> Our view is that we have to respect each other because we share a long history. We don't expect to change the Ethiopian style. For instance, in punctuality we are always on time. But student attendance is different; they don't like to observe time – the majority. Another example is labour work in the compound. The Chinese staff all participate including the Chinese Dean; he does labour work in the compound. The local staff don't like to do labour work – thinking it is humiliating; but we are having some effect; ideas are changing. (Chen Xiaoxi to KK, 7 April 2010)

Our other concern was about reciprocity in South-South cooperation; and here is where an Ethiopian Minister of State recognises that China promotes an ethic of equality but not of charity:

> But they have one major advantage *vis-à-vis* the West (USA) and it is an example of soft power – they are always prepared to engage with African countries theoretically and in principle on the basis of respect and equality. This, for a continent and for a people colonised, and used to the double standards of the West, has a lot of impact.

> There is a different quality to their engagement with Ethiopia. One important fact – the Chinese are not here primarily to help Ethiopia. They are not altruistic. No place for morality. It is a win-win situation they promote and project. A question of mutual equality. A transparent relationship. They are here to promote their assistance, but not with a

lot of hypocrisy which you can get with the West. (Minister of State to KK, 12 February 2009)

*From a two-way scientific collaboration to a Kenya-China partnership in the 20+20 programme.* Not surprisingly, not all China-Africa partnerships have followed the same road. Just over half (12) of the new 20+20 partnerships are based on partners that do have a Confucius Institute. But the long-standing twinning between Nanjing Agricultural University (NAU) and Egerton University in the Rift Valley of Kenya had developed without this CI dimension until 2012. There are a number of aspects which are certainly worth noting in this particular collaboration.

One of these is long-term staff commitment from the Chinese side; the professor from NAU who initiated the link in 1994 after the initial study by a Chinese team is still there in Kenya 19 years later; and his colleague who came in 1997 is also still there in 2013.

Even though, secondly, the principal focus of the link has been the introduction of horticulture into Egerton University along with relevant laboratory and equipment, Chinese language classes were introduced as early as 1998 through the support of Hanban. This did not develop in due course into a Confucius Institute in the mid-2000s, possibly because Njoro, where Egerton is located in Kenya's Rift Valley, is a rather small farming town with little in the way of Chinese businesses or other institutions which would have created a demand.[19] On the other hand, there were students who acquired Chinese language skills in Egerton and who went on, after training in China, to teach Chinese in Nairobi (see Chapter 3).

Third, one of the aid modalities which Egerton has been able to develop is a variant of the short-term training programmes that have taken thousands of African professionals to China over the 2000s. Instead of taking a group of twenty to China, there have been several regional training seminars held through the support of the Chinese Ministry of Education, bringing a regional Eastern African set of participants to Kenya. There is of course a debate about these *sur place* alternatives to training in China itself. A great deal depends on whether the purpose is to present some dimension of China's development expertise or to illustrate Chinese-influenced development within Africa. For the moment as we shall see when we come later in this chapter to this massive short-term training programme, the current emphasis is principally on exposure to Chinese experience. One of the Ministry of Education's resource bases in China for these short-term courses is actually in Nanjing Agricultural University with an emphasis on agricultural education.

Again, as with ECPC, there has been a sustained programme of staff development, and like ECPC, the staff from the African institution have gone to their Chinese partner predominantly. In other words there have

[19] On the other hand the Confucius Institute in Rhodes University, South Africa, is situated also in a relatively small town.

been a whole series of Kenyans trained, including to the doctoral level, in NAU, and as part of this process, they will routinely have picked up Mandarin through their first year of language immersion. This, then, is a tighter programme of staff development than when many of the staff in the new African universities in the 1960s and 1970s were provided with staff development funding from Ford, Rockefeller and other bodies. There are doubtless good reasons for most staff receiving their post-graduate training in the same university; it will tend to build a common base and help to encourage institutional development rather than just individual development.

A last question for NAU and Egerton would be: what would the additionality of being part of the 20+20 programme bring to this long-standing partnership? Will it dramatically increase the intensity and scope of the existing partnership? As with all FOCAC IV pledges made in November 2009, this programme has already been launched but the detail of its ambitions, trajectory, and financing are not readily accessible except at the level of the individual partnership. We shall note in Chapter 5, however, that the 20+20 bilateral partnership may have become a trilateral partnership through UNESCO.

Intriguingly, in late 2012, it was decided to develop the language and culture component which had been formally missing, and an announcement was made that Egerton would become the site of the first so-called Agricultural Confucius Institute, linked of course to Nanjing Agricultural University (Egerton staff member to KK, 4 September 2012). It will be fascinating to see in what ways this new CI will relate to the rural and agricultural context.

*From a first African visit in 1996 to becoming China's main Institute of African Studies*  Illustrating the speed with which institutional transformation can take place in China, with dynamic academic leadership, is Zhejiang Normal University (ZNU). Like the Ethio-China Polytechnic College, ZNU exemplifies most of the existing modalities of China's higher education cooperation. It started with a request from the Chinese Ministry of Education to support the development of a Chinese Language Centre in the International Relations Institute of the University of Yaounde II in Cameroon in 1996 (Nordtveit, 2010). It must have shown a policy interest in the teaching and study of African education thereafter, because when the Ministry of Education was looking where to locate the professional educators coming from Africa in the wake of the establishment of FOCAC in 2000, it turned to ZNU. Its first professional seminar on basic education management was in August and September 2002, and its second was a year later in September 2003. Every year thereafter several short-term seminars of two to three weeks would be offered by its School of International Education, many in the field of higher education management (for rectors and university presidents) from the first Presidents' Forum in 2006.

Its original resource base for the Ministry of Education (MOE) on African Educational Studies was folded into the new Institute of African Studies (IAS) when that was established in August 2007; and in the same year the Language Centre in Yaounde II became that country's first Confucius Institute but with its partner designated as ZNU. Internationalisation for ZNU was not only towards Africa; soon there was a second Confucius Institute partnership with a university in Ukraine. But one of ZNU's most ambitious initiatives has been to carry out a series of no less than sixteen intensive research studies on higher education in as many African countries. The project, referred to above, has as much been used to build the capacity and awareness on Africa of ZNU staff in many different departments as it was to pursue research on higher education. Some 32 staff and doctoral students have gone to African countries as different as Algeria and Botswana for periods of two months to research this topic. As a group, this series of studies should provide a fascinating lens on Chinese academic views of African higher education.

A very different IAS project with a strong policy aim was to produce a just-in-time volume on *Fifty years of Sino-African Cooperation* for distribution just before the FOCAC IV conference in Egypt in November 2009 (Liu and Yang, 2009). This was not just an attempt to get a relevant academic product into the hands of key policy-makers in a way that has become commonplace internationally in connection with major regional or world meetings. It was, in addition, a significant opportunity to lay a claim to the study of Africa with Chinese characteristics. In seeking to distinguish from the West the particularity of China's approach to Africa and African Studies, it comes very close to our concern in this chapter with the question of whether there is any difference from the West or from Japan in China's approach to higher education cooperation with Africa.

Liu Hongwu, one of the editors of this volume with 37 Chinese contributors, and also the IAS Director, seeks to capture the different dimensions of such a Chinese approach, to Africa in general and not just to higher education. First, there is an essential ethical concern about Africa, but we shall need to bear in mind how that differs from the ethical concern of the West about Africa:[20]

> We should have respectful and tender feelings towards the African people as well as their history and culture, appreciate them and care about them. (Liu, 1999: 22)

Second, and based on the unchanging principles of engagement, China, it is claimed, should be able to work with Africa across all spheres, including the social, the cultural, and the exploitation of its natural resources. This explicit illustration of win-win cooperation captures something of the difference between Western and Chinese approaches to partnership:

[20] See Mawdsley (2011 and 2012) for a valuable discussion of the different Northern and Southern ethics of development cooperation.

Based on the principles of mutual benefits and win-win cooperation, we should launch all-round strategic cooperation with African countries, and work with them to exploit the abundant natural, social, cultural and strategic resources and develop this vast land as well as its huge market potentials. (ibid.: 10)

Third, China's 'soft' cultural outreach in Africa cannot be separated from its 'hard' economic and aid engagements,[21] even if Confucius Institutes may not appreciate being bracketed with Chinese restaurants in the following:

When China's products, aid programmes and economic influences become omnipresent in many African countries, its cultural elements (such as traditional medicine, acupuncture, acrobatics and martial arts) and organisations (such as Chinese language schools, Confucius Institutes, and Chinese restaurants) have also started to spread in different scales across the continent, even in some remote villages and tribal neighbourhoods. (ibid.: 18)

Like twenty other Chinese and African higher education institutes, ZNU competed to be part of the 20+20 programme along with its earliest partner, the University of Yaounde II in Cameroon.[22] And it has established, as part of the FOCAC IV pledge to establish 'a China-Africa joint research and exchange plan to strengthen cooperation and exchanges between scholars and think tanks' in China and Africa, a collaboration with the Centre for Chinese Studies in Stellenbosch University in South Africa. Finally on the crucially important cultural side, the Institute has developed a major African Museum of sculpture, masks, costumes, music and household items, opened in October 2010, with 'the aim to substantially advance the dialogue and cooperation of Chinese and African civilisation' (IAS, 2010).

These multiple Africa-related activities all connect to what we are calling a series of aid modalities in higher education. In fact they cover all the different modes mentioned in the Ministry of Education's volume on *China-Africa Education Cooperation*. In summary, our analysis of ZNU above covers the following:

Despatch of teachers; support of language laboratory; receipt of professionals on short-term training courses and seminars; receipt of long-term scholarship holders and privately-funded students; Confucius Institute partnerships; development of a major resource base for the study of Africa, and of its cultures; participation in multi-country research; participation in 20+20 partnership programme; and participation in joint research and exchange plan.[23]

[21]  We return to discuss the soft and hard dimensions of China's aid in Chapter 6..
[22]  Surprisingly ZNU was allocated Yaounde I as its partner for the 20+20 scheme, although this university had historically been partnered with Zhejiang University.
[23]  To cap the range of modalities, ZNU just signed in late 2012 a framework agreement with the University of Stellenbosch to establish a China-Africa School for International Business.

We return therefore to our earlier questions: do these, whether individually or together, constitute a new way of working, different from traditional partnership approaches in OECD countries? Is there any sense in which they illustrate the characteristics claimed for South-South cooperation?

Historically, it could be argued that with the exception of the Confucius Institute partnership (to which we shall come later on) most of these modalities have at some time been present in institutes or centres concerned with development or area studies in several of the major universities of Europe. What is unusual is that, at least in ZNU, they are all going on at the same time. They are not all the responsibility of the Institute of African Studies of course but they are being supported across the university as a whole.

The ethical claim, however, is not so much about whether these activities exist but how they are delivered. Liu's language above about 'respectful and tender feelings' is a tall order, and in the next chapter on African students in China we shall look critically at that along with the Ministry of Education's claim that 'The Chinese government has taken great care of African students in every way it can. The institutions where they study understand and respect fully their cultures, ways of life, and religions and customs' (China, 2003: 17).[24]

The challenge to partnership of China's fundamental principles of mutual benefit, equality and common good are not exactly new. Nor are they unique to South-South partnerships, but have been a continuing concern of North-South partnerships for several decades (King, 1985). There have been debates about whether there can be knowledge symmetry if there is financial asymmetry between Northern and Southern partners. Equally there have been long-standing discussions about the ownership and control of research partnerships, including the division of labour: how to avoid the research design and analysis being done in the North with the data collection being left to the South (King, 2009b; Holm and Malete, 2010; *NORRAG News* 41, 2009).

Some of the same issues may well arise in South-South partnerships, even when the overall principles, as is the case with China, are mutual benefit, equality and co-development. Financial asymmetry will still arise between richer and poorer Southern partners. But in such cases where there is clearly asymmetry and lack of reciprocity at the level of the HRD project, does it make it any better to be able to point to reciprocity and symmetry over the whole of the China-Africa engagement at the country level? In other words, is it useful to distinguish project-level reciprocity versus reciprocity at the level of the whole bilateral relationship?

---

[24] The more academic analysis of China-Africa education collaboration presents this care as a two-way street, with China providing the students with 'comprehensive care and concern' but with many African students 'caring about and supporting China's modernisation' (China, MOE, 2005: 19).

## 2. Chinese teachers in Africa

When we turn to another of the modalities of China's education cooperation, the 'Chinese teachers' active involvement in teaching in African
countries' this may also turn out to have several potential partnership
links, and not just be a question of individual teachers going to Africa.
First, it is clear from the photographic record, of black and white photographs, in the *China-Africa Education Cooperation* book that teaching in
Africa by Chinese went back into the 1970s and earlier, and was not
restricted to countries which were nominally socialist. What was already
evident from the photographic record was that Chinese teachers were
teaching in a range of countries, and by no means only Anglophone.
Indeed the very first group of teachers went to Egypt in 1954, and by the
early 2000s, there had been over 500 teachers despatched to some 35 countries (He, 2006: 5–6). This is not of course a large number compared to the
Teachers for East Africa in the 1960s and 1970s (from UK/USA) or the
volunteer schemes such as the Peace Corps, VSOs, or JOCV from USA, UK
and Japan respectively,[25] but for a country like China which remained very
poor during the 50s, 60s and 70s, it was something of an achievement in
the early decades.

On the other hand we should note that in the medical sphere, the
numbers of Chinese going to Africa have been very much larger. Possibly
the mechanism of twinning between a particular Chinese province and a
state in Africa made a difference, as mentioned in Chapter 1, but world-
wide the number of medical team members is said to have been over
20,000 over a period of almost 50 years, and of course a majority of these
have served in one of some forty four African countries (Li, A. 2011: 122–
13). However, numbers are not the only criterion of effective aid as
Brautigam (2012b) and Yin (2012) have suggested in their critical
comments on China's health aid to Africa. Transfers of expertise are hugely
dependent on language and local capacity.

As we have hinted above, the messages brought by these teachers
would have differed greatly in the 1960s, 1970s and 1980s; and there is no
better analysis of these dramatic changes in China's political relations with
Africa over these 30 years than Snow's chapter: 'The Chinese as
missionary' (1988: 69–104). But in terms of the ethical development
agenda already mentioned, the Chinese Ministry of Education would
certainly want to claim for a broad impact:

> The friendship they cultivate among the local people helps promote
> the understanding between the Chinese and African people, thus facil-
> itating the exchange and cooperation between China and Africa in the
> areas of politics, economy and culture (China, 2003: 83).

Currently, we just do not have for Chinese teachers the kind of data available for Peace Corps, VSOs, or JOCV. For example *Never the Same Again:*

---

[25] VSO (Voluntary Service Overseas); JOCV (Japan Overseas Cooperation Volunteers)

*A History of the VSO* discusses the very different experiences of VSOs during the 1960s, 1970s, 1980s and 1990s (Bird, 1998). There could be valuable research and narrative accounts carried out on these first 500 Chinese teachers in Africa, just as the VSO book has a chapter on 'Opening in China' on the history of the first volunteers to arrive in China in 1982 (133–140).

Increasingly, it is likely that the teachers tended to come from Chinese universities which had begun to have connections with Africa. Hence it would not be surprising to find that the 25 universities referred to above are the source of many of the individuals who decided to go to Africa, and that these teachers then got drawn into some of the early projects for teaching Chinese language, to which we now turn.

*3. Chinese language teaching and research in Africa*
There is a short, but extremely important section, emphasising the fact that language was becoming 'a centre of attention in China-Africa cooperation'. These words were a prophetic comment in December 2003 because within a few months the first memoranda of understanding were being signed for the development of Confucius Institutes, and in particular for the inauguration of the first Confucius Institute in the world, in Seoul in November 21st 2004. But from 1954 up to 2003, there had already been some 150 teachers sent to teach Chinese in 15 African countries.[26] This number will have changed dramatically over the past five years since the first Confucius Institute in Africa opened its doors right in the central court of the University of Nairobi on 19 December 2005. But even if there are in 2013 more teachers present in one year now than there were in total over a period of 50 years, the aspiration for them to play a crucial role in China's cooperation more generally was already present, but in a less structured way. As for Chinese teachers above, we currently only have an assessment from the official Chinese side of the language teachers' impact in schools and universities in Africa. This too is a research challenge if we are to broaden the analysis beyond the official Chinese view:[27]

> The development of Chinese language teaching and research helps create a most favourable situation which enables China and Africa to assimilate the best of their cultures respectively, and makes it possible to promote the understanding and friendship among the peoples of China and Africa, thus facilitating the exchange and cooperation

[26] The history of China's language initiatives prior to the launch of the CIs would be fascinating. One element of that is the plan of November 1986 by the State Education Commission to set up a number of training centres in Africa to instruct young Africans in the Chinese language (Snow, 1988: 211).
[27] There is a good degree of detail on the development of Chinese language teaching in Egypt, Tunisia and Cameroon in the more academic assessment of *China-Africa Education Cooperation* (China, MOE, 2005: 58–4, in Chinese). But there is no mention of Chinese university partnership arrangements in the language section.

between China and Africa in the areas of politics, economy and culture (China, 2003: 99).

We shall shortly note that the mechanism for delivering Confucius Institutes to Africa and other regions of the world has been the university partnership between China and Africa. But it will be worth exploring whether many of these early Chinese language projects in Africa, for example in Egypt, Tunisia, Cameroon and Mauritania, were already using the university partnership mode. Certainly, as mentioned earlier, the Chinese Language Training Centre in the University of Yaounde II in the Cameroon benefited from a continuing and close cooperation with Zhejiang Normal University right from the period of its inception in 1996.[28]

*4. Professional seminars in China: one of the four largest programmes in the world*
Like the Confucius Institute (CI) development from the earlier support of a few Chinese language teaching centres to 33 CIs today, there was a similar transition from a series of specialist seminars for Africans in the late 90s to what would become a massive FOCAC programme, through the African Human Resources Development Fund.[29] Already between 1998 and 2003, there had been a whole series of seminars in China organised by the Chinese Ministry of Education (He, 2006: 11–12). These had brought almost 300 participants from 42 different African countries in courses of educational management, vocational education, distance learning, Chinese language teaching (China, 2003: 71). Doubtless other sectoral ministries such as Health and Agriculture were doing likewise. As with so much else in China's educational cooperation package, the obvious mechanism to deliver this specialised, intensive training was the university. Hence as early as 2003, the Ministry of Education had begun a process of designating university resource bases in China for these very short-term professional training courses. Amongst the first were Zhejiang Normal University and Tianjin University of Technology and Education, both of whom have been mentioned in the section above on Cooperative Education Programmes.

There begins then to be a complementary relationship developing for a series of universities which have had a) programmes or projects in Africa (or Asia), b) have supported Chinese language training, and c) now find themselves as the resource base for specialist training in China. Of course this last modality is not strictly speaking in the partnership mode, as there are often some 25–30 participants coming from many different countries in Africa. However, as the Ministry of Education argues, the very process

[28] For more detail on the transition from Chinese language training centre to Confucius Institute, see Nordtveit 2011.
[29] The FOCAC meeting of 2003 would pledge to train no less than 10,000 African professionals from 2004 to 2006.

of undertaking these courses in a university setting helps 'African participants understand China's education, politics, economy, history, and culture, while at the same time, enabled them to establish and strengthen ties with Chinese universities' (China, 2003: 71).

China's short-term training programme, organised by the Ministry of Commerce but delivered in relationship with other sector ministries, has expanded dramatically during the twelve years of FOCAC from a few hundred before 2000 to a target for 2013–2015 of no less than 30,000 African professionals to come to China. This makes it with India, Japan and Germany one of the largest short-term training programmes in the world.[30] The total number of courses is continuing to expand, and has now reached no less than 509, of which 440 are multilateral, drawing participants from many different countries, and 69 are bilateral, drawing all the participants from a single country. This modality will have brought to China in the twelve years from FOCAC III in 2003 to the end of FOCAC V in 2015 a total of 63,000 African professionals. Even though this is much larger than the figure of some 16,000 long-term scholarship holders over that same period, a good deal less attention has been given to this scheme than to the China Scholarship Council's (CSC) longer term awards. Even Brautigam (2009) comments that they 'will do little to build capacity' (ibid.: 158).

The fact is that we know very little about the operation of this, one of China's largest chunks of HRD official development assistance to Africa.[31] As far as is known, there has been no overall evaluation centrally done by the Ministry of Commerce, although every course is routinely evaluated at its completion. One of the very few examples of commentary on these short-term courses comes from a review of the education management courses held for university presidents in ZNU (Yuan, 2011: 246–256); this produces a very positive set of reactions to the courses from the participants as well as the organisers.[32]

By far the fullest and most detailed comments come from a feedback

[30] Germany runs both the largest long-term scholarship programme worldwide through DAAD, and also the largest short-term programme through GIZ. In 2009 from Africa alone, there were almost 10,000 GIZ trainees went for training, many of them to Germany (Jung, 2011: 43).
[31] An official responsible for these courses at the country level has commented: 'Though Chinese training programmes have featured strongly in their overwhelming scale and range, they are almost unknown by the world. This is partly because of the traditional Chinese policy which does not give priority to drumbeating. To be honest, I never consider this as a kind of virtuous modesty; it is what we need to do to make improvements with our assistance' (official in Commercial Councillor's office in Africa to KK 17 May 2011). There is a parallel with Japan here which has been noted by Maeda Mitsuko: 'The aid workers' cultural up-bringing is no exception to the general populace of Japan. Therefore, in the field, they are often admired by the people in developing countries more because of their helpful personality and their low-key and non-threatening approach, rather than the fact that they control the purse strings' (Maeda to KK, 1 May 2012).
[32] There is also a review and analysis of the education management courses in ZNU by Li et al., 2010, and three seminars are described in detail in *China-Africa Education Cooperation* (China, MOE, 2005)

form used by the Commercial Councillor's Office of the Chinese Embassy in Kenya. This was designed deliberately, with the help of the author, to encourage both quantitative and qualitative commentary by returned participants. In 2010, when this feedback began to be adopted, no fewer than 198 Kenyans had gone to China, which had risen from 130 in the previous year. These are roughly five times the numbers going on long-term CSC awards. The sheer number and variety of the seminars offered out of the total package of seminars is hard to exaggerate; the choice of which ones are relevant to Kenya is taken by the key ministry concerned in conjunction with the embassy. In 2010, there were 135 different seminars provided on which these 198 Kenyans were despatched for periods of between three weeks and three months. Here are just a few of those that were utilised in that year:

> Small hydropower technology; Hybrid rice technology for developing countries; Marine organism culture technology; Chinese acupuncture and moxibustion; Pollution-free tea production; Small hydropower technology; Hybrid rice technology for developing countries; Cotton breeding and management; Modern hotel management; Bamboo and rattan sector; Medicinal plants; Corruption prevention; Radio communications and digital TV technology; Forest law enforcement and governance. (Chinese Embassy, Nairobi)[33]

As with all training, the hard questions are about what can be learnt by the individual in a very short period that can be applied at an individual, institutional or even societal level. It seems worth exploring, for example, whether the bilateral courses which take 25–30 people from the same country may be institutionally more effective than just one or two individuals going on the multilateral courses. Equally, there are questions to be asked of China, as of Japan and Germany, about what are their principal motivations in providing such a large number of awards for such short periods, involving very high transaction costs. But, for China, some of the trainee reactions are, in public relations terms, unbeatable:

> The perception of the Chinese before visiting the nation is of a people living in a politically closed society, without regard to divergent political views, solely pursuing profits in a rigidly controlled economic system, and having no interest in developing partnerships with other peoples and nations. All these are fallacious assertions and appear credible only to those that have not endeavored to understand China, or visited China to observe first hand the pursuits of the PRC. The courses help place these in the right perspectives. (2010 feedback form)

[33] Courses differ by country. Thus South Africa has had two bilateral courses (where all the participants came from South Africa) in 2012, one on Security and the other on Aquaculture. A third would be in Textile Manufacturing.

Like the reactions of the long-term students which we shall analyse in Chapter 3, there is very considerable admiration of the discipline and ethos of hard work in China. Or as one participant put it rather charmingly: 'Chinese people have very high integrity and are self-disciplined i.e. I didn't see people drunk and wandering about. I didn't notice any idlers' (2010 feedback form). We shall return to reflect on the soft power aspect of such courses in our final chapter.

In terms of knowledge transfer, there are many examples in the forms of where individuals have seen possibilities for knowledge transfer. An obvious question here is what if any are the mechanisms for encouraging policy transfer to become policy learning in Kenya. Those courses which relate very directly to Chinese projects in Africa like 'Management of agricultural technology demonstration centres aided by China in English-speaking Africa' may have higher knowledge transfer potential.

These, however, are in very small minority. The great majority of courses concentrate very directly on exposure to what may be called best practice in China. They do not analyse poor practice in Africa; rather, the participants can make their own inferences and conclusions. So in this sense they emphasise what analysts such as Mawdsley have commented on as a feature of South-South cooperation: the direct and recent successful development experience of the host country. But there seems also to be a less formal dimension to some of the courses as well, encouraging people to people contacts, even if language may make it difficult.[34]

We should not imply that despite this massive programme being relatively unknown, including by development agencies, there is no criticism of it. Inevitably, as the participants on these courses are treated very well in China, there is considerable interest in some ministries to get included even for a second or third time. Care is certainly taken in embassies to ensure that this hugely labour intensive task is carried out effectively.[35] But there is sometimes slippage.

We have not addressed here the extent to which this huge programme by China differs from that provided by Japan. One of the main differences is that Japanese JICA has a whole series of JICA training centres across Japan where many of the trainees would come during the year, whereas China has to a very great extent relied on its sector ministries such as Education to provide training through a set of university resource bases. India, as another middle-income non-DAC donor to offer short-term

[34] One South African on one of the courses in 2012, a Mandarin speaker, found she was able to talk to workers in the evening and admire their meeting at the end of the day to discuss how to improve their business (Participant to KK, 1 October 2012).

[35] 'Our assistance is derived from Chinese taxpayers, and China is a developing country itself, so the work requires diligence and a meticulous approach. From annual planning meeting with local government to year round small-scale meetings with each functioning department, from tons of telecommunications to tons of paper work back and forth between our office and nominees and government departments, from interviews with nominees to annual evaluation survey, each procedure receives careful attention and great efforts.' (Official to KK, 17 May 2011)

courses, also relies principally on tertiary institutions for this form of development assistance.[36]

According to the university authorities who have been consulted on the question of why they should offer what is an extremely time-consuming activity, and not least when it is a question of providing these intensive courses in French, they admit that there is little financial incentive to do so (unlike the case in the UK where short courses can bring in very significant fee income from the sponsors or the trainees). Rather it is maintaining good working relations with the funding ministry (Commerce) or the particular sector ministry that has identified the university as a resource base.

There is one further difference from the long-term awards, where a very small number of African countries offer reciprocal scholarships to China, including Egypt, and that is that there seems no parallel offer from African countries of short-term specialist training to China.

Lastly in respect of research, there would be value in exploring what are perceived as the rationales for India, Germany and Japan continuing with such large-scale, short-term training when so many other DAC donors have abandoned this modality, and whether these are different from the training rationales of the two largest non-DAC partners, India and China.[37] As we shall see in later chapters, there are powerful soft power reasons for maintaining these courses.

## 5. African Studies and the training of professionals in China

One of the last pieces of the puzzle, before coming to the specificity of the Confucius Institutes as a modality in their own right, is the further development of African Studies in China; it was a logical outcome of all the other items just mentioned. China's own capacity to be a genuine partner with Africa, especially in areas of professional training and support of African students studying in China required that China should build up its own capacity in African Studies. More than ten universities in China now have specialist African research institutes, and they continue to increase in number (China, MOE, 2005: 65).

> With more and more exchange programmes established between Chinese and African universities, scholars from both China and Africa are interacting on a more regular basis with more on-going cooperative projects since the 1980s. The increased academic events shall further facilitate the growth and prosperity of African studies in both China and Africa. (China, 2003: 105)

---

[36] See the course brochures of Indian Technical and Economic Cooperation (ITEC): http://itec.mea.gov.in/ India relies on a network of some 250 institutions and universities to deliver around 6,000 civilian and military awards annually, both short- and long-term. See further Grover (2011).

[37] The Netherlands has long had a very substantial international training programme dedicated specifically to developing countries, but this is currently being affected by budget cuts.

This has nowhere been more true than in the development of the Institute of African Studies in Zhejiang Normal University (ZNU) since 2007. But it is noteworthy that other centres and institutes of African Studies have been expanding or starting in China, often taking advantage of a link that has been made with an African university through, for example, a Confucius Institute connection. This has been the case with Rhodes University and a new focus on African Studies in its partner, Jinan University. Other older centres in Yunnan, Shanghai Normal, and Peking University have also been strengthened. African Studies is also present in China Foreign Affairs University, Tianjin University of Technology and Education, and Xian Tan University, to mention just a few others.

The earlier tradition in China was that doctoral research in African studies was essentially desk research. This has only just started to change in the last few years, with ambitious field-work projects being launched in Africa with funding from sectoral ministries, such as the Ministry of Education.[38]

It is worth noting that while China has been setting up African studies centres, African countries have not been setting up centres for the study of Africa in China. No African cultural centres either have been set up in China. There is, Bodomo argues, an asymmetry in the cultural diplomacy of China and Africa which some of the more powerful economies of Africa could help to set right by setting up Pan-African cultural institutes in China (2009), using the phrase 'Africa-China' instead of always China-Africa.

A further support for the strengthening of African studies in China has been the FOCAC IV initiative of the China-Africa Joint Research and Exchange Programme. This led to the establishment of the programme and its launch in Beijing in March 2010.[39] But allied to this has been the launch of the China-Africa Think Tank Forum, launched in Hangzhou and Jinhua in 27–28 October 2011, under the auspices of the Institute of African Studies and China-Africa Business School of Zhejiang Normal University.[40] These official partnerships between China and Africa bring academics and analysts from China and Africa together in very different ways from the regular Western academic international conferences. Thus the Declaration at the end of the Think Tank Forum talks of setting up:

...links among Chinese and African think tanks, and scholars from other parts of the world with an interest in Sino-African relations to conduct dialogues, exchanges and studies on Africa's political and economic situation, Sino-African relations and related issues, in a bid

[38] A good example would be a 16–country study of higher education in Africa, already referred to, which is being carried out by Zhejiang Normal University.
[39] See: http://www.focac.org/eng/dsjbzjhy/t676571.htm State Councillor, Dai Bingguo's launching speech for the Forum mixed the celebration of China-Africa friendship's 1000–year history with a series of highly practical proposal for academic, people to people engagement.
[40] The China-Africa Business School is another partnership which is actively going ahead between ZNU and the University of Stellenbosch.

to promote mutual understanding, consolidate friendship, present recommendations and give a better play to the role of Chinese and African think tanks in boosting the comprehensive cooperative relations between the two sides ( http://www.focac.org/eng/xsjl/zflhyjjljh/).

*6. High-level exchanges and 7. Exchanges of students*
In the Chinese system, high-level visits and delegations have played a key role in initiating some of the agreements just discussed above, as well as agreeing to African students and professionals coming to China. The Ministry of Education claims that since the 1950s and the beginning of education cooperation, there have been no less than 100 educational delegations going to Africa, and more than 90 delegations and groups coming to China from Africa (China, 2003: 7). What is not so clear is whether China paid for only the Chinese delegations, or whether they also contributed to the costs of some of the African delegations to China. For instance in the high-level 2011 UNESCO-China-Africa University Leaders Meeting of 24–25 October 2011, which brought to Paris most of the 40 heads of universities participating in the 20+20 partnership programme, it would appear that China basically sponsored the meeting. Also in the Shanghai Expo of 2010, the huge Africa Pavilion which included all but a handful of the larger African countries which provided their own pavilions (e.g. Egypt, South Africa, Angola, Nigeria etc) was basically a Chinese aid project with the whole structure being provided by China, and individual African countries being given $US 650,000 each in support of their being present and developing country pavilions within the overall structure (King, 2010e).

Equally on the side of 'exchanges of students', the MOE states that between 1952 and 2002 they accepted 15,333 'person-time African students' of which 80 per cent were on China government scholarships, but although the term exchanges is used, there is no information on how many Chinese students went to Africa on government scholarships. We do know that under Mubarak's regime some 20 government scholarships were offered by Egypt to China, and 50 the other way round, but elsewhere on the continent the numbers offered to China have been minute. Just one was offered by Kenya for example (King, 2010d). In respect of this student exchange dimension, therefore, there would seem to be a very considerable asymmetry between China's scholarship offer to Africa and vice versa.[41] But the whole question of African students in China is taken up in the next chapter.

---

[41] See further *NORRAG News* 45 for the politics of scholarships and awards.

## Locating and categorising the unique[42] and dramatic case of the Confucius Institutes (CIs)

It may be useful, in concluding this analysis of China's higher education modalities, to comment on how this particular CI initiative, which is now a global phenomenon, illustrates many of the facets of China's HRD cooperation with Africa. However, as mentioned above, the CIs were not noted as one of the seven main modalities of China-Africa education cooperation by the Ministry of Education in 2003, since they were only launched in November 2004. But conceptually they can be seen as the continuation, on a much larger scale, of the sending of Chinese language teachers abroad, and including to Africa which was discussed earlier.

First and most crucially, the CIs are not intended to be a supply-side modality, driven by the ambitions of the Chinese government. Unlike the analogous language and culture institutes such as the Alliance Française, British Council, Cervantes and Goethe Institutes whose numbers and locations are determined by their respective governments, the rhetoric is that the CIs are demand-driven.[43] In other words, their numbers reflect the demand at the highest level of universities for a Confucius Institute. This doubtless explains why the largest number of CIs are to be found in the USA (over 70). By contrast there are just 33 in Africa as of 2013 in 26 different countries.[44]

The CIs also differ from their European comparators (above) as they do not operate on the high streets of capital cities. Instead they are located right inside their host universities,[45] and they operate as close partnerships between particular higher education institutions (HEIs) in Africa, for example, and appropriate partners in China (often proposed by the initiating university). They are clearly seen by the Chinese Language Council (Hanban) in Beijing as a response to the many requests coming from universities world-wide. This puts them in a rather different category from the other pledges in the FOCAC agenda, since, significantly and appropriately, there are no triennial targets for CI expansion laid out in the FOCAC action plans, in the way that there are, for instance, for long- and short-term training.

---

[42] None of the other obvious BRICS nations, such as India, Brazil or Russia, has sought to promote its major national language in the way that China has done. Nor has Japan done so during its own economic ascendancy, perhaps not least because it did so unsuccessfully during the 1930s in its military expansion in South East Asia and the Pacific.

[43] Although the great majority of the CI initiatives may indeed be demand-driven, there do seem to have been occasions where the visit of the top Chinese leadership may have encouraged the idea of a new CI.

[44] Some African countries have more than one CI: South Africa has four; Kenya has three, Nigeria and Zambia have two. New CIs have just been agreed for Mozambique and Kenya.

[45] In the case of my former university, Nairobi, the CI is located in the main quad with a link to its partner, Tianjin Normal; and Edinburgh University has allocated part of one of its fine old buildings to its CI, with a link to Fudan University in Shanghai.

Second, the CIs are increasingly operating as an additional focus for exchange and cultural cooperation between China and Africa. Through their parent body, Hanban, the Chinese Language Council Headquarters in Beijing, there are a wide range of short-term and longer-term scholarships available for African learners of Chinese to be exposed to China. For the African CIs alone there was a substantial number of longer term scholarship opportunities offered in 2010. This makes the CI scholarship window a significant addition to the offerings from the China Scholarship Council. These CI awards are not reflected in the FOCAC triennial targets. Nor are these degree and one-year awards the largest part of the CI opportunities to go to China; various shorter term awards including for study tours and summer camps have larger numbers. Thus Nairobi University's CI had 26 students going for shorter periods than a year in 2009, and the second Kenyan CI, at Kenyatta University, had 16 going for these shorter periods in 2011. By contrast, in South Africa, the CI at Rhodes University had 19 going to China in 2011 on shorter-term training. The Stellenbosch CI sent 16 in 2011 for a short-term visit. In other words, these four CIs alone had over 75 students going to China in the course of just one year for short-term language and cultural exposure.

For a single country such as Kenya, therefore, the CI window provides a substantial additional exposure to China when the short-term and longer-term CI awards are put together. The Kenyatta and Nairobi CI numbers can be added to the regular CSC scholarships of over 40, and the short-term training awards of 198, making a total of over 300 Kenyans going to China through these three channels in any one year. In addition every year, the two Vice-Chancellors along with their Chinese and Kenyan co-directors of the CI will go to the huge annual CI Convention in Beijing.[46]

Third, as to locating the Confucius Institute as a particular cooperation modality, there are clearly problems with identifying it as a form of official development assistance (ODA), for the good reason that perhaps as much as 50 per cent of the support from China to CIs is going to so-called developed countries, such as Australia, France, Japan, UK and USA. That does not alter the fact that it may be regarded as ODA in respect of the CIs in Africa. Yet all Confucius institutes, including in OECD countries, currently receive a generous annual subsidy from Hanban for their work, apart from receiving language teachers and volunteers, and the offer of the short- and long-term scholarships just mentioned.[47] Furthermore, it seems that there is scope for the Confucius Institute to become a mechanism for widening the inter-university cooperation beyond language to include

---

[46] This annual convention brings to Beijing from each participating university, North and South, their president or vice-chancellor along with the Chinese and host country co-directors of the Confucius Institute. The convention has well over 1000 delegates from the c 390 CIs worldwide.

[47] The fact that all CIs, regardless of their location in the North or the South, receive this subsidy, makes the CI a rather special institutional development. The subsidy has differed over time, but has been US$100,000 for many CIs, and much higher in the case of some CIs in Africa.

Chinese studies and culture. It will be interesting to see if in certain university settings in Africa, such as Nairobi and Rhodes Universities, this process may develop into larger Centres for Chinese Studies.

Where there already is a Centre for Chinese Studies in Stellenbosch University, the very active presence of the CI with its teaching links to the Modern Foreign Languages Department as well as its outreach to no less than 13 satellite schools and college in the surrounding towns and villages, has meant that there has been built up a very substantial academic research and Chinese teaching presence in the university along with a major extramural dimension.[48]

On the African university side of the CI, however, it is expected that the host university will provide accommodation for the CI itself, as well as for the staff coming from China. In addition, there is an expectation that some salary for the visitors will be provided, beyond whatever they and their families may continue to get back home in China. So there is a degree of symmetry in the support of the CIs, both in cash or in kind.

Fourth, and at the more general level of our concerns with South-South cooperation, reciprocity, and difference from traditional donors, the CI modality can be distinguished from other language and cultural promotion agencies by its being embedded within universities across the world. This has produced much greater media interest in some quarters about the CIs' potential influence (for good and for ill) than the almost invisible movement of some 50,000 African professionals through the short-term training programme just discussed. Of our seven different modalities for China-African higher education cooperation, this language promotion modality has been by far the most widely contested and discussed. Would the CI become a vehicle for propaganda, for stifling debate, or for promoting particular versions of Mandarin? Sometimes, as in the University of Cape Town, these concerns effectively held up the start of the CI for years after the initial memorandum of agreement had been signed. But as more and more leading universities sought to welcome CIs (some of those in 2010 being Stanford, Chicago and Columbia), and as those which have had a CI for several years found there was no interference with support for critical seminar programmes, the concerns have remained muted.[49]

There have been at least two different ways in which CIs have become institutionalised within universities. First, where there was no tradition of teaching Chinese, as in the University of Nairobi, or the University of Cape Town, the CI has been directly responsible for getting Chinese adopted as a degree subject. Second, where there has been a Chinese language department already, as in Stellenbosch in South Africa for instance, the CI has played a supplementary and supportive role, offering opportunities for

<hr>

[48] See further Kotze on the integration of CI into the university and community (2012).
[49] See however the concerns: with the CI impact on non-simplified Chinese characters (Churchman, 2011); and with the hesitation about opening CIs in Japan except in the private universities (Zhe, 2010). Note also that there is only one CI in the whole of India. We discuss this further in Chapter 6.

additional Chinese learning, links to special seminars and activities, and not least the increased possibility of going to China itself. A third approach is illustrated in the Ethio-China Polytechnic College where all the students take Chinese as a compulsory subject, but staffing prevents this being much more than elementary.

The CI movement may be loosely classified as a form of soft power, or cultural diplomacy. But it is also a very powerful mechanism for the further internationalisation of well over 150 mainland universities that are the China partners of CIs overseas. A few of these well-known Chinese universities have no less than ten CI link partners across the world. Xiamen, the partner of Stellenbosch, has 15 CI partners. This internationalising dimension was a point made very forcefully by China's Minister of Education, Yuan Guiren, who claimed in November 2010 that the global expansion of Confucius Institutes was an efficient way to promote 'soft power' and appeal to more overseas students to come to China. The Minister recognised that it was a combination of China's culture and history, its economic development, and its growing international influence that was drawing in more foreign students: 'China, with its rapid economic growth, will provide foreign students with not only a platform for learning but also employment opportunities' (Chen, 2010a).

But the terms 'soft power' and 'internationalisation' do not do justice to the demand side of the CI equation. The CIs are not so much creating and promoting the demand for Chinese language learning but are responding to a widespread vocational (and professional) interest in many countries for acquiring expertise in Chinese. This interest in Chinese is of course inseparable from the very visible presence of Chinese enterprise, industry and commerce, as well as new Chinese communities, in so many different countries, especially in Africa.[50]

The CI phenomenon underlines and illustrates, therefore, a good deal of what we have been analysing in this chapter. It is fundamentally a university partnership mechanism, with substantial contributions being made from both sides. It is not narrowly concerned with the promotion of language, but covers several other dimensions of the arts, culture, history, poetry and even technologies[51] and politics of China. And with the partner universities in China, there are now growing connections with new centres overseas. It is far from being therefore a stand-alone education project, as there are vitally important links and relations sustaining the initiative from outside the education sector.

Finally, in terms of South-South cooperation, it should be noted that as part of the CI presence in particular universities, such as Nairobi, Kenyan staff have gone to teach Swahili in the partner university, Tianjin Normal. Chinese students have also pursued the learning of Hausa in Bayero University in Nigeria, though this may not have been directly through the

[50]  See King (2010d) for further illustration.
[51]  In the Hanban headquarters, the exhibition area has a section on the technologies historically associated with China.

two CIs in Nigeria. However, we have said enough to make it obvious that the Confucius Institute phenomenon is far from being just a South-South movement of solidarity and engagement in language and culture promotion. If indeed China is South, then the CI movement is arguably as much South-North as South-South, given the sheer number of CIs in USA and Europe. It is a global initiative rather than merely an expression of South-South cooperation. But we shall need to return and interrogate some of concerns about the CIs and soft power in the final chapter.

## The FOCAC umbrella for HRD targets and the intensification of China-Africa higher education partnerships, 2003–2015

Before concluding this chapter, we shall now note how most of the modalities we have just been reviewing from the Ministry of Education's particular angle of 2003 are also supported in several different ways by the FOCAC process which we referred to earlier as the formalisation of many of the modalities which had been used prior to FOCAC. But first a word about the particularity of FOCAC itself.

It is interesting to reflect on the fact that the very year, 2000, in which the UN and other multilateral and bilateral agencies set out the six Education for All (EFA) goals in the Dakar World Forum on Education for All, and the UN set out the Millennium Development Goals (MDGs) following the Millennium Summit of September 2000, China launched its unique Pan-African forum for cooperation with Africa in October 2000. Although China's cooperation with Africa would continue to be an intensely bilateral activity, reinforced by very high-level visits of Chinese leaders to African countries each year from 2000, it was invaluable diplomatically for China also to have developed this Pan-African umbrella organisation.

China is almost unique amongst donors in having such a mechanism, the Forum on China-Africa Cooperation (FOCAC), that deals with virtually the whole of Africa.[52] Unlike many traditional donors e. g., France and Britain, China does not cooperate principally with a special sub-set of countries with historic, linguistic, geographic or economic ties with the donor country, such as the British Commonwealth. Or rather, it cooperates with the whole of Africa except the four states which still have diplomatic relations with Taiwan.[53] Also, China has sought to avoid these FOCAC engagements appearing like aid or development assistance. Rather they are presented as elements of a joint agreement between two partners,

[52] Arguably, Japan led the way on combining Pan-African and bilateral cooperation. But both countries have substantial bilateral discussions at the country level, leading to country programmes, and they also have continent-wide agreements through the Tokyo International Conference on African Development (TICAD) and FOCAC respectively.

[53] These are: Burkina Faso, The Gambia, São Tomé and Princípé, and Swaziland

'featuring political equality and mutual trust, economic win-win cooperation and cultural exchanges' (FOCAC, 2009: para. 1.2). China would also
argue, like Japan, that its cooperation is basically in the responsive mode,
as we mentioned above.

So when it comes to judgements, in Paris Declaration terms, about the
African 'country ownership' of the FOCAC pledges and commitments,
clearly the declarations and action plans from the five large FOCAC
conferences are shot through with references to 'the two sides agreed...',
as noted earlier. Even though more still needs to be known in detail about
how these different agreements are actually reached between China and
the 50 separate African countries, the outcomes are claimed to be owned
by both China and Africa. There is always a danger with quantitative
targets, which the FOCAC conferences initiated in 2003, that reaching
these becomes the central focus of the cooperation and that the wider
human engagement between China and Africa which we have been
discussing in tertiary education becomes less important.

It is vital, therefore, to underline also the fact that 'education' is not
identified as a FOCAC objective in a separate silo, like one of the Education MDGs. Former President Hu Jintao's speech at the FOCAC III summit
in November 2006 presented education within a much wider cultural,
scientific, medical and tourism agenda:

> Third, expand exchange for cultural enrichment. We will strengthen
> cultural and people-to-people exchanges to increase mutual under-
> standing and friendship between our two peoples and particularly
> between the younger generation [sic]. We will enhance exchanges and
> cooperation in education, science and technology, culture, public
> health, sports and tourism to provide intellectual motivation and
> cultural support for China-Africa cooperation. (Hu, 2006)

This is a very different world from the education MDGs of universal
primary education or gender equity in education, or the six EFA Dakar
Goals. In the former President's rationale it would appear that education
is simply one element in a broader goal of cultural cooperation, mutual
understanding and friendship. It is important not to lose sight of this over-
arching objective, which is itself part of the primary objective of deepening a 'political relation of equality and mutual trust' between China and
Africa. The 'targetisation' of these common understandings and their
translation into quantifiable targets often mean that the overall purpose
and the ultimate drivers of the cooperation are lost.[54]

This suggests that when we have looked at the different 'educational'
activities or modalities, we should recognise that they are not seen as
'education goals' in their own right. Indeed even in the translation of
mutual trust and solidarity into quantifiable human resource goals, education is not picked out for separate treatment; rather, education is part of a

---

[54] For the potentially distorting impact of target-setting in education, see King and Rose (2005),
and in that special issue the contribution of Jansen (2005).

much wider human resource agenda covering all professional fields but including agriculture, health and volunteering, as can be seen in the following 8th pledge from the Beijing Summit of 2006. Scholarships and school buildings are part of a larger HRD commitment, as we noted in Chapter 1:

> Over the next three years, train 15,000 African professionals; send 100 senior agricultural experts to Africa; set up 10 special agricultural technology demonstration centres in Africa; build 30 hospitals in Africa and provide RMB 300 million of grant for providing artemisin and building 30 malaria prevention and treatment centres to fight malaria in Africa; dispatch 300 youth volunteers to Africa; build 100 rural schools in Africa; and increase the number of Chinese government scholarships to African students from the current 2000 per year to 4000 per year by 2009. (Hu, 2006)

## The higher education focus of China's HRD partnerships with Africa

That said, what do the dimensions of higher education and HRD cooperation amount to, six years later, from the latest FOCAC V pledges of July 2012 in Beijing? They cover at least the following:

The specifically HRD and education pledges build on the format of the previous FOCAC commitments, with an increase in long term Chinese government scholarships to 6000 a year by 2015 and the continuation of the 20+20 cooperation plan for more intensive one-to-one cooperation between 20 Chinese universities or vocational colleges and 20 African counterparts. Within this modality there is support promised to African universities for establishing China research centres. Intriguingly, in FOCAC V there is no longer school-building as with the 100 rural schools of the previous plans (2007–2009) and 50 China-Africa friendship schools for the triennium (2012–2012). Finally, in the 'education' section, there is a strong commitment to continue to develop Confucius Institutes and Classrooms with teaching staff, personnel training and teaching materials. There is also a new form of trilateral cooperation with trust funding of US$2 million to UNESCO annually in support of education in Africa, especially higher education. Under human resources development, but not education, there is a very substantial rise in commitment to the already massive short-term training of what FOCAC calls 'professionals'. Now in FOCAC V an increase by no less than 30 per cent brings the total to 30,000 over the triennium (China, 2012).

In this way, at the higher education level, this focus on China being exposed to Africa and vice versa is central to the logic of China's cooperation. So when the FOCAC IV Action Plan (para 6.4.1) mentions: 'The two sides noted that people-to-people exchanges are conducive to mutual understanding and important to the deepening of China-Africa friendship. The two sides remain committed to promoting people-to-people exchanges', it is making a crucially important point about the nature of the cooperation process (FOCAC, 2009).

Reflecting on FOCAC from the ethical perspective of this chapter, the discourse is of course familiar, and much of it has a 50–60 year history. But what of the reality? Does FOCAC, with its Chinese follow-up committee to review the implementation of the targets, and on the assessment of their achievement, square up to the mutual benefit and political equality claims of this historical discourse? Most of the HRD commitments and pledges are official development assistance (ODA) in OECD Development Assistance Committee (DAC) terminology. But equally most of the HRD commitments are in fact tied aid, and the actual amounts of scholarships, awards, schools construction, and so on, are decided by China in a whole series of bilateral conversations; this is perhaps not very different from the way the TICAD commitments from Japan are implemented. But it suggests that FOCAC is really a Pan-African umbrella for continuing bilateral priorities in decision-making.[55] This seems to be different from the way that India has delegated to the African Union the decisions about the location of its various technical, technological and professional training institutes, promised to Africa, after the India-Africa Forum in New Delhi in 2008 (GOI, 2008; ITEC, 2011).[56] One consequence of this difference may be that FOCAC plus bilateralism leads to faster implementation than allocating the decision to the African Union in the India-Africa process.

Ian Taylor has concluded his useful, very short summary of what was agreed in each of the four FOCAC[57] conferences by a rather negative comment that 'Symbolism and spin then is (sic) at the root of the whole FOCAC enterprise, and works (sic) at various levels and is (sic) directed both toward Africa, toward the world *and* toward the Chinese population' (Taylor, 2011, 103). Much more needs to be known about the involvement of Africa's ambassadors in Beijing, the attitudes of foreign ministries in Africa, and the attitude of the African Union before we can be clear about Africa's joint ownership of the FOCAC process.

But as far as FOCAC's formalisation of the long-standing traditions of higher education cooperation between China and Africa is concerned, it has proved a useful vehicle for situating a set of activities within an apparently tight framework of co-ownership. The downside of moving from an historical tradition of providing assistance 'to the best of its ability' to one where assistance is set in terms of targets is that the targets begin to control the process. The expectation prior to the last FOCAC conference of July 2012 was surely that the HRD targets for FOCAC would have to increase

---

[55] This is perhaps partly what Taylor means by questioning the 'value-added nature of FOCAC beyond the symbolism' (Taylor, 2011: 103).
[56] The India-African Institute for Educational Planning and Administration (IAIEPA) is being located in the University of Burundi through the decision of the African Union.
[57] By July 2012, there had been five FOCAC conferences.

yet again. Otherwise, what would have been the message? In this sense, FOCAC may have become something of a strait-jacket from China doing 'the best it can' to China doing more on many of the targets. FOCAC and its targetisation has arguably moved China a long way from what Zhou Enlai talked about in Africa and Asia in 1963–4:

> On the character of China's solidarity at the time, it was often stated by Premier Zhou during this major tour of Africa and Asia that 'mutual economic assistance among the Asian and African countries was the kind of assistance between poor friends who were in the same boat pulling oars together' (China, 2000).

It is worth adding on the subject of goals and targets that so far China has avoided being drawn into the very intensive debate about the renewal of the global millennium targets. Currently, in April 2013, this still seems to be a preoccupation of the OECD donors and northern-based NGOs and think-tanks.

## Conclusions about cooperation, ethics and reciprocity

We end this exploration of the modalities of China's higher education cooperation with Africa with a number of insights from using the lenses of reciprocity and mutual benefit, and with some conclusions about how in practice this field of cooperation differs from the approaches of traditional donors.

First, the majority of HRD items of educational assistance from China would fall into the OECD-DAC definitions of official development assistance, such as school and university construction, short and long-term training, and even perhaps the Confucius Institutes in Africa.

Second, most of these modalities have been commonplace both with traditional DAC donors, and many of the new development actors. Thus, China and India are two countries which sponsor some of the largest number of short-term training courses world-wide, with only Japan and Germany competing in terms of total numbers (*NORRAG News* (NN), 45). Long-term scholarships remain on the agenda of many traditional donors, and they are very frequently one of the largest and earliest HRD items offered by new or re-emerging development actors such as Brazil, India and China, as well as the Republic of Korea (NN 45). Similarly, when it comes to school construction, JICA is probably by far the largest provider in the world of school buildings, including in Africa. When it comes to despatching teachers, language teachers and volunteers, there is little doubt that traditional donors have had very large-scale volunteer programmes for years, and that China just began sending volunteers to Africa shortly before the Beijing FOCAC III of 2006. During the ten to twenty years after the independence of most African countries, France, Britain, and also the USA sent very significant numbers of teachers to

Africa, both at secondary and university level. India also was the source of a large number of teachers at school and university level, though this tended to be at the initiative of individuals rather than through a government scheme.

Even the development of African studies centres is not something that is special to China. Just as China was celebrating, in 2011, 50 years since the foundation of the Institute of West Asian and African Studies, so Edinburgh University was doing likewise in June 2012. The only modality which seems clearly different from traditional donors is that China's mechanism for promoting language and culture is essentially based on a university partnership model, whereas all the major comparators, from Spain, France, USA, Germany and Britain, are based on stand-alone institutes in the national or regional capitals of both the developing and developed world, with no obvious partnership dimension. But we have argued that China's language and culture promotion initiative through the Confucius since 2004 is not just about South-South cooperation and exchange; it is certainly as much about South-North partnership, if we continue to accept that China is part of the South.

Beyond this difference in the modality of cooperation, the overall difference from traditional donors, if any, seems to come down to the ethical discourse about mutuality which we have picked out throughout this chapter. What difference does this rationale and these principles make to the delivery of the various items we have discussed? Is a scholarship or an award or a new tertiary level network different because of the background discourse under which it is offered? Perhaps not. From the perspective of the thousands of individuals who profit from scholarships and awards worldwide, the difference in the ethical discourse of many traditional donors, which claims to derive from unreciprocated giving and may currently focus on poverty reduction and good governance as opposed to the mutual benefit, equality, and common development, does not alter the quality of the training offered. Indeed, these different discourses may not be able to alter the racial attitudes of those who interact with the awardees in universities in China, as we shall explore in Chapter 3.

What difference then do the principles of mutual benefit and equality actually make to China's education cooperation? We have established that mutual benefit and common good or common development have been the explicit rationale for China's cooperation with Africa over 60 years. It is also clear that an ethical aid policy is not unique to China; South Korea for example has demonstrated that it feels a debt to those nations that supported it during the Korean war, and it illustrates a 'sentimental bonding' to many developing countries through its knowledge sharing programme (Kim, 2011: 12).

In China itself, it is possible to find analysts who acknowledge that these are the basic principles of China's aid, but they do not necessarily explain the implications of taking this stance. Here is an example from a recent paper on China's foreign aid:

*Insisting on the Principle of Equity and Mutual Benefit, and Common Development.*

China-Africa education development and cooperation always insist on the principle of equity and mutual benefits, and common development. They propose to form the multi-form and multi-level cooperation mechanism beneficial to each other by project cooperation, personnel and information ex change, aiming at advancing the capacity building of both sides and realizing co-prosperity. They frequently utilize the wording representing the bi-directional cooperation of equity and mutual benefits, such as cooperation, communication, exchange, dialogue, common development, etc., but not those of unidirectional assistance. (Li et al., 2010)

*China's Foreign Aid* reverberates with the same principles of 'equality, mutual benefit and common development' (China, 2011a: 4). Meanwhile, the historian, Li Anshan, has made the important point that though China's *policies* may have changed from the 1950s to the present, 'another look reveals the persistence of core principles that continue to underpin the relationship' (Li, 2007: 74). These are of course non-interference or a respect for sovereignty, equality, mutual benefit, and friendship. Despite being an academic analyst, Li Anshan can assert that 'China will never waver in its principles of treating Africa with equality, respect and mutual development' (ibid.: 87). We noted this also with Liu Hongwu, Director of IAS.

The result of this synergy between changing policies and unchanging principles is that a particular kind of academic analysis has emerged which maps the changes in the implementation of the modalities of educational cooperation over different political periods, but does not seek to assess changes in the core principles. Indeed even the modalities of cooperation remain remarkably unchanged over the period from the late 1980s till the present. So while Western analysts might review the history of educational cooperation with Africa against key milestones such as commissions, world conferences, influential World Bank reports, as well as Africa's own initiatives, Chinese analysts have used the key modalities such as student exchange, despatch of teachers, and university partnerships to map the quantitative changes over time, and then have used the framework of the five triennial FOCAC conferences to look at the quantitative implications for the different modalities of cooperation. He (2006), Niu (2009), Li Wei et al. (2010) have all very usefully applied slightly different periodisations of the last 50–60 years and have mapped on to them the quantitative changes in the key modalities. The model for this approach via the main modalities has been adopted in both the commemorative volume on *China-Africa Education Cooperation* which we have drawn upon in this chapter (China, 2003), and in the much more detailed *China-Africa Education Cooperation* (China, MOE, 2005, in Chinese) which has been one of the key resources on the periodisation of China's cooperation with Africa.

But they have not discussed how the principles themselves have constructed a cooperation regime that is not based on the unreciprocated generosity of the traditional donors but on a strategic reciprocal partnership. We have argued that the analysis of reciprocity and mutual benefit should not be carried out within the HRD silo alone; to look at mutuality only within the HRD modalities would suggest a highly asymmetrical China-Africa partnership with China doing most of the giving. Rather, the HRD modalities need to be set alongside what China is gaining from the China-Africa Development Fund, for example, or from other agreements made bilaterally at the country level.

There is one last point that needs to be made about reciprocity and academic analysis. What has been particular about this Chinese account of China-Africa education, and the same would be true of China-Africa cooperation more generally, is that it is highly China-centric; it is about African students and trainees coming to China, Chinese teachers and experts going to Africa, Chinese delegations going to Africa and vice versa, bilateral cooperation between Chinese and African universities, and more recently the development of Confucius Institutes in many of these university partnerships. In this respect it is reminiscent of Britain's account of *An Education Policy for British Aid* published twenty years ago (ODA, 1990) in which on virtually every page there would be a link to British resources and British organisations providing aid.[58] But there the similarity ends.

China's education cooperation, like cooperation in health, agriculture, infrastructure etc., is presented against an overall framework of core principles which we have been discussing in this chapter. It may be possible to interrogate and assess the different education modalities against these principles, and to an extent we have just begun to examine this possibility in this chapter; or it may be that the principles such as mutual benefit and common good cannot be understood completely within the HRD silo. Instead, the various HRD elements of cooperation need to be seen along with Chinese investment and macroeconomic engagement with Africa if the meaning of mutual benefit, and so on, is to be fully understood.

We started this chapter with a question mark after the sub-title: modalities for mutual cooperation? In conclusion, we might have to argue that in reality what these modalities reveal is an old voice, old values, and an old partnership, which China has embraced for 60 years. Much more work needs to be done on these 60-year-old principles in their relationship with policies and with practice. Perhaps this can only be done when African as well as Chinese analysts examine this synergy between principles, policies and practice, in the way that was done by Sweden in its examination of *A New Partnership for African Development* (Henock et al., 1997). The first stage of such a review has been completed with the publication of a book on *Sino-African Cooperation* with 37 chapters, each written by a Chinese academic (Liu & Yang, 1999). A logical next step after these *Chinese*

[58] This has changed dramatically since 1997 and with the untying of British aid.

*perspectives on Sino-African relations* would surely be *African perspectives on Sino-African relations,*[59] or better still, *Chinese and African perspectives on Sino-African relations.*[60]

[59] A book does exist with virtually the same name: *African Perspectives on China in Africa,* (Manji and Marks, (2007), but, unlike the Swedish initiative, that has not been supported and encouraged by China.

[60] See also Harneit-Sievers, A., Marks, S. and Naidu, S. (eds), (2010). *Chinese and African Perspectives on China in Africa,* Pambazuka Press, Fahamu, Oxford.

# 3

**African Students** Changing characteristics
**in China** contexts & challenges

African students are clearly a key foreign policy issue for China. Indeed, 'Exchanging students between China and Africa is one of the oldest forms of China-African cooperation' (China, MOE, 2005: 12).

In the White Paper on *China's Foreign Aid* they are mentioned as having been part of the aid agenda since the 1950s. The total number of students trained by 2009 is mentioned precisely as 70,627, and the total number on China scholarships in 2009 was 11,185 (China, 2011a: 14).

Students from Africa were not referred to as a category in Zhou Enlai's eight principles of foreign aid, enunciated in early 1964 in Accra on his African tour (China, 2000), but they are routinely claimed as an element in China-Africa education cooperation. Thus in the volume published in 2003 in conjunction with the Forum on China-Africa Educational Cooperation, the theme of 'Exchanges of Students' took by far the largest part (40 pages) of the seven modalities of educational cooperation used by China for Africa. Again, there was a special concern shown for the history of this particular mechanism, stretching back to the first students, at least in modern times, who came from Egypt to China in 1956. But there was also a powerful ethical claim made about this category of educational cooperation as we noted in Chapter 2, especially in regard to the great care to be shown them, the respect due to their cultures and customs whilst in China, and to their prospects on their return:

> The majority of African students work hard and score great achieve-
> ments in their schoolwork. African students who return to their home-
> lands have played positive roles in their nations' politics, economics as
> well as cultural development respectively. (China, 2003: 17)[1]

There are two main dimensions of this capacity-building cooperation

[1] Dr. Mulatu Teshome is used as an illustration of this in the celebratory volume; at the time of its publication he was Speaker of the Ethiopian House of Federation; and by 2010 was Ethiopia's ambassador to Turkey. He had spent some 9 years doing bachelors, masters and doctorate in Beijing University (King, 2011a)

according to *China's African Policy* (China, 2006). One is the training of African personnel, many of whom already have jobs but who have been coming to China for short-term courses under the auspices of the African Human Resources Development Fund since the early 2000s. This was looked at in Chapter 2. The other dimension is the continuation of the exchange of students between China and Africa (ibid:. 7).

In what follows, we shall see that there is not an abundance of sources on either of these two training modalities, short-term or long-term. But the few sources that do exist are much more concerned with the longer-term scholarship students from Africa than with the short-term training awards. We shall note that several of these sources are preoccupied with the problems of racist perceptions of Africans by Chinese students, and African student awareness of these attitudes, and to some extent also inadequacy of scholarship funds. In other words their focus is a challenge to the claim made above by the Chinese authorities. The issue of racial characterisation of African students appears to be sharply different, however, at different periods over the last 50 years.

On the other hand, we shall see that there is a tendency in several of the Chinese sources,[2] both government and academic, to focus on the quantitative dimension of African students and trainees. This emphasis is if anything increased with the formation of the Forum on China-Africa Cooperation (FOCAC) in October 2000. Particularly following the FOCAC meeting of 2003 in Addis Ababa and the Beijing summit of 2006, the African student and trainee modalities become principally represented as quantitative targets to be reached over the following triennium. There is still reference to the importance of encouraging more exchanges and closer cooperation between institutions of higher learning on both sides (China, 2006: 12). But the core message for instance in Beijing FOCAC III was the increase in government scholarships from 2000 awards in 2006 to 4000 awards by 2009, and to a total of 6000 by 2015. A similar commitment was made for the short-term training of African professionals from 10,000 to 30,000 in total over that same period from 2006 to 2015.

What is missing in this quantitative approach to students and trainees by the Chinese government is some sense of who these students are, where they come from, what their aspirations are, why they chose China as a destination for study. Apart from the brightly coloured pages of exchange students enjoying their classes in China, in the celebratory volume on *China-Africa Education Cooperation*, there is very little in the public domain that gives any sense of the quality of this experience of three, four or more years of study on scholarships in China.

Even though African students have been coming on government scholarships for over five decades, there has not been any formal evaluation of

---

[2] The Chinese sources consulted have been primarily in English such as FOCAC, but one of the key texts on China-Africa education cooperation is only available in Chinese. This has been translated for the author by Zhang Zhongwen in the Centre of African Studies, University of Edinburgh.

the individual, institutional or societal impact of this major training initiative. Intriguingly, the Commonwealth Scholarship scheme has also been going for over 50 years (since 1959), and in that period some 16,000 scholars alone have come to the UK.[3] Over that same time frame double the number of Africans have come to study in China on government support.[4] However, for the 16,000 scholarships held in the UK, a major review of this experience is available, and an attempt to assess impact in key development priority areas (CSCUK, 2009).[5] China is not alone in not having sought to assess the impact over time of their training provision in this area;[6] other major middle-income scholarship providers such as Brazil and India have not done so either.

Accordingly, in this chapter we shall seek to put some flesh on the skeletal African numbers for this long-standing major education scheme of the Chinese Government.

## Changing attitudes of Chinese and African students?

We shall start by examining the sources that document the apparently very negative feelings of African students about their reception and treatment in China. Firstly, we shall take note of a very personal account by a Ghanaian student, John Hevi, who came to China in 1960, and presented his experience under the title *An African Student in China* (Hevi, 1963), and also of two Canadian scholars, Sandra Gillespie, who examined the experiences of African students almost 40 years later, in 1997, in a book called *South-South Transfer: A Study of Sino-African exchanges* (2001), and Barry Sautman who published a critical article in *China Quarterly* in 1994 on 'Anti-Black racism in post-Mao China'. We should also acknowledge the pioneering work of Frank Dikötter on the long history of racial stereotyping in China, and the adoption by some Chinese intellectuals in late 19th and early 20th century of some of the 'scientific' racism of the West towards Africans (Dikötter, 1992).[7]

Interestingly, both Hevi and Gillespie discussed similar numbers of African students as part of their investigations; Hevi's book concerns the 118 students who had been brought from eleven African countries in

[3] The total number of scholarships across the Commonwealth, e.g. to India, Malaysia, Canada etc was 26,000 by 2009.
[4] The figure was 12,384 African scholars to China by the end of 2002, since when there have been FOCAC triennial pledges of 1500, 4,000, 5,500 and 6,000 respectively in 2003, 2006, 2009 and 2012.
[5] Of the total of 16,000, 6,000 were traced by 2009, of which 2,400 took part in the survey. 61% of the survey respondents were from Commonwealth Africa.
[6] In the case of the short-term training this would be the responsibility of the Ministry of Commerce (MOFCOM) and for long-term students on government support, it would be the China Scholarship Council (CSC) under the Ministry of Education which would be ultimately responsible for any such analysis.
[7] See also on the early history of Africans in China, Wyatt, 2010. *The Blacks of Pre-modern China*.

1961–2 to study Chinese initially at the Institute of Foreign Languages in Beijing. He records dramatically that within nine months of being in China, 96 of the 118 had returned to Africa. Allegedly, this vote with their feet against China was the result of 'undesirable political indoctrination', 'language difficulty', 'poor educational standards', 'social life', 'hostility', 'spying', and 'racial discrimination' (Hevi, 1963: 117–136, see also Gillespie, 2009: 212). For Hevi, racial discrimination is 'the first item on our list of grievances' (ibid.: 183).[8]

Gillespie's fieldwork in 1997, some 34 years later, also found that racial tension was a key lens for understanding the African student experience in China. From 1979 through to 1989 there was what she characterized as a 'decade of conflict across campuses' (ibid.: 213). This culminated in the 'Nanjing Anti-African protests' of 1988–9 in which some 3000 Chinese students maintained a week-long anti-black student protest which also included wider concerns on human rights and democracy. Gillespie sees the Nanjing Anti-African protests as heralding, four months later, the pro-democracy movement of 1989, 'as Chinese "democrats" used the anti-African sentiments to direct protest against the party regime (Sautman, 1994, p. 426)' (Gillespie, ibid.).

Although there were no more protests over the next almost ten years, by the time Gillespie did her fieldwork in 1997, she still felt it was possible to present 'colour and money' [i.e., discrimination and allowances] as 'the essential elements in the lives of Africans today' (ibid.: 223). She surveyed 133 students from 29 countries, studying in four major cities, Nanjing, Beijing, Hangzhou and Shanghai.[9]

In the very first section reporting on the fieldwork interviews, the first seven sentences are a series of critical comments about Chinese racial prejudice towards black Africans from students from seven different countries. The rest of the report on the interviews is unremittingly negative. A whole series of terms are used by the African students and the counsellors in African embassies to capture the anatomy of the discrimination in China towards Africans: black devils, dirty, stupid, non-human, ugly, alien, poor and much else. So far from this being a win-win exchange as in China's rhetorical discourse reviewed in earlier chapters, the Africans are seen to come to China empty-handed. They fail to make friends because 'you can never have a Chinese friend'. Relations between African men and Chinese women are impossibly difficult; hence abstinence or resort to prostitutes are the only options.

As if open discrimination was not enough, the great majority of the African students who were interviewed (71%) found that their 'so-called

[8] Snow's unique historical account of *China's Encounter with Africa* (1988) draws on Hevi's book and comments that 'Its appearance rang down the curtain on a brief and catastrophic experiment' (ibid.: 199). Snow's analysis of the next 20 years of African student experience in China is invaluable. See particularly his account of the anti-African upheaval in Tianjin in 1986 (ibid.: 202).

[9] Gillespie also carried out more qualitative interviews with 5 African students (2 undergraduates and 3 postgraduates), 4 graduates, and 3 Counsellors from African embassies in Beijing.

scholarship' from China was 'woefully inadequate' in terms of covering costs. Further, there was no way that they could make up for the inadequacy of their scholarship by part-time jobs, even during the holiday periods. Such jobs were said to be not allowed.

The paradox therefore was that at a time when China was growing dramatically wealthier, the African students felt increasingly poor, and not least because they were as a group perceived to come from a continent that had fallen behind and had lost China's respect. This picture from Gillespie's research has no lighter side; there is nothing positive said about China's attitudes towards these particular students. Nothing at all.

Gillespie's was not the only account of sharp racial prejudice against the African students in China. She drew also on an earlier article and survey by Sautman (1994) who had analysed educated Chinese attitudes both towards Africans in general and towards the Chinese peasantry. This survey, carried out five years before Gillespie, in 1992, covered no less than 461 individuals, the majority of whom were students and intellectuals.[10] The survey was unusual in asking the Chinese respondents to rate seven groups of foreigners, including Africans, on ten attributes, and also to rate the Chinese peasantry, intellectuals and entrepreneurs on the same basis. The ten areas of inquiry covered: cultural level, intelligence, industriousness, behaviour, role models from which one can learn, attractiveness, interest in education, honesty, capacity to manage their own political affairs, and interest in economic development (Sautman, 1994: 429).

There were many similarly disparaging comments made by respondents both on Africans and on Chinese peasants. But for our present review, it was the Chinese university student comments on Africans that were the most 'vitriolic':

> Africans were said to be undisciplined, wild, ignorant, uninhibited, primitive, uncivilized, lazy, foolish, ugly, weak, rude, incapable, backward, troublemakers, nuisances, not welcome, and the least intelligent tribe of black apes. They were held to lack the strength to resist suppression, to project a bad impression and lack a capacity for progress. A few students remarked that Africans are honest, but also simple and backward. Unambiguously positive characterizations were strikingly absent. (Sautman, 434)

It must be noted that the respondents were not being asked specifically about African students but about Africans as a group in comparison with Indians, Western Europeans, Japanese, etc. Nevertheless for most of the roughly 160 student commentators, their only direct experience of Africans would have been of them as students.

However, within just over a decade and a half, in 2008, Sautman and Yan carried out a survey of some 300 African students in the various

---

[10] There were also high school students, People's Liberation Army recruits in a 'Normal' university, staff of two research institutes, also from a municipal planning office, a trade mission, as well as technical and managerial staff from a factory.

universities of the city of Tianjin. Their findings on attitudes of these students towards China and the Chinese were generally rather positive:

the [results] generally showed that African students had overall positive attitudes toward China and Chinese, not substantially different from those of African students in Africa.[11]

Many had experienced occasional street-level experience while in China; that is, they overheard negative remarks about them made by Chinese as they passed them on the street, but no institutional racism and fairly positive interaction with Chinese faculty and students (Sautman to KK, 22.10.2011). [12]

How could this be? Had something happened to government and university policy on Africa in just over a decade to explain such a radical shift? The West has become used to very rapid and dramatic changes in values and orientations in China. Could this really be another example? Had there been any major policy change on China Africa in this decade? Had there been any significant changes in the Chinese universities' connections with, and awareness of, Africa since the late 1990s? Were the African students coming to China with different perceptions of China as a destination for study than in earlier decades? We shall review some of the possible influences on changing attitudes towards Africa and African students in China in what follows.

Interestingly, Sautman and Yan's Nigerian research assistant for this Tianjin survey was less sure about the claimed change in attitudes: 'If I would rate or summarise the attitude of African students towards China on a scale of positive, slightly positive, indifferent, slightly negative and negative, I will say NEGATIVE' (former student to KK, 9.11.2011). We shall return to this apparent contradiction later in this chapter.

Significantly, by the time Gillespie actually published her findings in book form in 2001, the Forum on China-Africa Cooperation (FOCAC) had just been established (in October 2000). This proved to be an invaluable Pan-African mechanism for China to engage with Africa. The series of FOCAC's triennial meetings had started, in which, as we have said, the quantitative targets for African students and trainees to come to China became a regular dimension of their Action Plans, at least from 2003. That summit offered 10,000 short-term training awards through the African Human Resource Development Fund, and 1,500 scholarships, over the next triennium.

FOCAC did not therefore immediately or dramatically alter African scholarship numbers. Indeed, scholarships were not even mentioned in the FOCAC 2000 Summary of Commitments (Taylor, 2011: 43). Nevertheless, over the 1990s the total number of African students in China had reached 5,569, doubling from the 2245 who had been in China during the

---

[11]  Sautman and Yan (2009) carried out a study in nine African countries of some 2000 students and faculty regarding their perspectives on the Chinese and on China's developments in Africa.
[12]  See further Sautman and Yan, forthcoming.

1980s (He, 2006). Even when the third FOCAC, summit in Beijing in 2006 doubled African scholarship numbers from 2,000 to 4,000 by 2009, it must be remembered that the figure of 4,000 is the total number of African scholarship holders in China, of all years, by that date. It was not a commitment to 4,000 per annum; the actual figure for new scholarships each year would have been closer to 1,000.

In other words, it would be difficult to argue that between Gillespie's fieldwork in 1997 and Sautman and Yan's in 2008, there had been a dramatic rise in African scholarship student numbers. The number of privately funded African students was certainly on the rise since 1989 when they were first allowed, and there had been a sudden rise, since 2003, in the arrival of the FOCAC-sponsored short-term trainees. Over the five years to 2008, probably some 17,000 such African professionals had come to China, and the majority would have received their training in the new resource centres based in the universities. Indeed, one of these centres, for the training of African professionals in vocational education, was in one of the universities in Tianjin.

By 2008 (the time of the Sautman/Yan survey), FOCAC had certainly put Africa on the aid policy map of China, and progressive academics with international interests could see that Africa could bring visibility and policy influence to their universities. Thus, Yunnan University set up its Centre for Afro-Asian Studies in 1999; Shanghai Normal University established its African Studies Centre in 2000; Zhejiang Normal set up China's first Centre for African Education Studies in 2003, along with Tianjin University of Technology and Education's Centre for Aid to African Vocational Education, just mentioned. At the same time, other universities such as Beijing Foreign Studies, and Beijing International Studies, were offering instruction in Hausa, Arabic and Swahili. They would be followed by others such as Tianjin Normal University, offering Swahili from the mid-2000s as we shall see below. Chinese scholars also began much more extensive publishing about Africa, (China, 2003: 106–117). Relatively large-scale research grants began to become available to carry out research in Africa. Doctoral candidates began to do fieldwork in Africa.

Illustrating the speed with which institutional change is possible in China, Zhejiang Normal University, as we saw in Chapter 2, had moved from setting up a very small Centre for African Education Studies in 2003 to launching a full-blown Institute of African Studies in August 2007. Some twenty new staff were hired to work on Africa, and a first set of masters students in African studies had started in 2008. For almost the first time, staff were travelling to Africa to undertake research, and it became possible even for masters students to contemplate carrying out some fieldwork in Africa.[13]

But the changing awareness of Africa was not just taking place in universities with named centres or institutes of African Studies. Following

[13] For more detail on the transformation of Zhejiang Normal, see Chapter 2.

the setting up of the first Confucius Institute in Seoul in November 2004, a series of African universities, literally from the Cape to Cairo, began to follow suit. In 2005, the University of Nairobi was the first to open a Confucius Institute, its Chinese partner university being Tianjin Normal University. Soon there were 30 other African universities (including Cape Town and Cairo) which were forging close links with their sister universities in China for the development of Confucius Institutes. But much earlier than the Confucius Institute partnerships with China, some 25 Chinese universities from Peking to Chang-an, and from China Agricultural to Beijing Language University, had developed links with partner universities in Africa in order to provide scientific laboratories. Many of these long-term partnerships from the mid- to late-1990s were formalised when the 20+20 scheme was announced in the Fourth FOCAC meeting in 2009, which again linked 20 Chinese universities more closely to 20 of their African partners.

But this growing awareness of Africa in the Chinese universities was not dependent only on institutional links. African celebrities such as President Nelson Mandela were to be heard addressing large audiences in Peking University just a year after South Africa initiated diplomatic relations with China in 1998.[14] Other heads of state from Africa such as the late Meles Zenawi of Ethiopia were recognised as the Co-Chair of the Second FOCAC summit in Addis Ababa in 2003. Beijing itself was the site of the largest meeting on Africa ever held outside Africa in November 2006, when almost 40 heads of state from Africa assembled in the capital for the FOCAC III summit. Beijing transformed itself into a celebration of Africa, from massive photographs of Africa in the metro to huge replicas of African wildlife in the best known shopping area. Banners and the media proclaimed 'Amazing Africa', and no fewer than one million ordinary citizens volunteered to be helpers and provide additional security on all street corners (King, 2006b).

2006 was also the year in which China declared its *African Policy* (China, 2006). And 2006 was widely hailed in the Chinese media as the Year of Africa. In terms of deliberate orientation of the press and the media towards Africa, this year of the Beijing Africa Summit was seen as a useful preparation for the even larger event of the Olympic Games two years later in August 2008.

The question we return to now, however, is whether the scale of these new developments relating to Africa, many of them affecting the universities in China, could have been responsible for a change in orientation towards Africa of the kind reported in Sautman and Yan's survey of African students in Tianjin's universities. Interestingly, no less than three of Tianjin's major universities had been drawn into substantial African partnerships in the decade before their 2008 survey. This included Tianjin Normal, Tianjin University of Technology and Education, and Tianjin

---

[14] President Hosni Mubarak of Egypt was awarded an honorary doctorate by Peking University in April 1999, and Mandela accepted one in May 1999.

University of Traditional Medicine which had links with Kenya, Ethiopia and Ghana respectively.

However, a further critical factor that could have made for a change in attitude towards China between the 1990s and the late 2000s was the dramatic alteration in China's status as a world power, with many of its universities aspiring to be world class, especially from May 1998.[15] Many Chinese universities, including Zhejiang Normal where the new Institute of African Studies was based, literally transformed themselves during the 2000s with massive investments in libraries, research facilities, student and staff accommodation. Deliberate internationalisation was part of this transformation, and the African elements in this process were a small part in a much greater movement to embrace a wide-ranging reorientation in higher education (Adamson et al., 2012; King, 2012b).

Recognition of these changes in China's universities was evident in many of the countries sending students to China; hence the worldwide interest in foreign universities partnering with Chinese universities through the Confucius Institutes when this became possible from late 2004. The change in status also meant that Chinese universities began to become destinations of first choice for a number of countries, including in Africa. Thus in Kenya, for example, sources in the Ministry of Higher Education recognised China as a priority destination along with Germany when it came to the popularity of its scholarships. This could well mean that there were different kinds of students drawn to Chinese universities from Africa during the 2000s than there had been in the 1990s. The internationalising changes in the Chinese universities and in the type of international students aspiring to come to them could translate into different attitudes towards their hosts by African students in the later 2000s and vice versa.

Be that as it may, it is now time to turn from speculations about the impact of internationalisation in general on African students coming to China, to the specific insights of Africans currently studying in China, and the perceptions of those who have studied in China but returned to Africa. We shall first look at a range of Kenyan students who have studied in China and returned, and then examine the insights of a number of African students studying in China from 2010.

In most of the discussions with Kenyans, one of the key issues that emerged was what could be learned from China for the improvement of work back home. There was often a particular comparative interest shown by the Kenyan students on China's work style, discipline and the quality of the working environment in China.

---

[15] Jiang Zemin's centennial speech at Peking University that year is widely taken as a launch point for China's world class university initiative (Li, J. 2012)

# Kenyans study in China

These discussions with Kenyans who have studied or hope to study in China were principally held in July 2009 except where otherwise mentioned,[16] and they covered a wide range of graduates of Chinese universities in the last twenty-five years. But the history of Kenyans studying in China goes a lot further back.[17]

We do know that Kenya was one of just five countries which had one or more students in China during the 1950s (He, 2006: 3). Intriguingly, the other four countries were Egypt, Cameroon, Uganda and Malawi (Nyasaland). We do also know that two Kenyans were amongst the 118 Africans referred to in Hevi's account of *An African Student in China*, which was mentioned above, and they were amongst the 96 who decided to leave prematurely in 1962 (Hevi, 1963:116). In addition, what we do know now for certain is that some of the other earliest Kenyans to travel to China in 1964 for a study tour were recruited personally in Makerere University in Uganda by the then vice-president of Kenya, Oginga Odinga. There were six of them, four Luo and 2 Kalenjin. Odinga's purpose was apparently to demonstrate to a number of well-educated Kenyan students that 'communism was not all that bad' and perhaps even better than the capitalist road being promoted by President Kenyatta. One of these six, interviewed in November 2011, has given us one of the earliest sets of comments by a Kenyan on the lessons from China:

> Overall, Mutai said he was impressed by the Chinese authorities' management of human capital in terms of total employment of the population with corresponding provision of welfare services to everybody on an equal basis. (Kipkorir to King, 11.11.2011)[18]

In due course it would be valuable to know a little more about these earliest impressions, coming from even before the Cultural Revolution. But as far as any impact of this safari to China was concerned, Mutai had

---

[16] Except where mentioned otherwise, all the direct quotations are from July 2009.

[17] Although the tradition is that one of Chinese Admiral Zheng He's fleets reached the current areas of Lamu and Mombasa on the Kenya coast in the 1400s, with some Chinese sailors settling after shipwreck, it was not until the celebrations of the 600th anniversary of this exploration, in 2006, that a Kenya–China training dimension developed from this early safari; Shariff, a Kenyan girl with claimed Chinese ancestry, was sent on a China government scholarship to spend seven years in Nanjing University of Traditional Chinese Medicine (PRC Ministry of Culture, n.d.).

[18] Dr Ben Kipkorir has mentioned that the party of six Kenyans who had been students in Uganda were offered a very special experience in Shanghai: In China, the Kenyan party were taken to many places including the Great Wall; and even when the visitors had become too tired of travel, their hosts still had another surprise for them: a visit to Shanghai where they were invited to meet a factory worker whose hand had been severed by a machine but had been re-joined by Chinese surgeons who claimed that that was the first such medical procedure in the world, accomplished thanks to the great leadership of Mao (Kipkorir to King, 11.11.2011).

the following to say: 'When we came back we forgot all about it – it had all been about Kenyan politics.'

*An early vocational safari with a comparative perspective on Kenya*
Our earliest direct interview was with someone who is now a senior medical officer in Kenya. He had hoped to study medicine in Nairobi University but did not get admitted on his first try. Instead of spending a year preparing to re-sit, he was advised to try Poland or China. It is interesting to note that the choices available to him, back in the early 1980s when he went to China, were Poland, still within the Soviet bloc, and China. At that time there were ten scholarships offered by China to Kenya, and he was one of three who went to pursue medicine. He entered Sun Yatsen Medical University in Guangzhou.

The key lessons from China for him were quite clear. Time management; if someone was late by two minutes, then repeat the job. The university syllabus was completely clear insofar as what was to be studied, prepared for and discussed; the system was transparent and if there was any problem on marks or grades, it was possible to go straight to the top and have it sorted. The machines related to medicine were already excellent. But when he had gone back to China fifteen years later the transformation was quite dramatic, 'an eye-opener'.

The contrast with Kenya was stark: 'Overall in China, while they are developing, we are deteriorating. Our discipline is bad. Our consultants come in, in the morning, but then go off to make money in private practice. Management is bad. In terms of promotion, there is a lack of merit. Even corruption.'

This set of comments is crucially important for seeking to understand one of the common threads of the debates about the advantages of overseas scholarship. The impact upon the individual is one thing, but the impact on the institution to which the scholar returns is something that is of great interest to many of the scholarship funding organisations. An indication of this kind of institutional impact is that this particular alumnus successfully managed to take a whole team of Kenyan doctors to China in 2000.

Identifying different kinds of institutional impact is what the survey of 50 years of Commonwealth Scholarships to the UK sought to establish. Thus they were able to claim that 'High numbers of respondents reported being able to introduce new practices or innovations at their workplaces' (CSCUK, 2009: 18).

*An early Kenyan female student in China; surprise at China's ignorance of Africa*
Our next Kenyan student in China went ten years later, in 1993, to what was then called Shanghai Textile University. She was one of very few black women in the city at that time, and faced a good deal of harassment which she put down to ignorance and because they had been 'closed in by

their government for so long'. She had expected they would be fascinated but it was rather different:

> They would block my way, so they could look at me with a closer view and of course would say things I didn't understand. But when I started understanding Chinese, then I heard SOME of the NASTY things they said. "Black devil" was a very common term. When they crowded around me they would try to touch the skin and hair to see if it was really dirty-and if their hands would get dirty after touching. Can you imagine trying to ward off many little hands from you as you would flies or other insects? I didn't take it all negatively because I thought they were ignorant and not exposed to a world outside theirs. They would, for example, ask if I came to China from Africa on foot or by bicycle, and if I told them I walked up to their capital where I was given a bicycle, they appeared to believe me. (Former student to KK, 20.11.11. caps in original).

She had gone there for technical expertise, which she received. But she was not impressed or influenced by their culture or work ethic although she recognised that they were 'work-aholics and followed the rules'. In fact she felt the Kenyans were more culturally advanced even if China was making more technological progress. She did note that when the African students had had to learn Chinese, there was more interaction with the Chinese students; she was in the first batch that studied in English. And the 'Chinese contact with foreign students in my university was limited or even prohibited'.

*Returning from China critical of Kenya*
Another Kenyan who went to China in 1996 and stayed for over a decade registered 'huge disappointment' and 'lack of incentive' on his return. Kenya by contrast with China lacks opportunities, has poor equipment and facilities in the public sector; and hence there is the attraction of the private sector, especially in medicine. But there is also, again, the work and governance culture:

> The people here are idle; they don't come in and work. And they lack the discipline. What could be brought in from China is good governance of the institutions; also of student behaviour. The students monitor each other and look after each other.

This doctor had been able to take additional jobs in China in order to supplement his CSC allowance. But for him the paradox was that the very apolitical character of student life in China had had a powerful effect on his return to Kenya: 'There is no politics in Chinese universities; yet you come back from China more critical of the Kenyan situation.' But he retained an overpoweringly positive view of the Chinese people, as good, honest and straightforward.

*Admiration for China's culture including its culture of work*
Another Kenyan who went to China, in 2003, on a provincial Chinese
scholarship rather than one from the China Scholarship Council, was very
clear about the lessons to be learned from China. He was very aware of the
direct impact of China on his own outlook, ethics and approach to work:

> The greatest impact was in understanding more of other cultures,
> including China's.

> It helped me to change the way I looked at something. The Chinese
> always look at the bright side. They have a can-do approach. They are
> very hardworking. And this affected me. At the weekend, all the Chinese
> went off to do part-time jobs. So I did likewise.[19] When it came to
> improving their English, they would go off and volunteer to teach English
> in middle school, to sharpen their practical skills. I did the same.

> All in all it had a very positive impact on my keeping time and doing
> the right thing. They were very time conscious and target driven. What
> I learned was to do things ahead of schedule or right on time. No
> excuses about missing targets. I can't remember any occasion when a
> Chinese student came late. So I came back to Kenya with these atti-
> tudes

This perspective on what can be learned from study in China, we shall
note in other interviews, is rather commonplace. The recognition that
there is a very powerful work ethic found in both teachers and students in
China is seen as something very positive by many overseas students on
scholarships or awards in China. The belief that hard work and effort (*luli*
in Mandarin) are crucial to academic achievement is very widespread in
China and in several other East Asian societies.[20]

*Fascination with the Chinese language and culture, plus a desire to
teach it in Kenya*
Another dimension of Kenyan interest in studying in China is less vocational but derives from an enthusiasm to learn this very different language.
In the case of a student from the Rift Valley in Kenya, it was the direct
impact with Chinese workers constructing buildings in an educational
institution that lit the spark. This was followed by some eight months of
part-time study of Chinese in Egerton University, and then suddenly there
was the chance to compete for a scholarship to China. It is noteworthy
that it was his very strong desire to teach Chinese on his return to Kenya
that probably improved his chances of getting a scholarship in 2001.

[19] This is in contradiction to what the students were saying in Gillespie's survey about not
being able to work.
[20] 'Teachers in China tend to believe that with due effort, a child should always be able to
achieve the expected standard. They believe that genetic factors are always secondary, so long
as pupils are trying hard. The motto "diligence compensates for stupidity" is seldom challenged' (Cheng, 1990: 165). See further, King, 2007c.

As far as impact on his own approach to work, it was a similar story to what we have just heard:

They are such hard workers. 24 hours a day! Very different from Kenya. On the subject of hard work, they have proverbs about this.[21] But they pay more attention to these proverbs about hard work making for success than we do in Kenya.[22] I was really impressed by their hard work; they worked perhaps twice as hard as we did. But I was also impressed by their sports, their strong family ties as well as their study. I noticed this when I was invited to their homes for some three weeks at a time.

On his return to Kenya two years later, there were already no less than five public or private colleges offering Chinese in Nairobi alone, and in a year's time the Confucius Institute would start in the University of Nairobi, right in the centre of the city. It was easy therefore to put into practice his ambition to teach Chinese. Soon he was teaching classes of twenty students. His longer term aim, in order to continue teaching Chinese more effectively, was to pick up a degree part-time in Nairobi, and then go back to China and get a Masters in teaching Chinese as a foreign language.

On the issue of racism towards Africans in China which we have focused upon in the earlier sections of this chapter, it is worth noting his rather balanced approach:

Yes, there was some stereotyping of Africans, and perhaps some teachers gave less attention to African than to other international students. But this was a question of individuals. And don't forget, we Kenyans stereotype the Chinese! The Kenyans readily say that the Chinese are eaters of dogs, snakes and frogs. And they also say that the Chinese cant see properly!

*Learning Chinese in a changing, enabling environment in Kenya*
The interest in learning Chinese and in studying in China is inseparable of course from an environment in Kenya where there are encouragements and incentives to become interested. This environment will differ greatly from country to country in Africa, and even within countries will differ from the capital city to rural and provincial towns. But already in Kenya in the mid-2000s, it was possible to access TV from China through CCTV9, the international channel. Also, China Radio International (CRI) had set up first a national centre in 1991 and a regional centre in 2006. Starting in

---

[21] Amongst the many illustrations of this emphasis on the crucial importance of effort and determination is the story told by Li Bai, the poet of the Tang dynasty, about the old granny grinding an iron pestle on a stone in order to turn it eventually into a needle. After the granny had explained that this could be done if she ground it every day, Li Bai thought: 'She's right. There is nothing that cannot be accomplished by perseverance. The same is true with learning' (King, 2011b: 4).
[22] For a rather similar set of proverbs about the role of effort in Kenya's Central Province, see Marris and Somerset (1971).

2008, this was broadcasting 58 short lessons in Chinese; and Xinhua, the official Chinese news agency, had set up its regional headquarters also in Nairobi. By the end of 2012, there were no less than 70 African professionals in the Nairobi office alone, with about 50 Chinese colleagues, and another 15 correspondents across the continent (Peter Wakaba to KK, 3.12.12).[23] Finally, *China Daily Africa Weekly* became available for the first time on the newstands across Eastern Africa from 7 December 2012 (Wekesa to KK 15.12.12).

These resources played their part in encouraging a number of young people to become interested in China and in studying Chinese. In the case of the sister of the Kenyan teacher of Chinese just mentioned, these multiple resources drew her to the study of China, but equally there was an awareness of China's success and its growing role in the world:

> My brother had gone to China in 2001. But I used to look at CCTV9 and listen to CRI. I admired China. I admired its culture. I got very positive images. So immediately after secondary school, in the gap before university, I studied Chinese intensively with the teacher attached to Egerton University. I did six hours a day for one and a half years. Looking ahead, after my BA, I am planning to study in China and get a chance to teach there. For me, doing Chinese is the key, and my parents are in favour.

Another factor which is likely to encourage similar responses to what are noted here with her is the start of teaching Chinese, as a pilot programme, in the primary schools of the Western Kenya city of Kisumu. This is the result of a request to the Chinese Embassy in Nairobi from the Kisumu East MP, Shakeel Shabir (King, 2010b: 493).[24]

*Switching from OECD countries to China?*
Kenya is not alone in having examples of students who were in USA for their undergraduate degree deciding that they should do their masters or doctorate in China. There is an example of another African student (from Senegal) who was actually enrolled in a Canadian Business Studies course deciding to abandon his studies and move to the Shanghai University of Finance and Economics for both cultural and professional reasons.[25] This

---

[23] See also Wu Yu-shan (2012) on China's state-led media dynasty in Africa.

[24] Wekesa, a Kenyan doctoral student from Western Province, has confirmed that Mr Yu was the Chinese teacher who came first, and who is still there; two further Chinese teachers have joined him, and other MPs are clamouring to repeat the initiative (Wekesa to KK, 12.09.12).

[25] 'There are more personal reasons that counted in his decision to move to China. He had for a long time an interest in this country and, even in Canada, he continued to read a lot on its culture and his emerging economic power. Since he is studying business, he considers that China is already counting and will continue to play an important role in this globalized world. So he decided to move there with the advantage of learning Mandarin and to continue his studies with a major on Chinese Business. He plans to do business with partners in China who target Africa for their business. Two of his friends from Dakar have decided to join him in Shanghai' (Father of student to KK, 11. 11.2011).

is not to suggest that higher education China is simply easier to access than some of the OECD countries. At least for the China Scholarships offered to Kenya, there is now stiff competition. According to the Minister of Education in Kenya in July 2009 it is necessary to have an upper second in one's first degree to be considered. Ministry staff indicated that the largest providers of scholarships in that year were Germany, China and India, and that first choices of destination, of the countries that relied on the Ministry to do the selection, tended to be Germany and China, as we mentioned above.

For the Kenyan student who elected to switch his host country from the USA to China in medicine, in 2008, one deciding factor, as a prospective engineering student, was that he had discovered, after a little research, that a great deal of the machinery in the Kenyan hospitals had come from China. An additional issue that students like him needed to bear in mind when competing to come to China on a government scholarship is that success usually means that the whole first year is dedicated to becoming sufficiently fluent in Chinese to cope with the terminology of a science degree. And it is primarily in the applied sciences that China's government scholarships are provided.[26] Hence the challenge is to reach the level of HSK 5 in Chinese which is the condition set for foreign students undertaking any science degree in China.

The wider picture for this student who elected to move from the West to the East is that there is a lot that Kenya can learn from China:

We are not the same as China; we are the Third World. We accept aid and we say 'Let them come and help us'. But we should be more self-reliant. We should not rush to be helped. Unlike China, we look at some jobs and say they are dirty jobs; we don't do them. The most important lesson is that China has developed. We need to learn from here and go back to Kenya.

The advantage of this immersion year in Chinese is that it offers a real opportunity to become part of another country's culture, like the best experience of the ERASMUS exchanges across the European Community, but even more intensive. The result is that this particular Kenya student found that '...he spent most of his time with Chinese students; they tell me that I am one of theirs.' This, of course, is in direct contrast with what the Gillespie survey had found much earlier.

*Self-sponsored Kenyans studying in English in China*
It is worth mentioning that apart from the China Scholarship Council (CSC) students whose degrees are in Chinese and who study alongside Chinese students, there are a growing number of Kenyans recruited by organisations such as China Information and Culture Communications (CICC) which has been operating in Kenya since 2006, and intending to

---

[26] In 2009, the disciplines prioritised were: medicine, surgery, aeronautical; aerospace, systems engineering; computer studies, telecoms, and megatronics.

open branches also in Uganda and Zambia. Within two years, it was sending 40 students to China to no less than eight different well-known universities. It has not been possible to secure a figure for the total number of self-sponsored students in China, but with fee levels, as of 2008, of as little as US$ 2,750 for tuition, accommodation and insurance even in a field such as medicine, few other countries may appear equally competitive as degree destinations.

In Chongqing Medical University (CMU), for instance, there were some 20 Kenyans in the first and second years alone. Two of these were would-be women doctors in their third year in 2009. They had checked out that CMU was certified by the WHO and was recognised in Kenya. They found that there were no fewer than 200 international students in their year. But the great difference from CSC students was that they were studying in classes which had no Chinese students at all. These were in effect separate classes made up exclusively of international students. But would this mean that the work ethic which other Kenyans have mentioned as a major influence in their time in China would be missing? Apparently not; the Chinese teachers 'kept encouraging us and saying "Work hard and you will reap what you sow"'.[27] In addition classes were compulsory, and they were well aware of the effort the Chinese students were putting into their parallel medical studies in Chinese medium.

One last Kenyan student, who already was working in the media, before going to China in 2010, illustrates the fact that expertise and experience of China may now be regarded as a comparative advantage in the competitive media business:

> The first thing I did was to look up the programme and the information provided on the website of Communication University of China; it fitted the bill for me – media literacy, theory of communication, communication research methodology, etc – these were courses I'd wanted to undertake and I reckoned China was now a global power and therefore media studies would be thorough-going – I was not unduly worried about China-bashing as working on the government paper had exposed me to the positive side of China's meteoric economic growth. Plus, I increasingly became convinced that an oriental perspective would be important as there were already many Kenyans who had studied in the West – a competitive advantage existed, I thought. I put in my application, the rest is history. (Wekesa to KK, 24.9.2012)

We shall return to the issue of whole groups of African students and professionals being separately taught from their Chinese counterparts when we review the Ministry of Commerce (MOFCOM)-sponsored Masters courses. But for now, it may be useful to draw together some of the threads that have emerged from examining this group of Kenyan

---

[27] For the widespread belief amongst teachers in East Asia that effort will lead to successful achievement by the majority of students, as mentioned above, see Cheng (1990) and King (2007c).

students and trainees who have been in China at different times over the last 25 years, or 45 years if the earliest recruits to China by Odinga are included.

First, of these students who have been in China (or are planning to be in one case), the theme of racial discrimination discussed in the first section of this chapter did not emerge as a critical issue. One reported that ten years ago some of the children they encountered in Beijing had never seen a black person; they wanted to touch to see if the colour came off. In another case, in a provincial university city, the children had wanted to know if their skin was black because of the heat of the sun in Kenya. Two others had been aware that there was some stereotyping of Africans by the Chinese but they were equally aware that there was similar stereotyping of the Chinese by Kenyans. There was little evidence at all that this group of Kenyans had found it hard to mix in China; indeed the reverse was true, and was much helped by having good Mandarin. One or two had maintained their links with Chinese friends after returning to Kenya.

Second, China has rapidly become a destination of choice for Kenyan students, and in the view of the Kenyan ambassador in Beijing in 2010, it had replaced India as a destination because of the readiness of the Chinese to transfer their knowledge and technology. This is not to say that many Kenyans might still prefer London or USA; but that might change, as in the case of the Kenyan who actually decided to switch to China from the US. Some evidence of this growing popularity can be seen in the embassy's estimate of there being some 500 Kenyan long-term students in China. There were strong clusters in Nanjing where there have been links with Kenya's Egerton University since the 1990s and in Tianjin where there has also been a link forged through the Confucius Institute partnership. Despite these numbers, there was not yet an Association of Kenyan Students in China, although there is a plan for one. However, apparently, there was already a Kenya Alumni Association of former graduates who had returned home (China, MOE, 2005: 21).

Third, since the Beijing Summit of 2006, the annual allocation of CSC awards to Kenya has been running at about 40, which over a five-year period would produce a figure of about 200–plus scholarship holders on central government scholarships. We have noted already that there are provincial scholarship holders as well, and we have seen in the discussion of Confucius Institutes, in Chapter 2, that there is a wide array of Kenyans coming for language and culture awards of varying length. Others too have been coming through the MOFCOM Masters scheme. But overall it probably means that there are about equal numbers of scholarship and self-funded Kenyan students in China.

Lastly, the dominant thread in the Kenyan student experience of China has been the exposure to a very powerful and influential work and study ethic. This theme is picked up and echoed by the Kenyan Embassy in Beijing. It is possibly reinforced by the relatively slow pace of the liberalisation of Chinese society; hence there is not to the same extent a whole range of activities outside the classroom like civil society, the churches, and so on. According to the Kenyan students, very little time is taken up in the discussion of politics as it would be in Kenya. In contrast to these Kenyan students with experience of China, there were in 2009 just one or two Chinese students in Kenya on Kenya Government scholarships. Discussion with one of these pursuing a PhD on the political thought of Thabo Mbeki revealed many problems with the award, the accommodation, access to the library, and even allocation to the most suitable department in the University of Nairobi.

## Other African students in China's universities

Apart from using a Kenyan lens to analyse some dimensions of student experience in China, it was thought valuable to look at the view of African students in one of the universities which has prioritized links with, and studies of, Africa in the last decade and longer. We had already mentioned Zhejiang Normal University (ZNU) above, and in Chapter 2, as an example of a provincial institution in China which had dramatically changed its international orientation including towards Africa in a very short time. Its first contact with Africa, with Cameroon, only goes back to 1996, linking with the International Relations Institute of the University of Yaounde II.[28] The first African student came to ZNU from Cameroon shortly afterwards. But within ten years, ZNU had a full-blown Institute of African Studies as described earlier. There were more than 70 African students by 2011, drawn from 29 different countries, and unlike several of the African studies centres in the UK, these students were drawn from Arabic-speaking North, Francophone West and Central, as well as Anglophone Africa. Here we shall consider in some detail two from Ghana and Nigeria respectively, two from Egypt, and through these students, several others from Ghana, Cameroon, South Africa and Nigeria.[29]

While considering these ZNU discussions in August 2010, with some of the same issues as before with Kenya, we shall pay more attention to the relations with the university itself and to the role of African student associations. Like the debate above on whether African views of China are positive or negative, so here too there is some controversy over the quality of educational experience of African students. Nor of course are these debates about quality restricted to African students in ZNU. The journal *Nature* has raised questions about the quality of China's degrees in science especially because of their allegedly being pursued in a Chinese medium at the same time as the language is being acquired.[30] This is not of course

---

[28]  See further on the relationship, Nordtveit (2010a: 102).

[29]  Unless otherwise mentioned, all interviews with ZNU students took place in August 2010.

[30]  'Other researchers argue that China's efforts aren't always tailored to Africa's needs. For example, China already sponsors long-term training programmes for African students, who move to China for several years, taking language courses while they study science in

the case; on the other hand it is certain that many African students on CSC awards continue formally to study Chinese after their initial immersion year of Chinese language training.

*Switching from French to Chinese language teaching*
In our discussion of the Kenyans, we had talked of examples of students switching from studying in OECD countries to studying in China. With the first of our ZNU students, the original intention had been to study at the Masters level in French in order to become qualified as a French teacher in Ghana. She had then heard about the Chinese scholarships and about the possible development of a Confucius Institute in one of the major universities in Ghana. Indeed, Chinese had begun to be taught in her university even before a decision had been taken on a Confucius Institute, thus illustrating the key role of the enabling environment for the spread of Chinese;[31] so she had come on a CSC award to ZNU, specifically to help build up Ghanaian capacity in teaching Chinese. Surprisingly, she had failed to be allocated to the masters on teaching Chinese as a foreign language for the whole of her first year, but this was sorted out in her second year. That aside, the facilities in ZNU were good; the computing very good. Also accommodation and food were fine. Shortly, there was a completely new hostel for international students, but again that would be separate from the Chinese students.

Beyond her professional development in Chinese, she had also thrown herself very actively into the seminars and workshops for African teachers who come to the resource base in ZNU for short courses in education. She had undertaken a study with one of the Institute of African Studies' staff of other African students in ZNU. Further, she had planned to write a joint research paper with a Chinese doctoral student working on China's aid to Africa. She had begun to think about China-Ghana cooperation and more broadly, China-African cooperation. Here her preliminary conclusion was that China's aid was different from other aid; it was win-win economic cooperation and not colonisation. On the other hand, she recognised that the Chinese clearly knew what they wanted. But she was not so sure that the Africans had worked out what they wanted from the relationship with China.

Chinese. Students see the experience as a good career move, but once they return to Africa, "the calibre of such scientists is very low", says Chinsembu, a molecular biologist at the University of Namibia, noting that the students struggle to assimilate scientific concepts in a foreign language. "Most cannot pass local examinations here in African universities'" (Cyranowski, 2010: 477).

[31] It was reported that an agreement had been signed between the Chinese Language Council in Beijing and the University of Ghana for teaching Chinese language and culture from the 2008/9 academic year. http://www.modernghana.com/news/160374/1/legon-teaches-chinese. html

*Country unions and scholarships in support of African students in China*

Perhaps because of the presence of an Institute of African Studies in ZNU, several of its students were aware of the place of African student associations.

Issues such as students being placed on apparently inappropriate courses in China raise the question of whether national associations of African students can play a role in sorting out such anomalies. Very few African countries with students in China have such associations, however. Those which do, such as Cameroon, Sierra Leone and Ghana, do not claim to have national coverage in China. Thus, the international branch of the National Union of Ghanaian Students (NUGS) in China is said by its current President to have about 1,000 members, and although every Ghanaian student, public or private, in China is automatically a member, only 250 have actually registered, of which 122 are active.[32] There are currently eleven branches in different cities on the Mainland. Interestingly, the eleven branches do not include either Hong Kong or Macao. There is an annual Congress, most recently on 24 October in 2012.

It is interesting to note that the current President of NUGS-China is not aware of the existence of any more general African students union (ASU) or association in China. This says something about its visibility; and one of the other executives of NUGS-China has said:

> I have not heard of ASU. I don't know how strong it is. If it were in Wuhan I would have heard of it by now. The association probably exists but is not very active, because China is still warming up to the idea of associations and gatherings; so they might be keeping a low profile.

In fact, there is just one known branch today of an Africa-wide association in China and that is the General Union of African Students in Tianjin (GUAST).[33] Earlier on, we know from Gillespie (2001) that there was a General Union of African Students in China (GUASC) which had played an active role in 1996 on the living allowances of those on CSC awards. We also know that the GUASC was involved in defending African students in the China-Africa Nanjing riots in early 1989.[34] It seems likely, however, given the year of these Nanjing riots, that the authorities would have discouraged the continuation of Africa-wide unions or associations.

It would be valuable to have a full tally of the active national student associations or unions in China. As mentioned, we are presently aware of

[32] See the active and well-developed website for the National Union of Ghanaian Students-China: http://nugschina.com/
[33] Over the last twelve years it has had presidents from Tanzania, Cameroon, Gabon, Mali, Nigeria and Sierra Leone.
[34] See the LA Times on the mention of the President of the Nanjing chapter of the GUASC being detained at the time of the riots: http://articles.latimes.com/1989–01–04/news/mn-140_1_african-students.

just three West African unions, Ghana, Cameroon and Sierra Leone;[35] there are also an Egyptian and a Tanzanian and Ugandan student association in China. Perhaps not surprisingly, there is no Nigerian students union of students in China, given the sensitive nature of China-Nigeria relations which we shall come to below. But there is an association called Young African Professionals and Students (YAPS).[36] This non-profit organisation only dates from 2009 but it is not clear from its website how active or widespread it is. Its most recent site visitors were many weeks earlier.

The other issue that surfaces is the overall composition of Ghanaian students in China. According to the current President of NUGS-China, about 95 per cent of them are said to be privately funded, and most of these are doing medicine. The small minority are on China government scholarships, or on Ghana government scholarships, or on both.[37] This last category raises an issue which appears to be of importance particularly to a number of Francophone African countries; there it is the government policy that, if students secure a China Scholarship Council (CSC) award, they are automatically eligible for a counterpart scholarship from the national government. Amongst the countries which have adopted this policy are Gabon, Benin, Chad, Senegal and Mali. Of course, what this suggests is that the CSC award is not sufficient to cover the costs of being in China, although CSC stipends for international students are more generous than local Chinese awards.

In the case of the Cameroon, for instance, this 'top-up' of China Scholarship Council awards is almost mandatory. Indeed, a great deal of the activity of the Cameroon Students Association in China (CSAC), which counts 200 members, is concerned with trying to ensure that the Government of Cameroon pays these allowances.[38] This issue is very visible on its website. Currently, the sum involved is some $US 160 a month from the Cameroon Government. This is said to be particularly important for postgraduate students in the sciences where there are additional costs of laboratory work.

Some of the most common issues faced by these national unions or associations, according to the President of the National Union of Ghanaian Students in China, are, first, transfer to another university in order to pursue a more appropriate course. Insisting on a transfer can incur a fine of some $160 US and the possible cancellation of the student visa. A second issue is the importance of pursuing practical training back in Africa, whether in medicine or in teaching Chinese. It is sometimes difficult to arrange this because of cost or of the absence back home of parallel

[35] For the Sierra Leone Students Union in China which was established in 1993, and which has a current membership of 121 members, on all of which there is full detail of university affiliation and discipline on the website, see http://www.slsuc.com/
[36] This is referred to in an interesting article by Ferdjani (2012).
[37] The president of the NUGS-China, for instance, is on both a China and Ghana government scholarship.
[38] See the website of the Cameroon Students Association in China: http://www.camerchine.com/home.php. CSAC was founded in 1996 and it too has a regular annual congress.

equipment as is found in Chinese medical faculties. Third, a continuing issue for students on CSC awards, despite many Africans being very good at second, third or fourth language learning, is whether one year of immersion in Chinese is really sufficient to deal with an undergraduate or graduate course taught entirely in Chinese.

*Egyptians studying Chinese and Chinese studying Arabic: a more equal partnership?*
Unlike the start of teaching Chinese in the University of Yaounde II in the late 1990s, in Nairobi from 2005, and in University of Legon in Accra from 2008, Ain Shams University in Egypt was teaching Chinese from 1958. It has been joined by four other universities since 2000, and there are now some 1,000 students studying Chinese in Ain Shams alone (Nordtveit, 2010b: 62).[39] Also, the provision of scholarships is more symmetrical, with Egypt providing 20 to Chinese students and China providing 50 to Egypt. It is not yet known if these arrangements have changed since the fall in 2011 of Hosni Mubarak. He had been a firm friend of China over many years, having visited there some ten times, and having hosted the Fourth FOCAC Summit in Sharm el Shaikh in November 2009.[40]

One of the Egyptian students pursuing the Masters in Teaching Chinese as a Foreign Language in ZNU said that this could be done instead of military service. Again, this may have changed. As far as the teaching and learning environment in ZNU was concerned, it was much superior to Ain Shams, even though the university was in a provincial city rather than the capital. There were no less than 10 Egyptians including himself following this same masters and two pursuing doctoral studies from their own university but in ZNU. His interest was vocational, as he had already worked for two years in a Chinese firm in Egypt, and now wanted to improve his language skills.

By contrast, the second Egyptian had already been studying Chinese for four years in Ain Shams. His interest was very different; it was in languages themselves and especially Asian languages. It is too easily assumed that foreign study is entirely vocational; so it is refreshing to recall that there are intrinsic rationales for study as well:

> My interest was in the way languages function – the mystery. For me it was like a moth to a flame – a magnet. So I am not sure that I came here for work or for jobs, but rather for interest, to learn more about the language.

[39] There is good deal of detail in *China-Africa Education Cooperation* on the dramatic growth of interest in Chinese in Ain Shams University, and in 2005 there were in the Department of Chinese Language: 8 associate professors; 18 lecturers, and six assistant lecturers. These are all Egyptian, but China had sent some 50 Chinese lecturers to Ain Shams since 1954 (China, MOE, 2005: 60–62).
[40] On his arrival for the FOCAC Beijing Summit in November 2006, he had declared: 'For me, visiting China is like going home. Egypt sees China more as a brother than as an ordinary friendly nation.' (Hosni Mubarak, former Egyptian President, 1.11.06) See further, King (2006b).

Ideally, he would have liked more time to study Chinese literature, go to films and read books. But he found he was studying the whole time. 'The Chinese religion is hard work!'.

This intrinsic delight in the Chinese language and literature was shared by another student from Cameroon, who was deliberately taking a second BA, this time in East China Normal University in Shanghai, in order to understand Chinese literature. This is an aspect of China-Africa cooperation that is too often neglected in the emphasis on win-win economic cooperation. In fact, cultural cooperation and exchange is also an integral part of *China's African Policy*.[41] The student explained his own position further:

> Since China is very positive about the African Union I thought it was important to know more about who the Africans were dealing with. The politicians know the politics, but the culture is so deep I thought I could be a bridge between China and Africa.[42] Like many Cameroonians, I had liked martial arts in Cameroon. Then I had studied history, world history, and Chinese history which is the oldest in the world. Right now I am focusing on the literature of China – novels, poems, *The Dream of Red Mansions*, Lu Xun, Ba Jin, – the evolution of Shanghai society. I know about Peking opera and the special dialect it is sung in.

In his view, there was however something profoundly unequal at the moment in this cultural exchange and cooperation between China and Africa. China was promoting its language and culture worldwide, including in Africa, through the Confucius Institutes, cultural centres and scholarships. But how many Chinese students and scholars were there in Africa studying the diversity of its cultures? He did not believe that Chinese had nothing to learn from Africa's cultures and history. On the side of African governments, he had noted that they had not promoted a single African Cultural Centre in the whole of China, as we note earlier.[43] His own personal contribution to this cultural exchange was to be involved in writing a book, in Chinese, on African tales and wisdom.

A last issue raised by this thoughtful Cameroonian student of Chinese literature was that there was still quite a large gap between many of the OECD student destinations and China. In many of these OECD countries, students who can manage to stay on and get work over a period of years can eventually secure citizenship, whether of Canada, USA, Sweden or

---

[41] 'China will implement agreements of cultural cooperation and relevant implementation plans reached with African countries, maintain regular contacts with their cultural departments and increase exchanges of artists and athletes. It will guide and promote cultural exchanges in diverse forms between people's organizations and institutions in line with bilateral cultural exchange programs and market demand' (China, 2006: 8).
[42] He was able to fulfil this bridge role by acting as compere in Mandarin to introduce the African musical groups to the Chinese audience at the Shanghai Expo in 2010.
[43] By contrast there are three Chinese cultural centres in Africa, in Mauritius, Benin, and Egypt. Gontin (2009) has also argued that 'The continent is culturally absent in China.'

another country. This is not possible in the case of China, and the same is true of Japan. Effectively, he argued, this reduces the brain drain out of Africa as far as China is concerned.

*Nigerian students in China: the promise and the challenge*
Our last discussion with a ZNU student was appropriately with a Nigerian. After a Bachelor's degree in education at Ibadan, he had taught, and then become involved with the private educational institutions (both university and secondary school) associated with the former president, Obasanjo. The company's intention had been for him to study higher education administration in China. However he was allocated a scholarship to teach Chinese as a foreign language. As Obasanjo Holdings was also involved with the Chinese in packaging and in agro-allied activities, business Chinese would have been a better alternative. Still, there were always possibilities perhaps of using his language degree should a Confucius Institute become linked to his university of technology in Nigeria.

His own considered view of his first year in China was positive; he felt he was well received in China and in ZNU in particular. If there were negative perceptions about Africa, he felt that on the whole these derived from lack of exposure to Africa; so he found the ordinary Chinese people had no problem with Africans. There was however a serious problem at the higher policy level *vis à vis* Nigerians in China. Because some Nigerians had been involved in criminal activity in China, there had been a tendency to generalise suspicion to all Nigerians. Thus, even in ZNU, his wife had not been allowed to study Chinese, though he had been ready to pay fees, and she had had to renew her visa much more frequently than would be the case with other Africans and their families.[44]

It is paradoxical that when it was Obasanjo who was responsible for making it very easy for Chinese businesses to come into Nigeria in very large numbers, someone working with Chinese employees in Obasanjo Holdings should find his family in such difficulty in terms of staying in China. From his own small-scale research and visits to other universities in China it would appear that several universities will not consider admitting Nigerian students. Illustrative of this becoming a major problem in China-Nigeria relations is that one of his Chinese friends who was in the Study Abroad business made a special point of going to Nigeria and seeking to interest young Nigerians in considering China as a student destination. After a long stay in Nigeria, he could not recruit a single candidate.

The crisis is widely described in blogs and other fora on Nigeria and China; which merely intensifies the suspicions on both sides. Thus 'The situation of Nigerians in China' posted in the Nigeria Forum[45] paints a very different picture from that of the Chinese ambassador in Nigeria's speech in *ThisDay* newspaper in 2011 under the title of 'Good brothers,

---

[44] For additional problems faced by Nigerian migrants, see Haugen, 2012.
[45] http://www.topix.com/forum/world/nigeria/TBGO83PK278FD

good friends and good partners'[46] or the Chargé d'Affaires' speech in August 2011 to China scholarship holders and other trainees departing for China.[47] The latter was celebrating the fact that there were over 300 officials and technicians going on short-term training seminars in China annually, and no less than 100 long-term scholars in China at any one time. Equally, he mentioned that 10 Chinese students had just completed their studies of the Hausa language in Bayero University in Kano, thus underlining that it was a two-way partnership.

It is worth noting that our former student in ZNU is now back in Nigeria and is happily involved in a joint energy venture with the Chinese. His concern regarding the widespread suspicions about Nigerians in China have not at all affected his own working relations with the Chinese.

*Former President of the General Union of African Students in Tianjin (GUAST) reflects on his experience*
The former president had studied in Tianjin University between 2003 and 2009, completing his doctorate, and had returned to the University of Agriculture in Nigeria. As a Nigerian who had played a leadership role in GUAST, he was very clear that African students 'most or all of the time face prejudice from the Chinese Government and especially Nigerians, even though China has strong business links with Nigeria. The reasons are not far to seek as many Nigerians have displayed dubious or unacceptable behaviour within the Chinese community which has produced stigmatisation' (Former student to KK, 6 November 2011).

We have mentioned earlier that his personal view about the attitudes of the African students responding to the Sautman and Yan questionnaire he had administered in 2008, and from his own individual interviews was that 'the majority of African respondents were negative about their experience of the Chinese.' Indeed, some respondents had added that they felt the provision of scholarships from China was a 'second colonisation of Africa'. His own personal view on racial prejudice in China towards Africa was that some African students never saw anything good about China because of the discrimination displayed by Chinese towards Africans while there. The racial abuse he felt was directed at skin colour instead of taking account of the positive contribution of the African communities in China. Overall, as was mentioned earlier in this chapter, his own view on this sensitive issue was clear: 'If I would rate or summarise the attitude of African students towards China on a scale of positive, slightly positive, indifferent, slightly negative and negative, I will say NEGATIVE.'

In this connection, it is worth underlining that the survey he was helping to administer was not based on just a handful of Africans in one university; rather it covered Tianjin University, Tianjin University of

---

[46] http://ng.china-embassy.org/eng/xw/t794324.htm The Nigerian ambassador to China admitted in 2009 that Nigerians were responsible for about 90% of the crimes committed by Africans in China (Taylor, 2011: 87).
[47] http://ng.china-embassy.org/eng/xw/t850456.htm

Traditional Medicine, Tianjin Normal, Tianjin University of Technology and Education, Tianjin Polytechnic University, Nankai University, Tianjin University of Finances and Tianjin Foreign Studies University.

He was clear that one could not strictly compare attitudes gained from a survey of African students in China in 1997 (Gillespie's survey) and from 2008 (Sautman and Yan). Much had changed, including many of the university rules, the former Communist ideology, and not least the influence of the market economy. But he felt that though there had been some positive responses in the survey he had helped administer, these were because the African students were making positive statements about the marketability and acceptability of Chinese goods in Africa rather than about Chinese attitudes towards Africans and African students in China.

Furthermore, he was certain that the FOCAC process and particularly the Beijing Summit of November 2006 had helped change African leaders' mentality about Chinese prejudice towards Africa. But on the ground, he felt that if it came to any dispute between African students and Chinese authorities, it was obvious that the law was on the side of the Chinese. For this reason, he added, 'many Africans, including himself, would not want to stay in China for a long time.' Nevertheless, despite the legal and racial problems, the sheer availability of Chinese scholarships and the relatively low cost of study and of living was continuing to draw students to China.

Moving from these wider issues of racial attitude to the crucial question of the impact of studying in China on himself, he would be the first to admit that the work ethic of the Chinese students and faculty had altered his own approach to his job: 'This had really changed my attitude to work and to my lectures as a lecturer. I hardly ever come to class late or to appointments; moreover I have banished that phrase "African time" from my diction'!

*From African student to African business in China and Cameroon*
Almost the last of our profiles in this section is also not with a ZNU student, but with a Cameroonian who had come to China in 1998. On the racial discrimination against Africans, he had a balanced view; of course many African students had experience of racism and were bitter about it. However, there was absolutely no point in pursuing this. On the other hand, African students recognised that China was a good place to see how development was actually working out in practice. There were also powerful messages to be learned in China about the value of hard work and the importance of discipline.

Not surprisingly, given the shortage of work back home, many Africans elect to stay on in China, and they explore joint business opportunities with China. This student had started a consulting company in 2005 which specialised in providing Africans with access to China and vice versa. He had also found a role in facilitating China-Africa business development after the 2006 FOCAC summit. His knowledge of Mandarin was vital in these ventures.

*A South African student in China*

Although the illustrations have come from Kenya primarily, they could have been drawn from Ethiopia or from South Africa. One of the South Africans, a graduate from Stellenbosch, spent five and half years in China. It was hugely influential on his later behaviour, not least because of the Chinese impact on his own work culture:

> I was never late for class. Except once. When I came late, the only place was right at the front. I went down there and the professor offered me a cigarette, and then lit it for me. I smoked it surreptitiously but I was never late again. Being in China affected my own behaviour later on. I will never forget this episode in my whole life.

There is a view that contradicts this positive connection between the gains of education and the move into China-Africa business. Rather it argues that the social and educational environment in Chinese universities does not impress the students. Allegedly this disappointment with the educational experience obstructs the promotion of Chinese values such as those just mentioned, thus obliterating the soft power potential of Sino-African educational exchanges. It is in part this discontent with the quality of the education in China that leads to African students turning to trade instead of their studies in China (Haugen, 2012b). There are examples of this, but most of our Kenyan and other students do not confirm this view.

# Aid-supported English medium Masters training in China

We have mentioned already that the mainstream government-supported scholarship scheme in China, associated with the China Scholarship Council (CSC) gives strong priority to learning Chinese in an intensive year of language training before embarking on the substantive degree. This emphasises the crucial importance of students getting inside the language and culture as well as their learning alongside Chinese students in their main years of study. However, as in many other countries providing scholarships, there is not a single highway for scholarship support in China. We have, for example earlier in this chapter and elsewhere, looked at the range of scholarships associated with the Chinese Language Council (Hanban) via Confucius Institutes in Africa.

Here we shall briefly mention the emergence of a very different modality, following the FOCAC IV of 2009 in Sharm El Shaikh. This was a Masters in Public Administration and it was offered in Tsinghua University and also in Peking University.[48] The aim was specifically to serve the needs of some 200 middle and senior level African officials. The medium of instruction was English and hence there was no major emphasis on

---

[48] It appears to have started in Peking University even earlier than FOCAC IV.

acquiring Mandarin before starting the course. Although some parts of the course were taken only by officials from developing countries, there were apparently some courses that were shared with Chinese students of international public administration.

At the same time in the field of educational administration two intensive International Masters in Education degrees were also initiated, one in East China Normal University (ECNU) and one in North East Normal University. These were delivered entirely in English, and the students from Africa who were on them were taught separately from Chinese students. Surprisingly for Chinese Masters degrees, the new Masters in ECNU was delivered in just one year, as compared with Masters of three years where there is a year of Mandarin as a precondition.

One of the Zimbabwean students on the ECNU masters found the course so influential that she decided to come back at her own expense but with a particular desire to catch up more on Chinese culture and language for she had not had the time during her first very pressured one-year Masters degree. She had not fully worked out how China benefits from all these students they fund, 'but one thing is certain: it is fast becoming a place where people want to be!' (Zimbabwean student to KK, 10 November 2011).

## Issues for further reflection and policy analysis

This tour around some of the history of African students in China and some of the debates brought up by our discussions in Kenya as well as in China suggests a number of avenues for further reflection.

*Contested perceptions on racial discrimination and prejudice*
We have noted from Hevi's, Gillespie's and Sautman's analyses and studies that there are very strong comments that Chinese and African students in China have been prepared to make about each other. On the other hand, in Sautman and Yan's more recent and not yet fully analysed work, there are signs of a discernible shift. At the level of the individual African student or graduate returnee with whom we have discussed this, we have encountered a good deal of maturity about this issue, and a recognition that prejudice is often related to ignorance. The pace of internationalisation of China's universities is certain to continue to have a positive impact on the awareness of Africa. But the fact that one of the recent presidents of the General Union of African Students in Tianjin should consider attitudes towards Chinese students by Africans still to be largely negative must continue to be a source of serious policy concern.[49]

Interestingly, one of the most recent publications on African students in China discusses many different issues but reserves just four lines for the issue of racial discrimination, as follows:

[49]  The fact that he is a Nigerian and must be aware of the critical generalisations about Nigerian students in China may be worth bearing in mind.

We're used to it by now but it's still annoying to be a black person in China on a daily basis. We have to endure the rudeness of taxi drivers, people in public transportation, etc. And it's not really a communication problem because I speak fluent Mandarin. It's not necessarily racism. But it's ignorance! (Ferdjani, 2012: 28)

*Very powerful positive impacts on attitudes and values at individual and institutional levels?*
One of the constant refrains from both present and past African students in China is their admiration of the work ethic of their Chinese student counterparts. This has also led to a fascinating set of claims about the impact on the individuals of being exposed to this particular culture of work. How these influences can in turn translate into the working environment back home is a very different issue. Civil service traditions are notoriously difficult to change, unless the incentive and management systems are changed.

These challenges to the transfer of attitudes and values, as well as of knowledge, were tackled by the Commonwealth Scholarship Commission's evaluation of impact in what they called key priority areas. The intention of the survey was to find some answers to the following questions:

- Did the award benefit you in terms of your individual knowledge and skills?
- Did the award, and those skills, benefit you in terms of your employment and career?
- Have you been able to pass on those skills and that knowledge?
- Has your award increased your ability to have an impact on your place of work?
- Have you maintained links with contacts in the UK?
- Have you been able to have an impact on wider society? (CSCUK, 2009: 18)

The Commission would acknowledge that individual assessments of these questions are highly subjective and notoriously difficult to demonstrate; nevertheless the great majority of returnees were able to point to very specific illustrations of knowledge transfer and influence.

There could well be a case for research in China to carry out something parallel. There has been an equally long time frame; there have been policy shifts over this lengthy period. Certainly, there would be an interest in how graduates of Chinese universities are received back in their own public and private sectors. Many of the questions about individual, institutional and societal impact are equally of concern to the Chinese policy and academic community as they are to the Commonwealth. There would be widespread interest within comparator scholarship agencies about the results of any such survey, whether Africa-wide or restricted to four or five countries in the first instance.

*Exploring impact via associations or unions of African students in China*

Although we have noted that unions or associations of African students in China still have a slightly uncertain legal standing, a few of them operate vibrant websites and have good data on their coverage and branches, and even on the individual members, in the case of the Sierra Leone Union of Students in China. This might suggest that they could play a role in identifying former members of their unions or associations who had already returned home. It is not immediately clear from their websites if there is an African students' alumni association operating at the country level. In the case of Ghana, 'Alumni' are referred to on the home page menu, but this is one of the pages still under construction. It is, however, known from our student discussions that Cameroon does have an active alumni association for former students in China. The most readily accessible associations seem to be Cameroon, Ghana and Sierra Leone, with Ghana claiming, at least amongst these, to have the largest number of members in China. It should also be recalled that former Kenya students in China had formed an alumni association as early as April 2003 (China, MOE, 2005: 20).

It would also be possible to use the good offices of the General Union of African Students in Tianjin (GUAST), which appears to be well organised, but only covers a single city.

Perhaps in these days of social networking sites, alumni associations may be replaced by other mechanisms. The numbers of graduates are presumably still too small for particular universities in China to be maintaining associations in Africa in the manner of leading US and UK universities.

*Exchanges of students or predominantly one-way scholarship flows and targets*

China historically has preferred the language of student 'exchange', as in its African policy rather than presenting itself simply as a provider of scholarships.[50] The reality seems to be that there are few countries in Africa, with the exception of Egypt, which independently send students to China on national scholarships. Rather, we have noted that in the case of several especially Francophone countries, their national scholarships seem to be added on to those candidates who are awarded a China Scholarship. They become therefore a kind of additional allowance, topping up the CSC award.

The introduction of targets for both long-term and short-term awards within the FOCAC framework reinforces the emphasis on one-way flows rather than exchanges. This particular focus for the presentation of scholarships and training awards dates from the Second FOCAC conference of 2003 in Addis Ababa, but it caught world attention in the Beijing Summit

---

[50] Thus in *China's African Policy* (2006), the term 'exchange' appears no less than 18 times in just eleven pages to describe different kinds of two-way collaboration. By the time of *China's Foreign Aid* (2011), the term 'exchange' was only used once in 18 pages.

of FOCAC of 2006. Up to a month before the Summit, the language in the draft declaration had been incremental: 'Gradually increase the number of scholarships for African students in China, which now stands at 1,200 per year'. Within a few weeks, it had become: 'Increase the number of Chinese government scholarships to African students from the current 2000 per year to 4,000 per year by 2009' (FOCAC, 2006a; 2006b. 5.4.4.).

The salience of target-setting in the discourse of international education in general has been sharply criticised by Jansen in his 'Targeting education: the politics of performance and the prospects of "Education for All"' (2005). There is a sense in which the targets become the policy, or become a substitute for policy. The same is true for the Millennium Development Goals (MDGs) and the whole evaluative apparatus that has been constructed around them.

We should not exaggerate the significance of the scholarships having become a key FOCAC target. But it does then mean that there has to be a mechanism for determining that the target has been met. This was duly put in place with the formation of the Chinese Follow-up Committee of FOCAC (King, 2009a). There is no parallel African Follow-up Committee of FOCAC, presumably because it would be difficult across 50 different African countries to track precise scholarship numbers. And in any case it could be argued that FOCAC remains a bilateral mechanism with a Pan-African face. As far as scholarship numbers are concerned, short-term training awards, or any of the other pledges such as hospitals or schools, these continue to be agreed through bilateral arrangements.

In summary, although targets in education remain a valuable yardstick, in these days of agency concern with 'value-for-money', 'results' and 'impact', it would be valuable, through focused research, to be able to go beyond the merely quantitative achievements claimed in this way for education by *China's Foreign Aid* (2011:14):

> By the end of 2009, China had helped other developing countries build more than 130 schools, and funded 70,627 students from 119 developing countries to study in China. In 2009 alone, it extended scholarships to 11,185 foreign students who study in China. Furthermore, China has dispatched nearly 10,000 Chinese teachers to other developing countries, and trained more than 10,000 principals and teachers for them.

The other side of student exchange is of course the question of symmetry in Chinese students electing to take up scholarships offered to them in Africa, or electing to go on their own resources to Africa, or accepting Chinese scholarships to study in Africa. We know from the Ministry of Education's review of educational cooperation between China and Africa that sending Chinese students to Africa was seen as critical in improving China's understanding of Africa. Hence a first group of students were sent to Egypt very early on. We have already mentioned that Egypt offered on its own account scholarships to Chinese students. By the end of 2000, some 270 Chinese students had gone on Chinese scholarships to Egypt, Kenya, Morocco, South Africa, Senegal, Tanzania, Tunisia and some other countries (China, MOE, 2005: 21).

An increasing number of self-funded students from China also went to Africa. Indeed, the Chinese Ambassador in South Africa claimed that there were 1000 Chinese students in South Africa (Ambassador to KK 12 October 2012). This is not the principal focus of this chapter but it might still be insightful to note the safari to South Africa of Iris Wu, even if this is just a single enterprising, privately funded student:

> After trying three times to go to the US, she found she could go and do English for half a year in the Cape Peninsula University of Technology. She then went to the University of Port Elizabeth, but found it too quiet, and she wanted to combine study with work. So she applied to the University of Western Cape, and was accepted in 2003, and completed honours and masters, and is now doing a PhD. In 2007, she started a Chinese restaurant in the university, and now has five staff, African, Chinese and white. The same year she started a Chinese Student Society to which any Chinese students can come. Shortly, she had organised a Chinese Education Exhibition which brought as many as 45 universities from China in 2007 and 62 in 2009 to advertise their courses, and offer scholarships to South Africa. Finally, and presumably to keep herself busy, she organised the first Confucius Classroom in the Cape Academy near Cape Town. In an opening ceremony on 2nd March 2010, the Chinese Consul General did the honours, and teaching of Chinese started on the 15th. (Iris Wu to KK 14 March 2010)

*Towards a political economy of China's scholarships or a scholarship policy with Chinese characteristics*
There are a number of issues that arise in the discussion of African students in China which are *sui generis*. First, there is the notion that the Chinese were the only people in the world to be free of racial prejudice (Snow, 1988: 204). This question of discrimination has been sufficiently raised in this chapter for it to be clear that there has been a continuing problem on this at different times, and at certain points this had threatened the wider political discourse about China-Africa cooperation and friendship.

Second, since the establishment of FOCAC in 2000, mentioned above, China appears to have pursued a genuinely Pan-African approach when it comes to the distribution of scholarships. Unlike some scholarship donors who focus on a particular subset of countries in Africa, China appears to offer scholarships in all of the 50 African countries with which they have diplomatic relations. This is not to say that there is exactly the same quota for each of these but, given that there have been roughly 1,500 new scholarships per year since the Fourth FOCAC conference, the order of magnitude is approximately 30 awards annually per country. It will, however, be invaluable to know more about the distribution process. Illustrative of its working out in practice is that in a university like ZNU there are no less than 29 different African countries represented in their African student body, half of whom are on CSC or CI awards.

Third, it has been argued that African student numbers were politicised following the events in Tiananmen Square in 1989, and that the visible absence of African government criticism of China was rewarded by doubling of scholarships (Nordtveit, 2011a:101). On reflection, this seems unlikely given that in Nanjing, just a few months before Tiananmen, there had been large-scale anti-African protests. It would have been difficult in the wake of this event dramatically to increase African student numbers. The evidence points rather to the increases taking place in the later 1990s. We revisit this issue in Chapter 6.

Fourth, we started this chapter with a very strong ethical claim made by the Ministry of Education in respect of African students in China. These principles about people-to-people exchange, mutual benefit and friendship remain central to China's discourse about cooperation with other developing countries, even when the policy reality is that scholarships have become FOCAC targets and when there is little evidence of symmetry in terms of Chinese students going to Africa in large numbers. Arguably, however, these fundamental principles are not dependent on exact symmetry. Win-win economic, cultural or educational cooperation does not depend on precisely equal activities within the education sector but rather on a shared appreciation that the other party is an equal, and that there is mutuality across the range of both economic and social cooperation.

Lastly, there is the basic question of whether scholarships and the offer of Chinese language training, in China or in Africa, constitute soft power. The very term, 'soft power', with its emphasis on obtaining what 'one wants through cooption and attraction' (Jian, 2009) sounds very much at odds with the fundamental principles just mentioned above. Indeed, at first glance, soft power as a concept seems to sit rather outside the 'symbolic universe' of South-South cooperation which Mawdsley has proposed, based on solidarity, direct development expertise, empathy from shared experience, and the virtues of mutual benefit and reciprocity (Mawdsley, 2011; 2012). But this too we shall revisit in Chapter 6 on soft power.

On the other hand, scholarships, whether from China, India, Brazil or South Korea, do give direct access to the development experience of countries that were until recently very poor. They may also be seen as a form of solidarity since they do not provide the host universities with very large fee incomes as UK and Australia do. Indeed, we have seen that the amount of the scholarship in China is such that some African countries deliberately top it up. As to mutual benefit and reciprocity, we have noted that there is no exact symmetry; 'student exchange' is actually more of a one-way than a two-way street. So too is cultural exchange, and especially since the development of the Confucius Institutes from 2004.

But the transfer back to Africa of some 12,000 CSC alumni or alumnae from China in the period from 2006 to 2012 alone is a substantial figure. As scholarship holders, they would have acquired Mandarin, and as we have seen in some of our student case studies, they find themselves teaching Chinese in both the public and private sectors, or getting involved in joint ventures with Chinese companies.

Assessing the reciprocity from China's point of view is complex. The explicit purpose on the China Scholarship Council website is short and applies to all international students, obviously, not just those from Africa. It is:

> In order to strengthen mutual understanding and friendship between the Chinese people and people from all over the world, and to develop cooperation and exchanges in fields of politics, economy, culture, education and trade between China and other countries. (CSC)[51]

How that ideal translates into practical action is not the responsibility of any Chinese ministry. But it obviously makes an enormous difference to the possibilities of using skills acquired in China, including the language, if there is a large and active Chinese presence back home. As compared to the pioneers who came back, and like our earliest Kenyan, might forget all about it, graduates are in some African countries returning to a situation where, as one Nigerian alumnus described it, the Chinese are 'in every nook and cranny' of his state. So the routine assessment of individual, institutional and societal impact of study abroad is very different if the graduate is returning to a unchanged or even disabling economic environment, as opposed to one where there are opportunities to use Mandarin skills as translators, interpreters, tourist guides or teachers. Thus the presence of large and growing communities of Chinese migrants is directly impacting on the utilisation of the language skills acquired abroad, not to mention other skills and knowledge.

The deliberate forging of links between graduates and China, in the manner of the Commonwealth's professional networks, has not yet happened, as far as is known. Chinese embassies in Africa tend to organise special functions when a large group of scholars or professional trainees is setting off for China.[52] But it would appear that active networking amongst the returned graduates has not yet happened apart from the case of Cameroon.

As far as reaching a neat conclusion about China's scholarship students from Africa is concerned, that is of course still possible, and eminently worthwhile, as it was in the case of the 2009 Commonwealth students' survey. But it needs to be remembered that it is now more than twenty years since privately funded students could apply to come to China. So whatever conclusions may be drawn about the 30 to 40 Ghanaians going annually on CSC awards to China, there are apparently around 1,000

[51] en.csc.edu.cn/Laihua/dd6ed814b3074388b197734f041a42bb.shtml
[52] See for example: en.csc.edu.cn/Laihua/dd6ed814b3074388b197734f041a42bb.shtml

Ghanaian students in China, as mentioned earlier, 95% of them privately funded, and many of these studying medicine. This presents suddenly a very different challenge to establishing what reciprocity between Ghana and China in aid-supported student numbers might mean. Equally, establishing the impact of Chinese study on the Ghanaian health sector would need to pay serious attention to the role of private Ghanaian students getting their medical training in China.

The same argument applies to those who would argue, as one of our case study students did in November 2011, that China is engaged in an undue degree of cultural diplomacy. He commented that, as far as China scholarships are concerned, 'some Africans are of the opinion that this is leading to a second colonisation of Africa.'

Back in 1989, the year that the South African cartoonist, Zapiro, did his famous sketch of the Fulbright scholars trekking back home with their American flags, there were no privately funded Ghanaians in China,[53] and the term soft power had not yet been used by Nye (1990). Now, just as 80 per cent of international undergraduate students in US higher education are self-funded, a similar situation is clearly true of Ghanaians in China (Belyavina, 2011: 67).

Fifty years after John Hevi, the Ghanaian author of *An African Student in China,* quit China in disgust along with 96 of the other 118 Africans whom China had brought to the Institute of Foreign Languages in Beijing, the Ghanaian students are back in China with branches of their national student association in eight cities. And unlike Hevi, the great majority are now paying to be there. More generally, of the 20,744 African students in China in 2011, no less than 14,428 are privately funded and just 6,316 are on government scholarships (Gu, 2012).

[53] Self-funded students were allowed to come to China for the first time in 1989 (China, MOE, 2005: 15).

# 4

## Chinese Enterprise & Training in Africa | A theatre for win-win cooperation?

In many contemporary accounts of Western aid and capacity-building in Africa, there would not be a close connection between aid and trade. The deliberate links between aid and trade provision, once very common, were broken in the UK, for example, with the 1997 White Paper on Development (DFID, 1997).[1] By contrast, in Japan, there still seems to be an expectation that there be a close connection between official development assistance (ODA) and trade. In the 2003 ODA Charter, for instance, it is stated clearly that:

> Japan will endeavor to ensure that its ODA, and its trade and investment, which exert a substantial influence on the development of recipient countries, are carried out in close coordination, so that they have the overall effect of promoting growth in developing countries. (Japan, 2003: 3)

In the revised version of the ODA Charter, which is significantly entitled *Enhancing Enlightened National Interest* (Japan 2010a), there is a great deal mentioned about cooperation with the private sector, including 'Facilitating participation by Japanese local companies and small-scale enterprises (SMEs) in ODA projects' (Japan, 2010: 15); indeed the term 'private' is used 24 times in just 21 pages.[2]

What of China? Where does enterprise figure in its own public statements about overseas aid? In the government's own first, historical account of its 'foreign aid' (China, 2011a), it is clear in just a few paragraphs that a key part of its reform of aid was the inclusion of the private sector. For example, the establishment in 1993 of the Foreign Aid Fund for Joint

[1] The deliberate linking of the donor's aid with the donor's own private sector interests (Aid and Trade) should be distinguished from Aid for Trade which is the encouragement through donor aid of recipients' trade development.

[2] Japan is not alone in aid cooperation with the private sector; former Canadian CIDA has been indirectly supporting Canadian mining companies in their corporate social responsibility activities through its support to NGOs working with those companies. See http://www.cbc.ca/thecurrent/episode/2012/01/26/cida-partnerships/

Ventures and Cooperative Projects 'was mainly used to support Chinese small and medium-sized enterprises to build joint ventures or conduct cooperation with the recipient countries in the production and operation spheres' (China, 2011a: 2).

We should also recall that one of the red threads going through Premier Zhou Enlai's Eight Principles of China's aid to foreign countries, set forth in Accra in January 1964, was the economic dimension. Premier Zhou referred constantly in his tour of ten African countries, not to the need for aid-as-charity but for 'mutual economic assistance'. In addition, the Eight Principles refer to 'economic aid', and to 'independent economic development' for China's partner countries.

*China's African Policy* (January 2006) takes a similar line almost 50 years later. 'Trade' is mentioned nine times in just eleven pages, whilst 'aid ' is used only once and then only in the context of humanitarian aid. 'Economic cooperation' and 'economic win-win cooperation' are emphasised as central to sustained China-Africa relations. As we noted in earlier chapters, economic cooperation is not something that China does to Africa; rather it is claimed to be a mutual benefit and essential to common development or to the achievement of common prosperity (China, 2006). We should be aware, however, that the construction of an aspirational discourse around common development may depend on a simplistic view of development-as-economic-growth (Mawdsley, 2012: 158–9).

While China's aid and African policies are full of the discourse of mutuality and reciprocity, there are few areas of China's presence in Africa that have proved more sensitive than business, labour standards, and labour practices. We shall turn to look at some of these instances in a moment,[3] but our principal concern in this chapter is with the impact on training and skills development in Africa of China's presence in so many different sectors, from agriculture, to construction, mining, manufacturing and infrastructure. Some elements of these activities are linked to formal development assistance from China implemented by Chinese firms; many others are contract jobs by Chinese firms won in the face of international competition.

There is, however, one unique dimension of China's business and labour practices in Africa that needs constantly to be borne in mind. This distinguishes China from all other expatriate national contractors in Africa. This is the sheer number of Chinese migrants, who have come to Africa over the last ten to twenty years. The exact numbers are not known but Park[4] estimates that the total may be at least one million. Many of these are regular employees in the Chinese companies operating in Africa, whether international brands such as Huawei and ZTE, or construction firms such as China Road and Bridge Corporation; others are contract workers on large infrastructure projects secured by China; others again are

---

[3] For a valuable account of China's aid in relation to OECD/DAC definitions of aid, see Brautigam (2011a).

[4] Yoon Park to KK, 8 January 2012. See also Park (2009).

individual, independent entrepreneurs, large and small, starting up factories in capital cities, in the large number of China Malls, or in export
promotion zones. But others again are very small shopkeepers, traders and
farmers. We should not forget the expanding numbers of those involved in
Chinese medicine.

This is therefore by no means a homogeneous group, but differs not
only in terms of type of employment (formal, informal and self-employed),
but also in skill levels. It has been suggested in this connection that the
great majority of China's temporary migrants are semi-skilled (Park, 2009:
6). This could have been the case in the earlier waves of migration,
whether in Zimbabwe[5] or in South Africa. But it must be recalled that the
very great bulk of the millions of young people migrating temporarily from
the poorer western provinces of China to the eastern seaboard have got
nine years of education, and many may also have had some three years of
upper secondary vocational education. Whether those migrating
temporarily to Africa have a very different level of education and training
must be a matter of further research but it is unlikely.

A similarly comparative point could be made about the training practices of Chinese firms in China and in Africa. In China, according to the
World Bank's Investment Climate Surveys, some eight out of ten Chinese
firms in China itself are training either through using their own training
capacity or buying these services from the market.[6] It would be surprising
if firm behaviour was dramatically different when the enterprise moved to
Vietnam, Cambodia or to Africa. But one of the key determinants of firm
behaviour being similar overseas might be the presence of appropriately
educated local African labour. Here there is clearly a very great difference
between South East Asia and much of Sub-Saharan Africa (SSA), with the
exception of South Africa. There are still relatively small proportions of
the SSA secondary school age cohort getting access to junior, let alone
higher secondary education. And unlike China where almost a half of the
upper secondary cohort would have access to vocational education, many
Sub-Saharan African countries have less than 5 per cent of their parallel
cohort receiving vocational education and training.[7]

The interaction of Chinese workers with host countries in Africa differs
greatly depending on government policy on migration, as well as on
different historical traditions of Chinese settlement; but there is a widespread tendency for Chinese migrant communities to remain separate for
social, economic, cultural and language reasons (Park, 2009: 10). This is
not enforced as it once was on the Indian communities in white settlement Africa by discriminatory colonial legislation, but is a matter of preference. Clearly, this affects the character of their interaction in the
countries to which they have migrated.

However, in their working relations with Africa, there are still some

---

[5]  Aeneas Chuma (UNDP) to KK, July 2009.
[6]  I am grateful to Van Adams for drawing this to my attention, Adams to KK, 11.1.12.
[7]  For detail by country see UNESCO, 2012b.

common patterns of influence. There are of course some transfers of skill, technology and knowledge, whether informally in the 'China shops' offering low cost consumer goods, or on the construction sites, in restaurants or in the formal factory settings. But there is also the influence of attitudes and values. There is, for example, the Chinese work ethic which leads to six and a half to seven day weeks, and to ten to twelve hour days. This is not just an ethic of hard work but an attitude to manual work that finds no problem with managers cleaning their own offices or the compound, or using similar transport and accommodation to employees. One agricultural expert from China in Ethiopia mentioned that his Dean in a particular agricultural college had told him: 'Don't just transfer knowledge to your students but also your working attitudes, like the readiness to carry containers etc etc' (Peng Dajun to KK, 10 February 2009). In the Ethio-China Polytechnic College, the Chinese Dean of the college had made a point of becoming involved in routine cleaning of the college grounds, as was mentioned earlier in Chapter 2.

It is important to underline the point that, in the case of micro-enterprises, these skills, technology and attitude transfers are not at all part of any training project. In the case of Kenya, for example, a great deal of the current technology and production methods used in the Kenyan informal sector today was transferred informally from small-scale Indian entrepreneurs in the 1930s, 1940s and 1950s. African employees painstakingly sought to pick up the technologies of welding, soldering, cutting metal and many skills from carpentry, to forging to vehicle repair (King, 1977; 1995). But this was in no sense a "training project"; it was effected informally on the job. There was no parallel to this transfer in agriculture. Indians were prevented from owning land in several white settlement countries, such as Kenya and Southern Rhodesia; hence there was little Indo-African transfer of agricultural technologies during the colonial period. By contrast now in Kenya, all the common vegetables, herbs and spices used in Indian cuisine are routinely provided by small-scale Kenyan farmers. The same is true of items of Indian cooking such as *chapatis* which are now widespread in thousands of small African eating places.

Doubtless there will be parallels with the Chinese migrants, and there will in due course be movement from the Chinese growing Chinese vegetables in farms in Ethiopia, as is happening now, to Ethiopians providing these for the Chinese and other communities. Patterns will be affected by context and culture. Thus in Kenya it was initially the Kikuyu who were most influenced by the Indian migrants because there were similarities between their cultures of work and enterprise ethics. There will be similar developments with China which will be affected by culture and context both in China and in Africa. Thus there are now very long-standing connections between the particular Chinese provinces of Zhejiang, Guangdong and Fujian, and particular countries or parts of countries in Africa. In the same way for Chinese medical teams, the historical connections between particular provinces and particular countries, going back to the time of Mao, may continue to be strong (Snow, 1988).

The sheer scale and diversity of the Chinese business presence in Africa may well mean that in terms of numbers, the in-plant, on-the-job training of Africans, formally or informally, in Chinese firms on the continent dramatically outweighs the numbers of those who are being trained in China, whether as long-term students, or as short-term trainees. If training is a key element in China's soft power, then the training of tens of thousands of Africans through Chinese foreign direct investment in Africa will need to be borne in mind.

We have seen, however, in the case of African students in China, there is still some measure of debate and disagreement about the nature of the experience (Chapter 3), but there is a great deal more in the case of Chinese business presence in Africa. We shall touch on some of the debates in this chapter, but they include the views that Chinese businesses are flaunting local labour laws, that they are not operating on the decent work agenda of the ILO, that they are using prison labour from China rather than employing Africans, and that they are flooding Africa with unskilled Chinese labour in preference to training and employing Africans.

Such allegations are difficult to dismiss. Some claims, like the use by China of prison labour, are extremely widespread, and doubtless derive from the separation of the Chinese workers from their African counterparts, their extremely long hours, their tendency, especially 30 to 40 years ago, to wear almost identical dress, and also from jealousy at the Chinese contractors winning so many infrastructure and construction projects in Africa. We heard these rumours from ambassadors in Africa to NGOs, and from senior academics to policy makers. The fact that serious scholars (Sautman and Yan, 2010), journalists (Michel and Beuret, 2010), and the Centre for Chinese Studies in Stellenbosch (2006) have all rejected these criticisms unequivocally may not have a rapid impact, as the allegations seek to explain China's extraordinary business success in Africa.[8] One of the ambassadors we interviewed admitted that he had no evidence for his views about this, except that he considered the whole of China to be a prison.

We shall review some of the other claims about Chinese labour practices in Africa as we proceed, but it is important first to establish the crucial relationships between the different kinds of formal education and training with which the first three chapters have been involved, and the role of Chinese business in Africa.

---

[8] 'To hamper the Chinese image, the dragon slayers and some NGOs have spread the rumour that most Chinese workers in Africa are actually prisoners. But in all our travels we have not met a single one and feel free to assert that this is anti-Chinese propaganda' (Michel and Beuret, 2010: 253). 'There are widespread rumours of Chinese construction companies in all countries surveyed using Chinese prison labour. We found no evidence to support these rumours' (Centre for Chinese Studies, 2006: 81). Interestingly, our contacts in the Chinese Embassy in Nairobi had not come across these rumours.

# China's support to short- and long-term training and the role of Chinese business in Africa

We have mentioned above that the presence of Chinese businesses, large and small, in most African countries is a unique factor in assessing China's cooperation with Africa. This is not to claim that Chinese business presence is somehow an integral part of China's foreign aid policy, even if it is possible to point to explicit connections between aid and trade. Rather, we would argue that the main training initiatives discussed in the first chapters of this book are very directly affected by the presence of dynamic Chinese businesses in so many parts of Africa.

Thus the interest in learning Chinese in the Confucius Institutes, as well as in many of the private language training centres, would not be the same without the Chinese business presence. This is not to say that all students in Confucius Institutes are driven by vocationalism. Some have more intrinsic reasons for study as the following suggests:

> When a beginners' class of language students in the Confucius Insti-
> tute in Nairobi were asked about their main reasons for deciding to
> learn Chinese, the attractions of Chinese culture and learning rated
> almost as frequent a response as those connected to business and
> employment opportunities in Kenya and China. Some saw the link
> between understanding the culture and history and unlocking the
> secrets of China's development path. One put it differently: 'Chinese
> culture is very diverse – like a hard nut that you just have to crack!'
> Another said: 'I find the Chinese language to be unique and interesting
> and they have a very rich culture which I enjoy learning about' (2nd
> year students in Confucius Institute, University of Nairobi, 5th August
> 2009). [King, 2010: 492]

Even if a majority of students in a Confucius Institute in Europe or North America would not necessarily have explicitly vocational orientations, in countries in Sub-Saharan Africa where often only 5–7 per cent of the work-force have formal sector jobs (Johanson and Adams, 2004), the increasing presence of Chinese companies in the last decade has been one of the significant changes in the formal sector labour market. It should not be surprising therefore that Kenyan education policy makers should assume that there should be a linkage between a Confucius Institute and the surrounding Chinese business community. Indeed, it was precisely the absence of such a community around Egerton University in Kenya's Rift Valley that led the Permanent Secretary of the Ministry of Education to declare that a Confucius Institute would not be appropriate there. This was perceived to be the important criterion despite there having been a higher education partnership between Egerton and Nanjing universities since 1994.[9] Interestingly, as we noted in Chapter 2, it has since then been decided to open an Agricultural Confucius Institute at Egerton, linked to Nanjing Agricultural University.

Similar aspirations and ambitions lie behind the thousands of students who have sought out China scholarships in recent years; it is doubtful if China would have become almost as attractive a study destination as Germany, in the eyes of Kenyan scholarship applicants, if China had not been so visible in the transformation of roads, provision of public buildings, development of other infrastructure, such as a new port on the Indian Ocean, and a pipeline across most of the country. The awareness of Kenyan traders beginning to go to China in large numbers, and the start of Kenya Airways flights to China would have reinforced this, as would the rapid rise in Chinese tourism and construction of hotels in Africa. In this sense, China's scholarship aid was more appealing because of China's trade and tourist presence. We shall return to the controversial side of China's presence on the streets of Nairobi later in this chapter.

Something of the same calculation would have been in the thinking of the 20,000 African professionals who will have gone on short-term specialist training courses to China between 2010 and 2012. The Commercial Councillor's Office of the Chinese Embassy would have prioritised courses, in discussion with the Kenya Government, which could link to particular investments in infrastructure, agriculture, small-scale enterprise, and so on. Even if the courses could not be exactly termed 'project-related training' with a close link to Chinese investments, it is clear from the trainees' evaluations that some of the participants regarded them in this light.[10] This is certainly the case with the interest in the aquaculture short course designed for South Africans by China, an interest in part derived from the Chinese aquaculture project in Gariep Dam in Free State.

Not surprisingly, the training and work aspirations of students in the Ethio-China Polytechnic College (ECPC) outside Addis Ababa are even more closely connected to direct experience of Chinese business. Several of the students who were interviewed had already worked alongside skilled Chinese in factories or in micro-enterprises in Ethiopia. Hence, their selection of the ECPC for further study was a deliberately vocational move.

Although there are these multiple connections and reinforcements between the formal support to training by the Chinese Government and the presence of Chinese business, we would not argue that this constitutes a coherent and explicit strategy of those in the Chinese aid policy community who have planned these forms of educational cooperation through the Forum on China-Africa Cooperation (FOCAC). Indeed it would appear that in many countries there has not been an attempt to join up even these major training initiatives with the various development projects supported

[9] Permanent Secretary to KK, July 2009

[10] I am grateful to the Commercial Councillor's Office of the Chinese Embassy for providing me with some of the trainee course evaluations (Embassy to KK, 17 May 2011).

by China, let alone with the role of Chinese business. In one West African country, in fact, the disconnect between the training policies on the one hand and the multiple Chinese projects on the other is only too clear:

> In fact, hundreds of young Cameroonians have been sent to study in Chinese universities since the 1960s. Many have returned home with degrees in medicine, engineering, technology, agriculture, management and a good mastery of the Chinese language. Unfortunately, these China graduates, who would have played an important role in bridging the language and cultural gap between China and Cameroon, have been less visible in China-supported projects. (A. Mahamat to KK, 7 January 2012)

Further confirmation of the absence of joined-up thinking between training policy initiatives and other development policies is evident in the decision in 2011 by Peking University's Centre for African Studies and UNDP to launch an analysis of the relationship between the Chinese government's formal scholarship scheme for Africa and its development outcomes. The project asks the question: 'To what extent has the implementation of this scholarship policy achieved the policy goal, both in terms of concrete as well as less tangible impacts?" and "What developmental or poverty reduction impacts in sending countries have been achieved through the scholarship programme?'[11]

We shall return to the coherence of the different components of the aid or cooperation policy in Chapter 5. But China would not be unusual in the development community in having some degree of fragmentation amongst the different elements of its cooperation. Equally, in the case of many other agencies it would be rare for there to be much explicit interaction between its human resource development (HRD) initiatives and its overseas business community. Our point was a different one: that there was certainly a relationship perceived by the African student community between China's HRD provision and the reality of Chinese business on the ground in African countries. The very presence of many different kinds of Chinese business gave a fresh meaning to the provision of scholarships, training courses and Chinese language courses.

## HRD dimensions of Chinese business in Africa

Apart from the perhaps obvious point that the very presence of diverse Chinese firms acts directly to increase the vocational relevance of many training options, our main concern here is to review the variety of ways in which Chinese business in Africa acts to transfer technology and to build capacities, if indeed it does so. Our starting assumption is that if this happens it can be formal or informal training. And we must never forget that training *per se* is very seldom a high priority in many business

---

[11] It should be recalled however from Chapter 1 that poverty reduction is less frequently the goal of China's than of Western aid.

cultures. Rather, it is a means to an end, a way of ensuring sustained income generation.

Our case studies will seek to give a flavour of how technology transfer and skills development are situated within the different kinds of business environment represented by China in Africa. Our interest is not princi-pally in whether the African workers in such firms are unionised, or are on permanent contracts, or receive the minimum wage. These issues have been valuably looked at in other studies such as those by the African Labour Research Network, and notably by Baah and Jauch (2009) in their ten case studies of the labour perspective in a series of mostly Anglophone countries.

## Chinese multinationals in telecommunications

It is probably important to specify the sector even for multinationals, since some of them, especially in the food and drinks field, may have much less need for elaborate training, trouble-shooting and capacity development. The quality of the product is secured by the manufacturing process which may be highly controlled. Only a handful of specialised technical staff are required. Other staff are in accounts, marketing and sales. The situation is clearly dramatically different when the entire telecommunication network of a country is being installed, or where Chinese telecommunication suppliers are in competition with other international brands.

What are some of the skill development and technology transfer issues that arise when firms once based in China go international, and in partic-ular when they begin operating in developing country environments? Training and very specific capacity-building on the nature of the company's products are very high priorities. Interestingly, in the case of ZTE in Ethiopia, one of the first announcements associated with its gaining its initial contract for a telecom spine across the whole country was the iconic number of 1,000 Ethiopian engineers from Ethiopia Telecom Corporation (ETC) to be trained by the company. These employees are not of course being trained from scratch but being re-trained to understand the ZTE tech-nology. Unlike China, where the knowledge base of new entrants to the firm would be known, but where there would still be the need for firm-specific training, the Ethiopia challenge was thought to be different. There was a specific solution laid out on the ZTE website:

> Considering the large requirement for training and weak knowledge background of ETC, ZTE provided progressive training services, from basic theories to product knowledge, practice with equipment and on-site practice, to the key technical personnel for ultimately improving the comprehensive skills of trainees.[12]

---

[12] www.en.zte.com.cn/en/cases/services/knowledge_services/201002/t20100203_180117.html accessed 12 January 2012.

Apart from installing the equipment to drive the whole national system, they have also at a cost of US$ 10 million dollars, necessarily set up a state-of-the-art training centre. Not all training is delivered in Ethiopia however; there is a ZTE University in Shenzhen in China, and some 100 Ethiopians are going there annually for more advanced training. Even though there are two human resources departments in ZTE Ethiopia at the moment, one for the Chinese and one for the Ethiopian employees, the ultimate target of technology transfer to Ethiopia is clear: 'Our goal is to train more technical personnel for Ethiopia and make Ethiopian engineers take over the whole network by our knowledge transfer' (Guo Jinyuan (ZTE) to KK, 12 January 2012).

As far as the Ethiopian staff in the firm are concerned, they are aware that the Chinese firm won the contract by putting in a more competitive bid than some of the European providers. Salaries might be higher if they were working for Nokia or Ericsson, but, in the words of the Ethiopian HR manager: 'The positives about being here are that it is a very good place to learn. Essentially it is on the job training, but there is also the possibility of virtual training' (Henok Woldemagene to KK, 8 April 2010).

One of the other differences between ZTE's operations in China and in Ethiopia is that there is a recognition of the need to bridge different cultural contexts. Hence Chinese staff historically received an orientation to Africa and to Ethiopia specifically. One particular cultural difference concerns the work ethic of the Chinese and the Ethiopians. For some of the Chinese staff, their purpose of being in Ethiopia is just to work: 'We have nothing to do except eat, sleep and work. And we don't charge for over-time' (ZTE staff to KK, 9 April 2010). Inevitably, there is something of a contrast with the Ethiopian staff who have family and social responsibil-ities and who cannot afford just to work on after 5.30 without overtime, or to work at the weekends.

Another feature of the larger corporations is that they do get involved in corporate social responsibility (CSR); so it is not surprising to hear that ZTE has begun to offer access to their training labs to students from college. This brings to mind a parallel in Kenya, where the multinational Huawei, one of ZTE's great rivals in telecoms in many African countries, has decided to open its training centre in Nairobi to Kenyan university engineering students. This will apply to the University of Nairobi and to the Jomo Kenyatta University of Agriculture and Technology, just outside Nairobi. The Kenya facility, which is one of no less than six regional training centres that Huawei has in Africa, is expected to be upgraded into a research and development centre to enable such graduates to develop and test their telecommunication inventions locally.[13] Students will not have to pay to use the facilities.[14]

---

[13] http://www.techmtaa.com/2011/06/02/huawei-to-open-its-nairobi-training-centre-to-kenyan-engineering-students/. This may be part of Huawei's decision to become more publicly known, see Garside (2012).

[14] For a more pessimistic account of China and CSR in Africa, see Knorringa, 2009.

Training can of course be a double-edged sword, since the telecom sector is extremely competitive. Apparently there is a good deal of poaching amongst the four leading firms. Hence high quality training has to go alongside firm loyalty.

But like ZTE, Huawei finds that for perhaps similar reasons there are really two sets of staff. In the view of the Kenyans, the Chinese staff have a more closed kind of life and they work together. They have set themselves targets and they have longer hours. They really believe in themselves, and seek to achieve their goals. They stay together and work in groups; they often work over the weekends, and there is no paid overtime.

In the Huawei training centre, most of the training is from Africans to Africans, the preferred mode. There is, therefore, something of a similar perception of the Chinese staff by Africans as there was in ZTE. But the overall view from the senior Kenyans in HR is that there is 'good symmetry, civility, freedom and responsibility; we all become target-driven' (Peter Thuo to KK, July 2009).

## Corporate social responsibility (CSR) and Chinese firms in Africa

CSR is not of course uncommon for multinational firms to engage in, and it is noteworthy that there other clear examples of it which link to our topic of training and technology transfer. For instance, China Petroleum,[15] which has gained the contract for the second oil pipeline from Nairobi to Eldoret across the Rift Valley, is planning to assist Egerton University (which is on the route) with a laboratory with modern welding equipment (already delivered to Kenya). A Chinese professor who has been in a partnership project between Egerton and Nanjing Universities for some 14 years is the official go-between on the project. Meanwhile, next door in Uganda, ZTE has initiated a pilot project of arming 300 teachers with mobile phones, to encourage lower cost networking of ideas with other teachers, as well as providing access to the Internet.[16]

The University of Nairobi has benefited from further scholarship support to medicine, geography, and to its Confucius Institute from Holley Cotec which is one of China's large pharmaceutical companies, heavily involved in herbal-based malaria drugs. Similarly, China Road and Bridge Corporation (CRBC) has been involved in Kenya in presenting computers, and has worked through a Kenya women's NGO on other projects.

---

[15] China Petroleum Engineering & Construction Corporation
[16] See Tumushabe (2012), 'Chinese company arms teachers with phones in bid to improve teaching.' I am grateful to Richard Webber for this reference.

# Training and development philosophy in the crucial infrastructure firms

China Road and Bridge Corporation (CRBC) is no newcomer to Eastern Africa; one of its earliest projects was in Somalia in the 1970s, and it was involved in the first China road project in Ethiopia, even during Emperor Haile Selassie's time. It is now a multinational, working in no less than 23 countries in Africa, and 35 world-wide, including Pakistan and Myanmar. Its managing director in Kenya has reflected on the contradiction between the absolute necessity of roads-for-development but the very low GDP of some of the countries in the East African region presents a real challenge of implementation. His view is that countries need to follow a development path of roads first, then rail, linking to ports. Further, on labour practice, while there was little difference in principle between Chinese and Africans, in practice it sometimes works out that the Chinese achieved 100 per cent more – perhaps again for some of the reasons we have alluded to above (Du Fei to KK, July 2009).

The old Chinese adage about the centrality of infrastructure for development and of roads in particular as a path towards growth and income generation is powerfully supported by a Nairobi university academic, Musambayi Katamunga, who appreciates the unique role that China appears to be playing not only in Kenya but in Africa more generally. He places this in an historical context, after noting China's road and rail developments in the Beira corridor, Congo, Zambia, Angola, Tanzania, Nigeria, Ethiopia and Kenya:

> China is an actor that is prepared to go into remote places where it has a comparative advantage. It provides infrastructure where it is needed. Without infrastructure nothing can take place. Road and rail are the most basic infrastructure but also communication. If you look at this, the current impact of the Chinese may be as large as the Kenya-Uganda railway a hundred years back. (Katumanga to KK, July 2009)

He goes beyond this to argue, in parallel with CRBC, that with the inability of some of the East African states to develop their own vitally important infrastructure, China in doing so is actually in the business of reinforcing African nations:

> This is why we are saying that infrastructure is critical. All these African states are very weak, and so their capacity is created by infrastructure; the Chinese are actually thus playing a role in state formation via infrastructure. There is therefore an interesting convergence of African leadership with China's objectives. (ibid.)

The key point about labour training on construction projects is that it is impossible to generalise. Worldwide, construction has had the reputation for using very poor standards, and drawing upon very large numbers of sub-contracted workers for whom the main contractor has no responsibility. A very great deal depends on the overall policy of the government of the country and the tradition of the particular company.

Thus, in Ethiopia, one of China's aid projects, in the form of a hospital promised under the FOCAC 2006, is being built through a contractor, the China Jiangxi Corporation for International and Technical Cooperation. It has a whole series of projects in Ethiopia, some aided and some directly commercial. According to the Chinese management, the work culture of the 26 Chinese and the 120 Ethiopians reflects the kind of differences which we have already commented upon:

> The Chinese work hard, but the Ethiopians and the Chinese respect each other. Training is only one month for the Ethiopian labour – which is semi-skilled. We have a high turnover, because as soon as they have learnt, they can go elsewhere. Thus, everyday there are several new faces. (Xiao Xin to KK, April 2010)

By contrast, but still in Ethiopia, a local entrepreneur, Messele Haile, who had been educated in the Tokyo Institute of Technology through Japanese scholarship aid, had developed a large-scale modern country club residential project, with every modern convenience. He reached an agreement with the Ethiopian government that he could import between 100 and 65 skilled Chinese workmen for all the key trades. They would have their own housing, their own food, and would grow their own vegetables. There was no immigration problem, and they would go home annually at Chinese New Year. However, the key to the agreement was related directly to training: for every Chinese skilled worker, ten Ethiopians would be trained. It was a major challenge since the training would go to the very peasants who had been working some of the land on which the new residences would be located. According to Messele, this is not an isolated scheme; there is a further scheme linked to the Shanghai Construction Company where 50 Chinese workers have been allowed on a similar training-for-immigration basis (Messele Haile to KK, February 2009).

Confirmation of some of these trends in our case studies, and of the overall, crucial importance of government policy comes from the Stellenbosch Centre for Chinese Studies' review of the state of affairs in the construction and infrastructure sectors in four African countries. The different policies of governments made a vital difference to the outcome. Thus in the case of Tanzania, Chinese companies did pay low wages, but not below the minimum wage. The Chinese engineers on these projects were paid approximately 10 per cent of what their counterparts in Western countries received. The usual reports were made on the companies operating a seven-day week, and sometimes, in tight deadlines, on a 24 hour day. But the great majority of the workforce was Tanzanian, and there was also evidence of Tanzanians in management roles:

The Chinese workers were generally found to be well-organised and their workers considerably better-disciplined than many of the workers in local construction companies. The majority of Chinese companies in Tanzania reported that up to 80 percent of their workers are local and one company reported that 95 percent of its total workforce is local. A good number of companies reported that they employed locals as managers and several reported local staff at senior management levels. (Centre for Chinese Studies, 2005: 58)

In concluding this discussion on construction and infrastructure which is such a central part of China's approach to development, we may suggest that, as with the Italians in Ethiopia,[17] so with the Chinese contractors, there may be a substantial transfer of skills and of technologies in this very critical sector of the economy. Much of the skills transfer will be on the job, but whether on the job or in colleges such as the Ethio-China Polytechnic College (ECPC), one of the most crucial elements of skills transfer may be in the attitudinal domain, in the readiness to take on both manual skills as well as technical and knowledge-based, and to avoid the temptation to consider that the higher the level of technical knowledge, the less the need to be involved in skills. In the words of the deputy dean of the ECPC:

> There is a big difference between Ethiopia and China. We Chinese are ready to do everything, manual or intellectual. The picture is of the Ethiopians in cars and wearing suits as engineers, versus the Chinese engineers getting into the lorry or whatever transport was available. The Ethiopian attitudes to work and to knowledge are rooted in their culture and are difficult to change. But here in the college, most of the college's administrative staff are from China, and so it is possible to influence them step by step. One of our missions – and it is the main mission – is training. So as administrators, our habits and ideas and ways of working and thinking can be an example. We hope our rules and regulations can change the local culture. (Chen Xiaoxi to KK, April 2010)

## The challenge of training for the smaller Chinese company

In many of the areas where the Chinese have entered the market, there has been very stiff competition. This would certainly be true of the telecommunications area which we have touched upon. The same would be true of construction, including in East Africa from Kenyan Indian contractors. However, in many other product lines China has brought in dramatically

[17] Senior Ethiopians frequently point to the Italians as a source of excellent technical skills, after which there was an enormous gap for 20 or more years with little or no skill development during the period after Emperor Haile Selassie.

lower cost versions of well-established lines, such as motorcycles. Sometimes the Chinese versions are a full third less in price than the Japanese brands.

The case of one Chinese assembler of motorbikes in Kenya illustrates some of the limitations upon training alone as a separate element in the success of business. It still does play a key role, but there is in addition the question of the enabling (or disabling) environment as will be discussed later in this chapter.

One of the characteristics of many of these owners of small companies is that they are already part of business networks, both in China, and in some cases also in Africa. In the example of this particular entrepreneur, he had already done oil exploration in the West of China, sold heavy lorries in China, and then decided to check out his brother's experience of working for a Hong Kong company in Nigeria for fourteen years. He went to explore Nigeria in 2000 and found it a little too like what Michel and Beuret had described in Chapter 2 of their book: 'How the Chinese found their Wild West and called it Nigeria' (2010: 29–44). He decided against Nigeria on the grounds of family life. A few years later another friend in his network suggested Kenya; so he came to explore in 2005 and found that it was indeed possible just to open shop and start selling, as opposed to having the much larger capital to do wholesale.

As a small-scale motorbike assembler, his key concern on the training front underlines the difference between the education and skill levels of Kenyans and of young people in China which we have referred to above. In Kenya by contrast, only a minute proportion of young people in the first eight years of basic education any longer have access to practical skills training; that strand was removed from the syllabus at the end of President Moi's regime in 2002.

In the words of our assembler in regard to on the job training, it was not easy:

> Why? The use of tools; you would tell them but they would still make mistakes. With putting down the serial numbers there would frequently be a mistake with one or two of the numbers. With tightening nuts, they would do it more on one side than the other. Or they would force it on against the thread. They kept on making mistakes right up to now. For office staff it was easier, but for the mechanics it was difficult; only 2–3 would have qualifications. (Assembler to KK, July 2009)

There were other problems such as pilfering from the premises and stealing tools. On the other hand, although there were the usual differences with work ethic, punctuality,[18] and overtime between Chinese and Kenyan approaches, there were nevertheless two of the Kenyan staff who could be entrusted with millions of Kenya shillings. Small and medium-

---

[18] But punctuality is a key issue –'"I'm coming" means that you are sometimes hours away. If however they are late three times, we don't accept [it]. They have to start on time' (Assembler to KK, July 2009).

sized businesses like this also face a disabling business environment.

One of the leading issues in undermining the investment climate in Kenya is the extent of corruption, both petty and large-scale. As has been pointed out in many surveys, any routine contact with officials for permits, licences and so on can become a corruption opportunity (World Bank, 2004; Iarossi, 2009). In the case of this assembler, these problems were rife, and then for every item related to the motorbike there is a series of corruption opportunities, such as getting the number plates, the registration books, the log books, and so on.

## The two faces of corruption

If one crucially important dimension of corruption is the disabling environment created by the all-pervasive local culture of both petty and larger scale corruption, whether in Kenya or in other SSA countries, the other side of corruption is the attitude of the Chinese firms to this expectation. We did not study this dimension in our analysis of skills transfer, but we should acknowledge that at least one senior African manager claimed that using corrupt practices strategically was itself one of the skills transferred from the Chinese:

> Since this communication between you and me is for real studies, and people who will get access to them should know about this, then let me say this: yes most of our engineers know about our products and to some level there has been skill transfer but I wonder if the Chinese in our firm really have good work ethics that we can learn from. Perhaps I'm biased, but believe me I'm in charge of all local HR matters I know each and every thing that happened in the office. So I would say we never got positive work ethics from them; rather they spoiled the good on our side by showing us how to bribe a customer to sign a contract. Even I myself I have attended project managers' training on how to bribe customers in the so called firm's theory of bribe — ABOVE TABLE AND BELOW TABLE — that is, give above the table the contract to be signed and the kickback beneath the table. So it is not that we are learning their good work ethic, but because everything is so corrupt, it is rather that we all are losing our good national work. So sorry for the hard words I have used to reply to you. (Manager to KK, April 2010. Emphasis in original)

## Training through different business modalities

There are clearly several different varieties of China-Africa business arrangement. The character of these makes a difference to the role of training and capacity-building. Connecting the experience of 'learning in firms' by Africans in Chinese firms in the continent with the history of *Technological Capability in the Third World* (Fransman & King, 1984) would be important, but only some very preliminary points can be made here.

### Wholly owned Chinese enterprise
A wholly owned Chinese enterprise such as the one we have just discussed will employ and train labour at their own discretion. Although there has been a levy-grant mechanism at work in Kenya for several decades to encourage training, few small-scale enterprises engage with it, as it is too demanding of form-filling for the small-scale sector. Historically, very few Indian-owned firms participated in this scheme either, except when they became very large-scale.

### Joint ventures between Chinese and Africans
A lot will depend on the proportions of the equity, but where the African share of equity is high (45% and higher) there will be African management along with Chinese. Will this make any difference to human resource policy? Not necessarily. In some situations, however, as with a case study in Nigeria, a joint venture with some Nigerian management may mean that the local managers take care of all the labour issues, almost like a subcontractor. 'Being a trading company, the Chinese handle management and sales, we take care of the finances, business locations, local mid-level cadre and low-cadre staff recruitment and some other local responsibilities the Chinese might not be able to easily handle' (Nigerian joint venture manager to KK, 13 January 2012).

### Turn-key installations and operations in Africa
When, on the other hand, the Chinese are supplying and installing machinery, then of course they undertake training for the client's personnel either in Nigeria or in China. In the case study of a corrugated carton factory, two sets of personnel were trained in China, but for any trouble-shooting, a technician has to come from China, with all expenses being borne by the Nigerians. Increasingly, as more and more Chinese machinery comes into Africa, this crucial form of maintenance training or training for sustainability will become even more important. The same challenge faces Huawei and ZTE as they sell and install whole systems into African countries. This is precisely why Huawei has developed no less than six regional training centres across the continent. Nor is it a very different challenge for the Ethio-China Polytechnic College, where all the machinery for all the different trades is from China. At present, in early 2013, there are four Chinese instructors still in the ECPC, but managing the transition to completely local responsibility will be a challenge, and especially so once all the Chinese instructors are localised.

*Specialised turn-key projects with government agencies*
There will be differences again when it comes to such Chinese projects. A notable example has been China's support to Nigeria's National Space Agency Programme. Very specific training conditions were laid down in the agreement. As noted by one key informant: 'A number of young technicians were sent to China by the government to study space technology and this crop of young engineers now constitutes a strong knowledge base in the national space centre' (Nigerian joint venture manager to KK, 11 January 2012).

But even with China's aid projects, whether in infrastructure, construction of hospitals, schools and so on, there will be significant differences towards the training of local people depending on the urgency of the project and the degrees of freedom workers have in moving to new jobs. Thus in the China Jiangxi Corporation for International and Technical Cooperation's building of the hospital in Ethiopia, there were fresh faces every day, as some workers tended to leave to search for new situations as soon as they had secured basic training.

## Chinese traders and China shops in relation to Africa's informal economies

At the smallest level of Chinese business in Africa, there are significant numbers of Chinese moving to Africa to search for business opportunities, however small. Again, it is difficult to estimate the extent of this migration but the sense that there is an opportunity in Africa has been disseminated at many different levels within the traditional provinces of migration and amongst thousands of workers in China who are looking for new opportunities. In these provinces there is almost an encouragement to migrate as part of growing up.[19] Two very contrasting commentaries on how Africa is perceived can be mentioned. On the one hand, long-established Chinese businessmen in Nigeria perceived Africa as a unique opening:

> "Africa is just one immense opportunity that came at the right time for us," Zhang says. Jacob Wood [also Chinese] goes even further: "I'm going to be honest with you. China is using Africa to get where the United States is now, and to surpass it. It is willing to do anything to achieve that, even build a Nigerian railroad that has not a hope of making money or launch a Nigerian satellite into orbit". (Michel & Beuret, 2010: 39)

On the other, a professor in an African Studies Centre in China told the author that he sometimes got calls out of the blue from would-be migrants saying 'Is it true that it is possible to get land to farm in Africa?' But what-

[19] 'It has become a rite of passage for the men (and more and more women) of these villages to spend at least some time overseas. Young people from these areas are under social pressure to go out into the world and return successful'. (Park, 2009: 5)

ever the motivation, and the networks and connections that facilitate migration, individuals are turning up in Africa's capitals, towns and markets, and setting up shop. There are naturally differences in government policy towards migration and towards who is allowed to trade. Thus, in Ethiopia, small-scale foreign traders may not set up stalls in the Mercato (market) in Addis Ababa. But in Dar es Salaam, in the main market, called Kariakoo (after the Carrier Corps of the First World War) the author, along with a Chinese colleague, has talked to traders from China who said they had just arrived and were already working in smallscale trade. The same is true of many traders operating in the Chinese Malls in Durban; some of them only arrived a few weeks or months ago.

At this level of micro-enterprise, the intention to set up a stall in the market or to open a 'China shop' will be affected not just by government policy on migration, but also on the vibrancy, spread and competitiveness of the local informal sector. Thus in Kenya, and particularly in Nairobi, the sheer dynamism and activity of the informal (*jua kali*) sector is such that it might prove difficult for outsiders to find a foothold. Nevertheless, the Chinese challenge at the micro-enterprise level did prove to be serious. Some *jua kali* enterprises were defeated by the competition, but others appear to have learnt from the Chinese, just as they did from the Indians several decades earlier.[20] Nevertheless, the intense competition between the *jua kali* and the Chinese traders flared into actual protests in August 2012 with 'Chinese must go' slogans being carried to the prime minister's office. Although this was just a one-day protest, it is not clear what level of *jua kali* were behind the protest; but it would seem that in part it was the Kenyan importers of Chinese merchandise who were being undercut by Chinese importers in Kenya.[21] This is confirmed by a local analyst:

> Rather than the manufacturing *jua kali,* it was the small scale traders (micro actually) like hawkers and small time peddlers of mostly Chinese goods termed *mali mali* here in Kenya (loosely translated as fast moving consumer goods and trinkets) that were worried that the Chinese were infiltrating that sector and using their personal relationships with Chinese suppliers to undercut them in business so that the indigenous guys couldn't compete. The protests were thought to have been orchestrated by larger scale traders who supplied the peddlers and suddenly found their own Chinese suppliers were competing with them on the ground. (Wakaba to KK.5.12.12)[22]

---

[20] According to Gadzala: 'two trends that were beginning to emerge: 1) some local ventures were going under; 2) jua kali enterprises were diversifying their strategies and learning how to hone their competitive advantages to remain afloat in the marketplace.' Gadzala to KK, 30th April 2012. See also Gadzala (2009).

[21] http://www.bdlive.co.za/world/africa/2012/08/23/kenyan-businessmens-protests-raise-tension-with-chinese

[22] Though there are notable exceptions (see King, 1995), Wakaba correctly points out that there is in fact little competition at the manufacturing level: Kenyan cottage industries remain rudimentary at best and show little inclination to scale up, adapt technology of any kind' (ibid.).

The same may not be true of Namibia, Zambia or Botswana where there is a much less dynamic local informal sector. It might be expected, however, that the same would be true of Ghana, Nigeria and other West African environments where there is a hugely dynamic informal economy with its long-established patterns of training and apprenticeship. Nevertheless, in Douala in Cameroon, interestingly, there is abundant evidence of Chinese street sellers of grilled fish as well as of doughnuts, both of which are very popular.[23] They sell vegetables and breakfasts on the street, and one Chinese, Liu du Camer, even started a band playing local Douala music.[24] In Dakar, the dramatic transformation of the main boulevard with Chinese shops was marked by it being called informally 'Boulevard Mao' (Gaye, 2008: 129).

In Ethiopia, where there are also dynamic trading communities, there appears to have been 'learning from the Chinese', at the level above the smallest micro-enterprises. Gadzala, drawing particularly on the competition in leather between Chinese and Ethiopian entrepreneurs reached the following conclusion:

> Therefore, there is an indirect training dimension of China's firms. Simply stated, Ethiopian (and I believe this can be extrapolated more broadly to most African) companies faced with Chinese competitors are being thrown into the deep end and must quickly learn how to swim. Those which do, float, and those which don't, sink. In a curious and indirect way, Chinese firms teach market capitalism to local industries. (Gadzala to KK, 30 April 2012)

However, also in Egypt where there is already a very large local trading community, it would appear that Chinese traders have managed to make a foothold, and are even marketing the traditional local foods:

> What about Chinese entrepreneurs? There are two groups – the larger Chinese entrepreneurs whose investment we all want. Then there are the Chinese vendors who want to go and trade in Egypt. We are very forgiving when it comes to work permits etc. So Chinese vendors come with products which cover high class to low class needs. They are even going to the countryside, and there are clips in Egyptian films of Chinese vendors on three wheelers selling Foul medames [Fava beans]. The situation in many African countries is that these Chinese entrepreneurs large and small are acting in a vacuum, but in Egypt the market place is already full with all kinds of traders. So there is less space. (Hany Selim, Egyptian embassy, Beijing to KK, May 2009)

We have briefly reviewed the training and human resource sides of the many different faces of Chinese business. On the one hand there may be the very formal training of local staff in a Chinese aid project or in a Huawei regional training centre. On the other, and particularly with the

[23] Eliane Nugent to KK, 15 January 2012.
[24] Adam Mahamat to KK, 15 January 2012

small and micro-enterprises, there may not be any formal training provided at all; what is available at most is training on the job, working next to Chinese skilled people. This is how skills and technology were transferred in Kenya from Indian to local small-scale business. It may happen again with the Chinese.

There is a parallel with the Jewish traders in South Africa who were trading at rock-bottom prices and who were also setting up little shops in the Karoo. Over a hundred years, Africans have been working for these Jewish shops, large and small, and have picked up skills. Now, in turn, these Jewish stores are faced with direct competition from Chinese traders, and it is the China shops which have replaced the Jewish shops in the Karoo.[25]

But there is a major difference between the role of the Chinese traders in the 21st century, whether in Cairo, Dakar, Bloemfontein or Dar es Salaam, and the Indian artisans who were operating all over Kenya's towns in the 1920s, 1930s and 1940s. Then, the Indian artisans were actually fabricating cooking braziers, cooking pots, utensils, small lamps, and cutting and bending iron to make a whole range of basic household commodities. Now, the China shops and China mall traders are mostly not fabricating; they are importing a massive variety of products which are ready-made. In some countries, for example, Nigeria, there are 'China shops' run by Nigerians with the same range of products.[26]

Richard Dowden of the Royal African Society makes the point well, sitting in a small village in Western Uganda in 2006:

> The tablecloths at the hotel are made in China, so are the lampshades, plates, cups and cutlery – and the little bunches of plastic flowers on each table. Even the rice they eat comes from China. The cars in the street come from Korea and Japan. In fact almost every manufactured thing I can see has been made in Asia. (Dowden, 2009: 484)

Before we move from our case studies to review the wider literature related to Chinese business in Africa and its implications for training and capacity development, we should acknowledge that there is a view in the African policy community that this conjuncture of Chinese investment in Africa is a moment of great opportunity. For instance, in July 2009, the then Kenyan Minister of Education was absolutely clear that the moment was ripe, with the Chinese, to go for greater technology transfer:

> Learning from the Chinese? We are facing hunger right now; we need to use their technology to develop hundreds of dams. That is what we

---

[25] One of the well-known Jewish stores in Bloemfontein showed the author a receipt for eight items bought in their store in 1911, including two suits, for a total of £5.00 sterling. Right next door, in the Chinese mall, garments were being sold today at a fraction of the price of the Jewish store. (Rabinowitz [82 year old owner] to KK, 11.10.12).

[26] Another interesting finding is that many Nigerians, especially those who cannot find regular employment and those laid off as a result of factory closures are daily turning into the operation of China shops' retail activities.

are going to do. Transfer of technology is the key. The nation that does not believe or participate in technology transfer is not a nation. (Sam Ongeri to KK, July 2009)

He was also very clear that there was a world-wide opportunity to outsource from China, including by Kenyans. But equally important, from the minister's perspective, there was a unique chance to learn from China's business presence in Africa: 'The main features of the Chinese interaction with Kenyans are. 1.Their attitude to work is perfect. 2. Their capacity to attain their goals. The speed of reaching their targets. 3. They achieve this without social upheavals' (Sam Ongeri to KK, July 2009).

This rosy view from the minister's office may need to be contrasted with the realities and limitations of skills and technology transfer at the level of the individual construction site, restaurant or China shop. After all, as the then Chinese ambassador to Kenya stressed: 'Take Chinese companies. Profit is the key. They want to cut prices to get bids; but we need to be aware of the regulations and intervene to insure propriety in Chinese business' (Ambassador to KK, August 2009).

Such individual policy approaches as that of the Kenyan minister and the Chinese ambassador, however, also need to be translated into overall government policies. This is extremely difficult to achieve when Chinese migrants are coming into countries in very large numbers; nor are all the migrants traders and business people. There are even academic entrepreneurs. One of these arrived with a delegation in early October 2012 in Johannesburg, and declared to the author that they were checking out where they would establish a Confucius Institute. But right there near China Town in Johannesburg, at 23 Marcia Street, there already was what could be called an informal sector Confucius Institute, even with the Hanban logo on the gate. Controlling such enterprising initiatives from Hanban in Beijing or from the Chinese Embassy in Pretoria is becoming increasingly difficult. We turn now to look at how human resource development (HRD) with a Chinese face looks in different HRD policy regimes.

# Orient Express, bulldozer, and locomotive in human resources strategy

Deborah Brautigam, in seeking to dispel some of the myths about China as a 'rogue donor', has discussed the notion of Chinese companies as a kind of 'Orient Express' transferring 'hordes of experts' to Africa. She admits that China does use more of its own people as staff and technicians than any other country (Brautigam, 2009: 154). But the idea that China just planes in its own experts and does not train locally, she argues, is simply wrong. As far as capacity-building on its aid projects is concerned, she points to the existence of five clear steps that Chinese experts are meant to follow in the implementation of all projects. The exact origin of this five-step guide is not yet known, but of course it resonates with the Eight Principles of foreign aid laid down by Zhou Enlai in January 1964 in West Africa:

> First, as early as possible, inform recipient country staff of the time when Chinese experts will be leaving, so that they can prepare. Second, Chinese experts should gradually transfer to the second line, letting the recipient staff work independently and practise solving problems on their own. Third, instruct recipient country's staff in repair and maintenance of major equipment, and focus on areas of weakness. Fourth, help staff organize blueprints and drawings about gas lines, etc., and the operating instructions for equipment. Fifth, make a booklet of the various standard parts, and their categories. Draw simple pictures of non-standard parts so that they can be ordered as needed. (Shi Lin, trs. Brautigam, 2009: 345–6)

We shall return to Brautigam later in this chapter, but the transport metaphor of the Orient Express is continued in a fascinating article by Tang Xiaoyang on the bulldozer versus the locomotive in China's capacity-building approaches in Angola and the DRC. The bulldozing perspective suggests a clean sweep, with the Chinese delivering the project exactly to time and to target:

> The first one brings a large number of Chinese technicians and emphasizes speed and cost efficiency. In this pattern it looks as if a whole Chinese company has moved to Africa. Like a powerful bulldozer, it cleans the ground very efficiently, but has no essential interaction with others and its impact is limited to the work it has done. (Tang, 2010: 13)

This model is illustrated particularly in post-conflict settings where there are serious shortages of skilled artisans, technicians and managers. The bulldozer approach may be particularly attractive when the Chinese project is awarded by politicians who perceive the strong two or three year advantage of the road, bridge, stadium or dam being completed to high quality on time, before the next election (ibid.: 14). Such projects do not have the luxury of long-term training approaches, including perhaps degree or diploma training in China. Situations where this approach is appealing are very short of local talented managers, and those that do exist can command much higher salaries than their Chinese counterparts. Other reasons that promote short-termism would include the fact that highly skilled Chinese workers do not want to stay for a second or third contract. As we said earlier, the comparative advantage of the Chinese in the rapid provision of essential infrastructure plays a key role in state formation in Africa.

> The other model focuses on establishing close links between Chinese and local people in order to integrate the Chinese company into the local community. The company is pursuing long-term profit by creating

synergic growth together with Africans. Using the strength of the Chinese side, such as capital, technology, efficiency, this model, like a locomotive, can contribute to a much larger scale of local development, including training, indirect employment and market prosperity. (ibid.: 13–14)

Tang's second model of the locomotive builds on a different aspect of China's comparative advantage: that they are in Africa for the long haul.[27] According to Katumanga whom we quoted earlier, the philosophy of Confucianism – of dedication, hard work, and long-term aims, not just for today – is strong in many Chinese migrants. The same point has been made by a Chinese ambassador quoted by Yoon Park:

One Chinese ambassador to a large African country argued that most of the Chinese migrants to Africa had one dream: that was to return home to build a three-level home or 'monument' to their success overseas. To them, hardships of life in Africa are worthwhile and surmountable because they are seen as temporary. He explained that there is a cultural value placed on suffering for the longer-term goals; without hardship, there is no gain. (Park, 2009: 9)

This personal philosophy suggests of course that there are powerful forces transforming the bulldozer into the locomotive. But there are some contradictions at the heart of this search for sustainability in Africa. Given that Chinese companies' success has been based on low-cost, high quality delivery of complex projects on time, the move to localisation of technical and managerial cadres is problematic in the short term. Not least this is because in most African countries, these cadres are in very short supply, and hence can demand higher salaries than their productivity may justify. As the Global Monitoring Report (GMR) of 2010 argued, the future of satisfactory skills development for much of Sub-Saharan African depends on a dramatically higher proportion of the age cohort entering both general and vocational secondary education than at present (King, 2011c; UNESCO, 2010). This could ease the challenge of sustainability facing many Chinese companies.

Capacity-building by the Chinese in Africa is not simple. For the aided projects, many of them of high political importance as we have mentioned, there are inherent difficulties to securing genuine capacity development along with the political commitment to deliver at high speed. This is perhaps one reason why Brautigam has said that 'Like other donors, the Chinese have not yet figured out how to build capacity or really transfer their skills' (Brautigam, 2009: 161).

But with the majority of non-aided Chinese projects, it will be crucial for African countries to continue to develop much larger cadres of well-educated and well-trained young people than at present. This is of course

---

[27] A third view, arguing that there is short-termism in the management of state owned enterprises, is supported by Haglund (2009).

also the case for other foreign direct investment than Chinese.

## China in Angola: The case of skills in the construction sector

Before moving to look at other dimensions of the skills environment in Chinese businesses, it may be worth looking at a study that relates directly to Angola, one of the countries considered in the above bulldozer versus locomotive analysis. Corkin's study of construction is unusual and valuable in taking skills issues very seriously but in a sector which we have noted is notoriously poor, worldwide, at investing in training (Corkin, 2011). She makes a number of key points which underline the crucial importance of context and skills culture rather than trading allegations about whether a company trains or does not train labour in Africa. The first of these is that there has been an historical lack of investment in education and skills training for the bulk of the population in Angola. The country lacks even the data on secondary and technical secondary participation rates to report to the EFA Global Monitoring Report (UNESCO, 2010); but when Sub-Saharan Africa as a whole has only 1–2 per cent of the age cohort in technical secondary education, and the continent as a whole has only two million technically trained people as compared to East Asia's 22 million, it can be seen that finding educated and skilled labour in Angola will be difficult.

The sheer scarcity of locally abundant sources of skilled workers and managers, and the political priority to employ these, has meant that such a premium has been placed on the few that exist they are more expensive to hire than many expatriate cadres.[28] With such a history of low investment in education, and with the very serious evidence of desperately poor levels of achievement for those who have attended basic education, there is no quick solution to the skills vacuum without fixing the quality of primary education and paying attention to secondary school numbers: 'One important policy conclusion to be drawn from the data in these regions is that no national policy for developing skills is likely to succeed unless governments dramatically increase the flow of students into secondary school' (UNESCO, 2010: 81).

Corkin gives considerable attention to the difference in the work ethic between Chinese and Angolan workers; it is an issue that has been a red thread through this whole chapter. Like the absolute scarcity of secondary-educated and skilled artisans in Angola, this is certainly not something that can be sorted out speedily. It must be remembered, however, that in countries like Angola the percentage of workers in the formal economy is very low, possibly less than 10 per cent. Only this group, and not all of

---

[28] Corkin quotes the example of someone in London with 40 years' experience being cheaper to hire than an Angolan local (59).

them, will receive social benefits, such as leave, sickness pay etc. Like the education 'elite' just referred to, this formal sector 'elite' is distinctly privileged compared to the remaining 90 per cent of the workforce, many of whom will effectively be in the informal sector, whether rural or urban. This then sets up a fundamental inequality in the work force, and arguably the informal sector has a work ethic much closer to that of the Chinese: typically, they will work all day, including weekends, and there is no concept of overtime, nor any social benefits. Many of the complaints that Corkin records about work ethic relate to work practices of formal sector workers. By contrast, if the Kenya informal sector is anything to go by, the 'Chinese workers' ability to "eat bitterness" or work extremely hard' may actually be paralleled in Angola's informal economy (Corkin, 2011: 61).

Another cultural issue of note is that the Chinese practice of bringing Chinese labour to Africa is actually based on a practice in China itself, in which contractors from one city or province will take workers from that location to where they have secured a contract in a different province. In other words, it is local labour that is preferred rather than Chinese.

In the Angolan setting, therefore, Chinese construction companies are being expected to operate in a rather different way from at home, and with a different level of education and skills than in China. They are also competing, in effect, for workers from the small formal sector. Or they may indeed be expanding the numbers of formal sector workers through the sheer scale of their infrastructure projects. The result may not necessarily be an increase in regular wage and salary workers with all social benefits; some of the new workers, and especially those working for Chinese or Angolan building sub-contractors, may actually not receive regular benefits. They may experience a kind of informal employment within the formal sector.

As in Ethiopia and in Kenya, the large multinationals like CRBC and Sinohydro do get involved in serious training policy, including overseas training in China. However, this kind of company will be acting very differently from some of the smaller Chinese contractors and sub-contractors. Currently, there seems to be some difficulty in linking the scholarship recipients back into work positions on their return to Angola (Corkin, 2011: 67). A similar problem was noted earlier in this chapter in the case of Cameroonian recipients of Chinese government scholarships on their return. Clearly, there needs to be some greater coherence and integration between Chinese companies and Chinese government-sponsored overseas training and integration into relevant projects after their return, but this could be very difficult to arrange.

## Other perspectives on skills and capacity development in Chinese business

Having looked at a series of case studies of approach to capacity and skill development in different sectors, it may be useful to examine the attitude towards Chinese business in Africa from two or three institutional perspectives, and then to end with a brief examination of how HRD policy in Chinese business is viewed in some of the new China-Africa texts that have emerged in the last few years.

*African Labour Research Network (ALRN)*
It should not be surprising that ALRN takes a labour (and trade union) perspective on Chinese investments in Africa. Chinese firms are measured against ILO's decent work standards, and on positive attitudes toward unions, social benefits, wages, as well as capacity-building and skills transfer. The flavour of the reports on the ten case study countries is captured in the executive summary:

> Although working conditions at Chinese companies in Africa differ across countries and sectors, there are some common trends such as tense labour relations, hostile attitudes by Chinese employers towards trade unions, violations of workers' rights, working conditions and unfair labour practices. There is a virtual absence of employment contracts and the Chinese employers unilaterally determine wages and benefits. African workers are often employed as 'casual workers', depriving them of benefits that they are legally entitled to. (Baah & Jauch, 2009: 13)

As far as skills transfer and capacity building are concerned, the reliance of many Chinese firms on imported labour is said to undermine 'the potential for job creation, skills transfer and human resource development' (Guliwe, 2009: 24). In some of the ten country cases in the edited volume by Baah and Jauch, just a few references will communicate a sense of how negatively training and skills transfer in Chinese firms are perceived. Thus in the Chinese mine, Chambishi, it is contended that training is less and less of a priority, and foreigners are employed in preference to Zambians (181).[29] In Namibia, it was a similar tale: 'The evidence collected during our fieldwork revealed that Chinese investors do not place an emphasis on developing the skills of their Namibian employees' (213). And in Zimbabwe, the same story: 'The research revealed that most of the workers employed in Chinese companies are either unskilled or semi-skilled' (257). 'Most companies have no policies, programmes or plans for

[29] The following five references are taken from the different case study country reports in Baah and Jauch 2009.

skills development and capacity-building for workers' was claimed for South Africa' (330). And in Nigeria: 'Chinese firms are notorious for relying on cheap Chinese labour for many of the major industrial projects and thus do not see the need for skills transfer to the locals' (346).

There is no ready response to this catalogue of complaints about the Chinese employers in Africa and their approach to training except to say that in traditional Chinese firms, the employee is expected to come with formal education and skills already and continue to invest in him/herself through evening school, while the employer offers very practical experience of learning on the job.[30] As we have said above, the Chinese employers in China can look to select from a cohort of young people with fully nine years of education and often some vocational secondary education.[31] The bringing of young people from China who are well-educated is simply a continuation of what firms are used to doing in China.

An alternative approach to the one taken by ALRN (which is to measure Chinese firms against an ILO decent work standard) would be to compare Chinese labour practice with that of the Indian business community in Eastern Africa. That community also basically believes in on the job training, and, like the vast business community in the sub-continent, it has traditionally had very little faith in formal skills training or qualifications (King, 2012b).

A second alternative to the condemnatory approach of ALRN is to argue that skills transfer need not be in terms of formal training or sending for specialized courses in China or South Africa. Skills transfer in Chinese firms may parallel the massive informal skills transfer in Indian firms in Kenya. Often this has gone unrecognised, and it is noted that Indian firms refuse to take part in the formal levy-grant scheme of the Government of Kenya. But in reality many of the key Kenyan African contractors and business people today acquired their skills and technology through working in the very tough, low cost, hard-working environment of Indian firms, and not in European or American multinationals that did offer formal training. Might this prove true of Africans working for Chinese contractors in due course?

It may well be also that many of the local firms in the countries we have picked out such as Kenya, Nigeria, Zimbabwe and Zambia operate in ways that are not dissimilar to what is said of many Chinese firms in the sphere of skills transfer and capacity-building. South Africa may, in this as in much else, be an exception, as it has one of the strongest trade union environments in any Sub-Saharan African country.

---

[30] I am grateful to Sanne van der Lugt for comments on the Chinese business culture (Van der Lugt to KK, 13 January 2012)
[31] The situation in China is changing as the formerly unlimited supply of educated migrants is reducing, in part through the one-child policy.

*African Economic Research Consortium (AERC) on China-Africa relations*

The AERC's set of eleven country scoping studies of China-Africa relations in Aid, Trade and Investment has naturally a very different feel than the analysis of China's investment from a labour perspective. One of the key dimensions where the two sets of studies differ is that the AERC are much more concerned with the role of government when they look at the issues of capacity-building, skills and technology transfer, or human resource development. In an overview paper, Ajakaiye, director of research for the AERC, points firmly to the responsibility of African governments to develop their own human resources, taking advantage of the new investments flowing in from China:

> *The challenge, therefore, is for African countries to invest the inflow of resources from the commodity booms in improving investment climate, developing human resources necessary to support investment in new industries and establish development banks necessary to provide financial support to nascent private investors.* (Ajakaiye, 2008: 11 emphasis in original)

Another of the overview papers concerned with Chinese investment in Africa points to the challenges of ensuring that local capacity is built and technology transferred; their concern is less with China and more with whether African governments have the capacity and capability to gain advantage from the many new investment deals (Ajakaiye et al., 2009: 9). When it comes to the AERC analysis of capacity-building at the country level in relation to the Chinese investment opportunities, they take a very critical stance towards government capacity, and most particularly in Zambia. At the most basic, the country is said to lack the capacity to supervise foreign investments and foreign consultants by their lack of relevant expertise:

> The country also lacks laws and systems which are results oriented and accountable. No one so far has been taken to task for failure to perform. There is lack of workable systems, lack of capacity to implement anything and regulate anything be it wild life, forestry, building, hospitals, etc. As one Minister put it, "Zambia is a place where you keep your job by not doing it". (Mwanawina, 2008)

When it comes to bilateral cooperation with China, the country needs to rethink the terms of agreements especially in respect of joint and sub-contracting arrangements, since that is where there could be more effective methods of furthering skills transfer and capacity-building (ibid.: 27).

Other countries reviewed are not so sharply criticised as Zambia for their lack of institutional capacity to manage investment. But there is clearly some degree of similarity in Angola when it comes to taking advantage of inward investment: 'Of concern, however, are the challenges posed by a lack of institutional framework and Government capacity to monitor and encourage direct investment in terms of local skills development and technology transfer' (Corkin, 2008: 26). In Angola, as was discussed above, the national skills base is so low that there are real challenges in implementing the discourse about ownership, joint venture and skills and technology transfer. In Nigeria, by contrast, there is an allegation that there is little transfer of skills and technology via Chinese firms, in part because of their reliance on expatriate expertise, but again the lesson to be learnt is that the country needs 'to design appropriate policies and regulation and ensure that these are implemented' (Ogunkula et al., 2008: 6).

## Skills and Capacity development in Chinese business in Africa – the lens of literature

We shall end this chapter by reviewing what a series of key authors and commentators think has happened on the human resources dimension of China's business engagement with Africa. The first of these is the classic account by Snow of the poor helping the poor in the era of TAZARA. Very soon after the completion of the extraordinary project it became clear that the Chinese had not left competent Tanzanian staff behind them. Partly it was the fault of the equipment but in large part it was the absence of a maintenance mentality in the local staff. 'Tanzanian and Zambian railwaymen were failing to perform the all-important work of preventive maintenance' (Snow, 1988: 170). Within five years of the project being completed in 1976 only 30 of the original 85 locomotives were still in service. Snow documents in fascinating detail the tensions around completing a project in Africa and continuing to advise and maintain it in some capacity year after year. By 1982, when President Zhao Ziyang visited Africa, the Chinese were much clearer about the importance of training, and about the more commercial approach that might be necessary if they were obliged to maintain a relationship with their projects and prevent them falling into ruin (ibid.: 170–183). TAZARA had not of course been a business, but rather an aid project. The same issue, however, of how to construct something in Africa, and be able to leave it in safe hands would continue to face Chinese contractors, as we shall see in Brautigam's account of Chinese projects and how they have fared over time.

After Snow, Alden was one of the first of the Western academics to produce a short, sharp, balanced account of China's engagement with Africa. Significantly, its starting point is the FOCAC III summit of November 2006 which brought most African leaders to Beijing, His book, *China in Africa,* pays quite some attention to Chinese business in Africa at different levels from multi-national corporation to small-scale trade. It acknowledges that the Chinese business strategy in Africa is in some measure based on low-cost bidding, facilitated by reliance on skilled and semi-skilled Chinese labour, and on lower management costs (Alden,

2007: 42). In noting the constant criticism by the West of China's labour practices in Africa, he reminds the reader that the absolutely massive foreign direct investment (FDI) by the West in China has been sustained by the low wages and comparatively lax labour standards in China, as well as the access to the iconic figure of one billion consumers (ibid.: 131–2).[32] Alden is aware that the use of skilled Chinese labour and managers is a critical element in China's economic comparative advantage, but also that this differs from country to country depending on the depth of skill in local people but also on government policy.

Alden also refers to evidence from Brautigam (2008) of well-networked Nigerian (Igbo) traders in Nnewi learning from their Taiwanese contacts to move from importing to manufacturing. The years of intense trade and interaction led to the Nnewi acquiring 'the skills and information necessary to source their own materials from China and enter into manufacturing of automobile parts themselves' (Alden, 2007: 47–8). The crucial point about this skills transfer was that it was not a government requirement; it was not a formal HRD project. Rather it was an informal process over time between two very dynamic trading communities, one Nigerian and one Chinese. It was a direct parallel to what had happened in the Indo-Kenya skills transfer some years earlier to which we have referred above. By contrast, often what is being referred to in the analysis of Chinese business in Africa is a very uneven interaction between a dynamic Chinese migrant community and a much less business-oriented host community. So it is not just African governments that need to have thought through their trade and technology policies; ideally there need to be receptive African business communities.

Another early book on the theme of China-Africa, a theme which was to turn into a flood over the next few years, appeared in 2008: *China Returns to Africa: A Rising Power and a Continent Embrace* [sic] (Alden et al.). The number of its contributors (25) underlined the fact that there was a whole community which had been working away on the study of China in Africa for some years already. Appropriately, the collection had a foreword from the person who had published in 1988 on *China's Encounter with Africa* earlier than anyone, Philip Snow. In terms of our concerns in this chapter with Chinese business and skills transfer, it is fascinating that one of the themes he chose to highlight was that in many of the well-known Chinese projects from TAZARA onwards 'Chinese skills were not getting transferred to the African recipients on the lines once laid down by Premier Zhou Enlai' (Snow, 2008: xix). He threw down a challenge to Chinese business as a consequence: 'Will Chinese enter-

---

[32] Alden could not put the contradiction between Western business practice in China and Western criticism of China in Africa more strongly: 'Indeed, the "no holds barred" approach of many foreigners towards working in China and Chinese society generally certainly set a remarkable standard of blatant arrogance, overt decadence, and even at times outright depravity that Chinese entrepreneurs in Africa have yet to visibly aspire to, much less achieve' (Alden 2007: 131–2).

prises in Africa be able to overcome their reluctance, apparently as widespread and resented as it ever was, to employ local people in responsible posts and their preference to do things by themselves?' (ibid.).

This challenge about Chinese business and Chinese workers being quite separate from their African co-workers runs through at least one of the key articles on labour practice in the collection. The article, by Monson, describes how African labour was treated during the great rail project, and also what the expectations of the Chinese were for the work standards of the thousands of African workers from Tanzania and Zambia (Monson, 2008; see also 2009). In spite of the rhetoric of brotherhood amongst the workers, life in the railway camps was essentially segregated. Yet there was something very different in working alongside the thousands of Chinese workers compared to the experience of British rule. But when the Chinese workers were signing on to undertake fourteen-hour days to help complete the project well before time, there was some diffidence from the Tanzanian and Zambian sides in doing likewise. Nevertheless, though demanding and difficult, this unique experience did transfer an awareness of modern work in what could be called the formal sector of the economy. It was not of course the same as working in a Chinese state-owned enterprise or private company 30 years later, but the exposure to the Chinese work ethic was memorable, and the impact of new skills on individuals was powerful,[33] even if the project as a whole did not sufficiently create an institutional culture of maintenance.

While Monson's is the only extended account of labour relations between Chinese and Africans in the whole collection of articles, there are others which touch on our theme, notably that by Brautigam, which has already been mentioned in passing, but we shall look at her perspective on human resource development and skills transfer in her major book, *The Dragon's Gift*, rather than through her article.

Before we leave this useful collection, we should acknowledge the importance of the sheer disparity amongst the Chinese in Africa, and even within the business community. Stephen Chan, who is an Africanist rather than a Sinologist, argues in a valuable set of ten caveats on China-Africa, that the failure to distinguish the very different characters amongst the Chinese business community is a mistake. He argues that it is the recent waves of Chinese businessmen and traders that have created most problems:

...it is very often the newer "privateers" and entrepreneurs who create racial tensions most. Under-briefed and under-educated about Africa, assiduous in Chinese work habits and risk-taking – sometimes blatantly exploitative – Chinese make demands of African workers that can be illegal and demeaning... The profile of resentment, and whether

---

[33] The case histories of workers on the railway constantly refer to the acquisition of new skills and new trades (Monson, 2008: 215–17).

it can be corrected, differs again from country to country. (Chan, 2008: 341–2)

Most of the authors in the Alden collection were from the West, though two were from Africa (Senegal and South Africa) and two from China (including Snow in Hong Kong). A very different approach to the position of Chinese business in Africa may be evident when all the authors are from the so-called global South, including China. The collection by Guerrero and Manji (2008) has sixteen separate chapters, and although none of them is explicitly concerned with labour practice and skills training as their main theme, it is a thread that is picked up in more than a few contributions. One of the most succinct of these is by Corkin whose analysis of construction we reviewed earlier. Here we simply add a few of the characteristics of the Chinese construction companies that were not mentioned before. First, in Chinese work-sites, usually all levels of workers live on the site with little visible difference amongst them; it is a system that dramatically cuts down the costs of communication. Second, the bulk of Chinese workers are not only well educated and skilled; often they are multi-skilled, and, by tradition, participate both in manual labour and in a range of skilled artisans' tasks. This speeds the work process and reduces the number of workers required on the site. Third, there is widespread use of double-shifts with day and night workers using the same accommodation (and beds). Fourth, and connected directly to the first point about all workers living on site, there is very low absenteeism (Corkin, 2008: 142–3).

We have already encountered Sautman and Yan in their analysis of the convict labour allegation, but they have a contribution in this collection which argues that there are two factors, China's approach or 'model' of development and their aid as well as their migration, which make China distinctive in Africa. We note briefly here the labour force implications of these approaches. Unlike OECD countries whose expatriates in Africa are primarily well-paid professionals and managers, China's temporary migrants to Africa cover a wider range, from self-employed, to artisans on labour service contracts, and to professionals. Their wages and salaries are much less than the West, as Chinese firms plan to secure much lower profit margins, and to have lower staff costs (Sautman and Yan, 2008: 109).

Another distinctive human resource dimension of China's engagement with Africa relates to the comparative analysis of the brain drain. The haemorrhaging of African professionals to the West is already very well established. By contrast, most of the African students and trainees in China, sent by governments, Chinese companies, or by private finance, actually return to Africa after four or five years.

Sautman and Yan have for at least a decade been conspicuous for interrogating critically the widespread Western media and academic allegations about the role of the Chinese in Africa. We have noted earlier their analysis of the very widespread claim about China's use of its convicts in infrastructure projects in Africa (Sautman and Yan, 2010). We should also point to their critique of the historically and theoretically unsound allegations about the Chinese being the new imperialists or new colonialists (Sautman and Yan, 2006). But on our specific theme of China's business community and human resource development, they have weighed in to comment very critically on the report by Human Rights Watch (HRW) about the labour abuses in the Chinese-owned mines of Zambia (Human Rights Watch [HRW], 2011).

First a word about the HRW report. The situation of the mining sector in Zambia is analysed without any attempt to position the wage employees in Zambia within the wider economically active population. Thus there is no attempt to discuss the size of the Zambia labour force, and the position of the miners in it, compared to the bulk of Zambians in the informal economy (i. e., approximately 90 per cent of the workforce). Indeed, the terms formal and informal sector do not appear in the HRW report. The possibility that a small proportion of the working population in the mines is treated much better than the bulk of the population is not considered except in a quotation from a Chinese manager:

> [The laws are] really 'too sound'—the standard of the legal system is a little too ahead of its time… Almost 50 percent of the people are unemployed and yet they still want to have so many housing allowances, education allowances and transportation allowances. Also, employees can't be dismissed without good reason. They can only be dismissed when their work record is poor…. It is necessary to have some laws in the early stages of development; equality gets sacrificed. Inequalities are a reality at every stage of development. They should learn to accept this. (HRW, 2011: 22–3)

Further, there is insufficient consideration of the fact that within the so-called formal sector, there are large amounts of informal employment. In many apparently formal industries, not just in Zambia but worldwide, there are permanent and casual workers with fundamentally different benefits. This is of course the case with the mines in Zambia and also elsewhere in Africa.

Sautman and Yan have little difficulty in showing in their response to the HRW report that there is considerable bias in its focus only on the Chinese rather than the other international mining operations in Zambia. The attempt to target Chinese mines in one country and then generalise this to claim that that its report 'begin[s] to paint a picture of China's broader role in Africa' is also shown by the authors to be quite unacceptable methodologically.[34] Equally, there is insufficient attention given in the report to the status of the interviewees, given the massive differences between permanent and contract workers in many mines. This is crucial

[34] It would be interesting to consider what would have been the international media reaction if the Marikana mine in South Africa, with its many associated fatalities, had been Chinese-owned.

if many of the 95 Zambians interviewed were in fact not permanent workers.[35]

The wide-ranging discussion on the HRW report which was carried on around the Chinese in Africa–Africans in China Research Network abundantly confirms that the issues surrounding a firm's labour practices need to be understood against the culture and context of the industry, its traditions, its comparators in the country, and the policies and practices of the government.[36] International labour standards are extremely valuable but they are more honoured in the breach than in compliance.

*The dragon's gift of skills, technologies and capacities in Africa*
There are of course many other collections on China-Africa as well as single-author monographs that have appeared over the six years from 2006 to 2012 during which we have been examining our topic. However, they pick up for different countries and different sectors some of the same red threads we have identified in the four books which we have glanced at briefly.[37] Deborah Brautigam's *Dragon's Gift: The Real Story of China in Africa* (2009) is in a different category. At first glance and because of the title it would appear to be about China's foreign aid, and indeed seven of the eleven chapters are explicitly about some dimension of 'aid'. However, it is also about the particularity of China's economic engagement with Africa, and the four other chapters deal directly with China's building business in Africa. It has the advantage of being based on some 30 years of scholarship, and can connect in the mid-2000s with aid projects or industrial initiatives visited 15 or 20 years earlier. In one way, the book's industry side is an extended answer to the question Snow had put in 2008: 'Will Chinese enterprises in Africa be able to overcome their reluctance, apparently as widespread and resented as it ever was, to employ local people in responsible posts and their preference to do things by themselves?' (Snow, 2008: xix).

What Brautigam terms 'a robust mythology' has developed around the question of China shipping in large quantities of its own labour to Africa (Brautigam, 2009: 156). Her considered opinion on Snow's question is that *it depends.* There is no black and white answer; it depends on how long the firm has been in the country, on the government policy on work

---

[35] The HRW report does not give any breakdown of the employment status of the Zambian miners interviewed.

[36] See the emails to the network from Wells (HRW), 19 December 2011; and from Yan Hairong, 19 December 2011, and Sautman, 10 January 2012.

[37] Other obvious titles would include: Manji, F. and Marks, S. (Eds), 2007. *African Perspectives on China in Africa.* Fahamu, Oxford; Rotberg, R. (Ed.), 2008. *China into Africa: Trade, Aid and Influence,* Brookings/ World Peace Foundation, Cambridge, Mass.; Van Dijk, M.P. (Ed.), 2009. *The New Presence of China in Africa,* Amsterdam University Press, Amsterdam; Taylor, I., 2009. *China's New Role in Africa,* Lynne Rienner, London; Cheru, F. and Obi, C. (Eds), 2010. *The Rise of China and India in Africa,* Zed Books, London. A further book which is clearly relevant to Chinese labour practice in Africa is J.P. Cardenal and H. Araújo (2013) *China's Silent Army: The Pioneers, Traders, Fixers and Workers Who Are Remaking the World in Beijing's Image,* Random House, New York.

permits, and, crucially, how easy it is to find skilled labour locally, but it also depends on whether the company is a multinational like those we have discussed, a state-owned enterprise, or a medium, small or micro-enterprise. Local flexibility on the use of Chinese labour will also differ a great deal, depending on whether the company is delivering on a highly visible project whose timely completion would be politically attractive.

The issue of the availability of really skilled local labour and of differing Chinese and African work ethics comes up throughout her account. The productivity of local labour in the factory setting is a key issue in some countries, as is the relatively high cost of formal sector workers. The rigidity of labour regulations, and the contrasts between the wages and benefits of permanent employees versus contract or casual workers, all play their part in the decision to use more or less local labour.

Brautigam is not concerned, *per se*, with the kind of dispute about the labour practices of particular Chinese firms, like the debate about Chinese mining in Zambia we referred to above. Her preoccupation with these human resource matters connects to the much bigger questions of how they relate to the sustainability of China's aid projects, on the one hand, and of African industrialisation, on the other. The fundamental question for her is what role foreign, minority economic groups can play in industrial transformations (ibid.: 192), looking back to the crucial example of Japan's influence on its neighbours including China and South East Asia. The accessibility of the imported technology, the potential for the new skills to spill over into local firms, or to be carried out by employees who 'graduate', and the scope for sub-contracting, and innovation are all critical to this process becoming embedded in a new country.

In other words, access to skills and transferable technologies are vital to the process of indigenisation. Of course, something similar can happen with aid projects which involve the development of agricultural or industrial institutions, but the challenge of spinning off sustainable aid projects is enormous, as Snow's TAZARA and Brautigam's Urafiki Friendship Textile Factory in Tanzania demonstrated only too clearly (ibid.: 197–201). Paradoxically, industrial relations, rigid labour regulations, and international standards can all get in the way of skills and technology transfers, and particularly when the Chinese (or Indian) firm is competing on profit margins, productivity, and speed of completion. A Chinese work ethic that is based on reaching the target or finishing the job rather than counting the hours is a vital component in this competitiveness. Often, as we have seen in the ALRN studies, there is a disconnect between the necessity of sustained hard work, and particularly so in an environment where there are problems of supply of regular electricity, water etc. and the standards aspired to by the African employees.

What we have noted throughout this chapter is that it is the work ethic in some of Africa's informal sectors, such as Kenya's, Nigeria's or Ghana's, that comes closest to the ten-hour day seven days a week which can be found in many Chinese companies in Africa. The synergy in Eastern

Nigeria between the existing work ethic of the Igbo around Nnewi and their Asian clients (Japanese, Taiwanese and Chinese) has been power-fully written up by Brautigam to illustrate the potential of learning and technology transfer from importing to local production. However, the key factor in this success is the dynamic business orientation of the Igbo. This markedly contrasts with the many examples Brautigam gives of where the recipients or the counterparts to the Chinese company or project are on a different wave-length. Internationally, in the aid literature there has been a long-standing problem with the status of counterparts; they are frequently of low status and it is perhaps understandable that sometimes they are not even assigned to the project (see Brautigam: 159). On the other hand Western aid projects are also responsible for a very different kind of local expert which is drawn out of the line ministries into donor projects on a salary at least two or three times more than their government salary. The problem is that their expertise is only available during the project cycle of the Western donors, and hence does not contribute to long-term sustainability. This is one reason that JICA tries to resist sourcing experts in this way.

It is a very different matter in the case of a private company or a state-owned enterprise. Joint ventures ought ideally to be the meeting ground of common business interests, as in the case of the Nnewi autoparts devel-opment. But too often, local employees are appointed to foreign compa-nies as managers for political reasons, such as meeting national quotas. In Brautigam's research in Mauritius and Nigeria on skills and technology spillovers, she found that 'in both countries the local people who learned from the Chinese were already entrepreneurs for the most part' (ibid.: 224).

The question of whether China's presence and FDI can catalyse African industry is one on which it is not possible to generalise. Many more detailed studies are needed of the sort that Brautigam has done for Nnewi and Mauritius. These need to be done both at the level of the formal sector factory, as well as at the small and micro-enterprise level. But they also need to take careful account of the wider investment climate encouraged by government and of the crucial role of what Brautigam calls 'African agency'. We do not want merely a set of individual case studies of joint ventures between Chinese and African entrepreneurs, but rather how these particular accounts are affected by the government's aid, trade and investment policies, and by the parallels on the Chinese side. A good if very brief example of this is to be found in a recent discussion by Brautigam of 'Ethiopia's partnership with China', tellingly subtitled: 'China sees Ethiopia as a land of opportunities, but the African country remains in charge of any deals' (Brautigam, 2011b). It is a very different account from what many Western media channels offer on Ethiopia, with their focus on aid, poverty and famine. By contrast there is a key role for Chinese and Ethiopian private investment and training, as we saw in the country club scheme which built training into the enterprise's joint devel-opment.

A similarly critical role for Chinese private enterprise can be seen in Brautigam's fascinating account of how the Agricultural Demonstration Centres, announced as part of the pledges at the FOCAC III summit in Beijing in 2006, are exploring an innovative role for Chinese private sector management in Africa (Brautigam, 2009: 247–252). These fourteen institutions promise to be an important illustration of some answers to the age-old development question in Africa: How can aid projects really become sustainable? Here too the key determinant will be the character of African agency.

*A further angle – from the perspective of the Chinese Academy of Social Sciences*
Appropriately, a last set of comments on the human resources side of Chinese companies in Africa comes from a former member of the Institute of West Asian and African Studies, Liu Haifang, who had carried out field studies on this in Angola, Mozambique and Uganda, and who brought to the analysis her own strengths in the understanding of culture.[38] Intriguingly, the spark for her research was a series of challenges in Angola about the Chinese and their alleged use of convict labour.

Like Brautigam, she does not look narrowly at Chinese companies as an item on their own, but positions them against a history of the waves of Chinese migration, and of the formal encouragement by the state and the different provinces in China for companies to go global. She is refreshingly frank about how Africa is seen as a last frontier for Chinese 'gold-diggers', as a place to make a fortune, or to gain six or seven times more pay than as a migrant within China (Liu, 2009: 312–7). With her background of cultural concerns she is interested in the wider issue of the social integration of Chinese firms, including evidence of intermarriage between some Chinese entrepreneurs and local women.

However, at the level of the Chinese firms and African labour, her social and cultural interests lead her to note the predisposition of Chinese firms to draw their labour from the same part for the country as the main contractors, for reasons of communication and convenience (ibid.: 317). Equally, these same strong cultural ties discourage the African workers on the rebuilding of the Benguela Railway from working more than 100 kilometres from home; the human resources side of this disposition is that there has to be a constant capacity-building because of the mobility of the labour. Hence it presents a challenge to technology and skills transfer (ibid.: 318).

Even the pressure for Chinese firms to participate in corporate social responsibility (CSR) is presented as something of a challenge to the traditional hesitations about Chinese firms' involvement with civil society and with the support of non-governmental organisations. The fact that few Chinese firms claimed to be engaged in CSR formally does not mean that

---

[38] Liu Haifang has moved from African Studies in CASS, and is now a member of Peking University's Centre for African Studies.

there have not been firms that supported the building of schools or of technical training facilities, but the tradition of keeping a low profile, and of modesty, discouraged firms from claiming to be doing so much for their surrounding communities (ibid.: 320).

For our key issue of utilising and training African employees, she argues, along with others whom we have discussed, that it depends so much on the state of education, training and other critical policies in the particular country. But she has no doubt over the future direction: Chinese firms will have to increasingly ensure that they abide by so-called international best practice. This process is a trend that is irreversible (ibid.: 322).

## In conclusion

Human resources and Chinese enterprise in Africa are a vast landscape, and only parts of it have been mapped, such as the skills and technology impact on Tanzania historically of TAZARA (See Snow, 1988; Monson, 2009). The sheer scale and suddenness of the appearance of Chinese state-owned enterprises, private companies, would-be entrepreneurs, and petty traders in most African countries are such that no regular programme of research work has been able to do justice to this issue yet. It would require a sustained analysis over time to capture the complex of human resource issues connected to policy borrowing and policy learning within Chinese and African firms. Like policy learning, technological capacity-building is not a project but a process. It is not something that is done to African firms by Chinese; it is more of an interaction but one that is made up of a myriad of pieces over time.

In the case of Indo-Kenyan skills and technology transfer, it was possible to point to an informal transfer process at the level of the *jua kali* (informal economy) over a period of 30 years (King, 1995). It is much less clear what has happened at the next level of Indian firms which have taken a major role in the formal industrial areas of Kenya's main towns and cities. Kenyan African firms have been conspicuous by their absence in these industrial zones. Despite the very strong business interests of some of Kenya's communities such as the Kikuyu, there does not appear to have been a learning or transfer process in what many have called the 'missing middle' of small and medium-sized firms.

Will it be different with China? It is already different. China has employed many more modalities of interaction than the Government of India was prepared to use after Independence. It is only in the last four years, since the India-Africa Forum Summit of 2008, that there is clear evidence of major decision-making in India affecting Africa. Many of these India-Africa initiatives almost seem to copy measures that China had taken earlier.[39] By contrast, there is an armoury of different measures

[39] India has offered a whole series of Pan-African training institutions to be allocated through the African Union, however (King and Palmer, 2011).

already sponsored by China from the economic processing zones to the agricultural technology demonstration centres that are going to be pivotal in any skills and technology transfer process.

It will not be possible even in ten years' time to generalise about this extraordinary development, made more so by the tens of thousands of petty traders, peddlers and street-sellers that have already made their way onto the main streets of many of Africa's cities. But Brautigam should have one of the last words on the likely outcome:[40]

> Ultimately, it is up to African governments to shape this encounter in ways that will benefit their people. Many will not grasp this opportunity, but some will… They [the Chinese] believe in investment, trade and technology as levers for development, and they are applying these same tools in their African engagement, not out of altruism, but because of what they learned at home (Brautigam, 2009: 311).

[40] A similar position on African agency is taken by Gu Jing (2009: 585): 'From the African perspective, in the final analysis, whether or not the development impact of Chinese private investment in Africa can be effectively realised rests with African governments and the wider policy-making community, including civil society.'

The other side of the equation is Chinese agency, portrayed so powerfully by Cardenal and Araújo:

China benefits from an army of astonishing human beings with a limitless capacity for self-sacrifice, who venture out into the world driven only by their dreams of success and who go on to conquer impossible markets which Westerners never dared to tackle – or if they did, they failed. (Cardenal and Araújo, 2013: 5)

# 5

## China's Aid & Traditional Donors — Convergence or divergence?

It has been said that people's brains are conditioned by the communities they are living in; therefore only people looking on from outside can give really constructive ideas for the former society. I believe that Professor King is one person who possesses significant insights and who looks in on China from outside. His suggestions will be by definition very valuable in helping us lay a solid foundation for the 5th Ministerial FOCAC Conference. It would be great if the Professor can let us know how does he view the implementation of previous conferences? How does the future of China-Africa cooperation look from his perspective? Should China continuously formulate and announce a new set of 8 measures at the 5th Ministerial Conference? If it should do so, what would be an appropriate magnitude of the new 8 measures? And to which areas should we give more priority? (From a Commercial Councillor's Office in Africa to KK, 20. 12.11)

The view of many traditional donors towards China's role as a development partner in Africa was that it was 'unclubbable'; it did not want to be part of the donor club or the very large number of donor working groups, or donor task forces found at the country level in Africa. This was thought to be because China did not want to present itself to Africa as a donor. As has been mentioned in earlier chapters, China preferred to see itself much more as the largest developing country helping, to the extent it could manage, the continent with the largest number of developing countries. In other words, its stance, which has a long history, is that it was engaged in South-South cooperation (SSC), and not in North-South cooperation.

As China's priority was with mutual benefit and common good rather than one-way provision of charity to Africa, it should not be surprising to learn that China has traditionally taken very little time engaging with other donors or development partners at the country level. In none of our case study countries did China participate in the Education Donors Coordination Group (in Kenya), or in the Technical Working Group on Education (in Ethiopia); neither, at the more general level in Ethiopia, was China a member of the Development Assistance Group. The latter group has no fewer than 26 members in Ethiopia, and it is intriguing to note that of the non-DAC donors, Turkish International Cooperation Agency and the Indian Embassy are represented, but China is not.[1] In Ethiopia, the Chinese have been invited to participate both at the level of the Technical Working Groups, of which there are ten, and the four multi-donor programmes, as well as the overall Development Assistance Group, but they have not accepted so far. The main reason is almost certainly what has been already mentioned, a powerful reluctance to present themselves as part of the mainly OECD donor club. But a further consideration must surely be the sheer shortage, in the two sides of the Chinese embassies,[2] of personnel with specialist expertise on Education, HIV/AIDS, Governance, Nutrition, Gender Equality, to mention just five of the fifteen specialist groups or programmes in Ethiopia's donor groups. China in this respect may be rather similar to Japan which has historically relied on generalists circulated every three or four years to staff their embassies and their development agency, JICA.[3] Such generalists in JICA have found themselves at a considerable disadvantage when it comes to participating in an Education Sector Working Group, where all the other development partners had specialists discussing education (King and McGrath, 2004).[4] It will be remembered that China only has two Education Councillors in the whole of Africa, and their original mandate was not connected to educational aid at all, but to the presence of large numbers of Chinese students in South Africa and in Egypt where the two Councillors are based. This can be contrasted with DFID which has not less than twenty-five Education staff based in Africa.

The questions we have in this chapter are concerned with the distinctiveness of China's aid or development assistance, and especially of course in the field of education and training. How different are these really from the approach of traditional western donors, and in particular, from the way that the western donors delivered their aid several decades ago? Are the assumptions behind aid different in the case of China and the west? Has the rise of the aid effectiveness discourse in the west, especially since the Paris Declaration of 2005, had an impact on China's attitude towards aid?

On the other hand, is there any evidence that there is some growing convergence between China and western bilateral and multi-lateral agencies? Is there an interest in China in learning from the west, and in parallel an expectation in China that the west may learn also from China?

[1] www.dagethiopia.org/index.php?option=com_content&view=article&id=26&Itemid=9
[2] In many African countries, China has its main Chinese Embassy, but also its Commercial Councillor's Office
[3] For further similarities between Chinese and Japanese aid, see King, 2007d.
[4] See particularly Chapter 7, 'Experience, experts and knowledge in Japanese aid policy and practice', pp. 130–154 in King and McGrath (2004).

We started this chapter with a quotation from someone representing the Ministry of Commerce in a Commercial Councillor's Office in Africa. I was surprised to be asked in December 2011 for my opinion about past FOCAC meetings and my views about the priorities for the then forthcoming FOCAC ministerial conference in July 2012. Ever since I started researching China's educational aid to Africa in early 2006, I had been told by Chinese scholars and policy makers, and by heads of development agencies in Beijing: 'Don't even think of getting into the Ministry of Commerce (MOFCOM), where the Department of Foreign Aid[5] is based. You won't succeed.'

Now, suddenly in 2011 it looked as if there might be something of a change underfoot. In April 2011, the State Council produced for the first time a White Paper on *China's Foreign Aid* (China, 2011a). We shall examine this in more detail later. But over the course of the year there were a series of collaborations involving bilateral agencies, multi-lateral agencies, and Chinese ministries, including the Ministry of Commerce.

Before considering the evidence, if any, for increasing convergence between China's aid policy and that of western donors, we need to be clearer about the substantial differences that exist between China's assistance and that of many western donors. Our concern in this continues to be with its implications for China's human resource strategies towards Africa.

## Distinctions and differences in China's aid to Africa

*Cultural traditions*
There are perhaps some relevant cultural dimensions of giving and receiving that lie deep in China's traditions, but which may be worth acknowledging when it comes to a discussion of development aid. For instance there is a famous story going back several hundred years BC, about 'Never eating a handout'. There is a parallel in the story from the Book of Rites about it being better to die a beggar than live a beggar (Tan, 1989). This emphasises, in the words of the starving man, 'I don't eat relief food handed out in contempt. I won't accept your humiliating pity.' The notion of preferring hunger to loss of dignity has been explained as follows: 'Chinese preferred to work much harder rather than receive aid or donation during hard times in the old days, like during Chairman Mao's period. If you are not a friend, and you give your help without proper respect to the receiver, we do not accept that; instead we choose to die in dignity.'[6]

The parallel but better known HRD adage about 'Give a man a fish and

---

[5] The Department is called 'Department of Aid to Foreign Countries' on the website of the Ministry of Commerce: http://yws2.mofcom.gov.cn/ . We shall use these titles interchangeably.
[6] I am indebted to Zhang Zhongwen for the reference to refusing handouts: Zhang Zhongwen to KK, 29.02.12

you feed him for a day' can also be applied to some of the contradictions in the approach to aid.[7] This too can be seen to criticise aid as a handout compared to the sustained, long-term effect of teaching a man to fish, and thus feeding him for a lifetime. These crucially important notions of avoiding charity and handouts, (see 'unilateral alms' below), and respecting the independence of the other party are of course the first two principles of Zhou Enlai's eight principles of foreign aid (1964):

1. The Chinese Government always bases itself on the principle of equality and mutual benefit in providing aid to other countries. It never regards such aid as a kind of unilateral alms but as something mutual.

2. In providing aid to other countries, the Chinese Government strictly respects the sovereignty of the recipient countries, and never attaches any conditions or asks for any privileges. (China, 2000)

These cultural foundations for the approach towards development assistance may also help to explain China's diffidence about declaring too publicly all that it is doing in support of other developing countries. It may now be the second largest economy in the world, but it still ranks 99th in terms of per capita income worldwide (World Bank and China, 2012: 64). Arguably China has not changed its status as a developing nation. This crucial fact and the continuing presence of millions of poor people in both rural and urban China may help to explain the absence of rich data sets on what China is providing to Africa. One scholar has commented:

Actually China's per capita GDP is lower than a lot of African countries. In reality there are a great number of poor population living in China's rural areas even in suburbs of big cities like Beijing and Shanghai, and many Chinese don't understand why the government gave aid to other countries when it is not so rich itself. That is also why the aid becomes a sensitive issue in China. Thirdly, most African governments prefer bilateral aid to multi-lateral, and the Chinese government respects African choices. (Academic in CASS to KK, 1 February 2012)

*Learning from China's own history of development?*
We noted in Chapter 1 that one of the distinguishing features of several Asian nations' accounts of their development assistance is that they have learned from their own successful development experience, and desire to pass this on. This is certainly the case for both Japan and South Korea, and these claims are by no means old history; they can be found today on the respective websites of the Korea Overseas International Cooperation Agency (KOICA) and the Japan International Cooperation Agency (JICA). Thus directly in the Mission statement of KOICA is the following:

[7] See Taylor (2007) '"Give a man a fish" and foreign aid.' I am grateful to Yuan Tingting for this reference.

In particular, Korea has the unique experience of developing from one of the poorest countries in the world to one of the most economically advanced, as recently demonstrated by Korea's entry into the OECD/DAC (Development Assistance Committee) on November 25, 2009. The know-how and experience Korea gained from this transition are invaluable assets that allow KOICA to efficiently support the sustainable socio-economic development of its partner countries and to offer them hope for a better world.[8]

Japan too has frequently drawn attention to what it learnt that could be relevant to other nations in the period of the Meiji Restoration, from 1868, as well as in period after the Second World War.[9] These experiences of modernisation in the 19th century, and of recovery after 1945 included understandings of being a recipient of external expertise in the Meiji period, as well as of massive external aid after the war. The Japanese axiom that captures best the balancing of Western technology and assistance with Japanese values is *Wakon Yosai* – Japanese spirit, Western knowledge (Sawamura, 2002: 343). These core values turn out to be hard work, commitment and clarity about what should be prioritised for borrowing and adapting to Japan. This cluster of attitudes is central to the Japanese emphasis on ownership and self-reliance (King and McGrath, 2004: 158–9). It is noticeable that Japan accords a particularly crucial role from its own historical experience to education in the development process:

> JICA believes that education is at the core of all development issues. This is rooted in Japan's own experience. Recognizing the importance of education as the base for its development, Japan advanced scientific and technological development and industrial growth by enhancing people's capacity through education – especially during the process of modernization from the mid-19th century. Through that process, Japan also created an equitable society by ensuring the equal right for all people to receive education. Based on Japan's own experiences, JICA will support developing countries to strengthen educational systems and institutions, develop human resources, and extend human networks in order to promote social and economic development. (JICA, 2010: 2)

China's account is different, however. For one thing, it does not believe that it has succeeded yet in transforming the country and moving all of its people out of poverty. Hence there is the constant refrain that China is still a developing country. The emphasis therefore is not on what Africa's developing economies can learn from China, but rather on what China

[8] http://www.koica.go.kr/english/koica/mission/index.html
[9] 'Japan will support the sustainable growth of developing countries, while sharing with them its own experience with post-war reconstruction and growth as well as Japan's expertise, technologies, and systems' (Japan, MOFA, 2010b: 21).

and Africa can both learn from each other. This is an absolutely central message of *China's African Policy:*

Learning from each other and seeking common development. China and Africa will learn from and draw upon each other's experience in governance and development, strengthen exchange and cooperation in education, science, culture and health. Supporting African countries' efforts to enhance capacity building, China will work together with Africa in the exploration of the road of sustainable development. (China, 2006: 3)

Rather than developing countries learning from China, in the manner of South Korea and Japan, the emphasis is on the fact that China and Africa have shared parallel challenges; there is therefore no sense of a one-way learning process:

China-Africa friendship is embedded in the long history of interchange. Sharing similar historical experience, China and Africa have all along sympathized with and supported each other in the struggle for national liberation and forged a profound friendship. (ibid.: 2)

In other words, China emphasises much more the common experience between China and Africa, of occupation and invasion, than of developing countries learning directly from China. The same is true of the International Poverty Reduction Centre in China (IPRCC); its mission statement does not point to the potential of learning about poverty reduction from China, but rather of collaboration worldwide in poverty eradication.[10]

In terms of difference from other donors, therefore, China is not only different in this respect from Western donors, but also from the two Asian DAC donors, who do certainly emphasise the scope for others learning from their development experience. By contrast, as we noted in Chapter 1, China remains a developing country with many challenges 'a low per-capita income and a large poverty-stricken population' (China, 2011a. 1). Furthermore, even when there are very obvious arenas where transformation has been quite dramatic, such as poverty-reduction, or nine years of education for all, there is a strong hesitation about claiming a 'China model'. If anything, there is an inclination to argue that China's progress has been the result of not directly copying others, but developing solutions that fitted their own particular context.

Despite this modesty of approach towards other developing countries learning from China, there is the obvious question of why China is supporting 30,000 short-term trainees from Africa to visit China between 2013 and 2015. As was mentioned briefly in Chapter 2 the majority of the trainees are simply exposed to one out of a huge range of specialist courses, from technical and vocational education and training or university leadership, on the one hand, to high-yielding varieties of rice or

---

[10] See www.iprcc.org

managing small scale enterprises on the other. The courses focus on how China arranges these and several hundred other specialist areas; but there is no attempt critically to analyse the strengths or weaknesses of these thematic areas in Africa itself. Nor is there a 'China model' promoted; it is more a case of saying: 'Here's how we do this in China. Take a look, and see if there is something that you might learn from this.' Such an approach which does not sell a particular model is of course deeply embedded in China's aid discourse:

> China upholds the Five Principles of Peaceful Coexistence, respects recipient countries' right to independently select their own path and model of development, and believes that every country should explore a development path suitable to its actual conditions (China, 2011a: 3–4).

What is intriguing about China's very clear position on this, in the foreign aid White Paper, is that there is really no counterpart on the Department of Foreign Aid website, in either English or in Chinese, of this discussion in the 2011 White Paper. Indeed there is no discussion of anything in English beyond a few lines about the role of the Department, while the Chinese version of the site merely has a listing of the eight functions of the department. Given the significance and sheer scale of the short-term training courses, it might seem surprising that these are not laid out publicly, along with the location of the providing university or research institute in China. This is what is readily available in the case of the very large number of courses offered by the Government of India, as we mentioned in Chapter 2.

The explanation for this not happening is that currently the decisions about who goes to China from which university or ministry are taken bilaterally between the Economic and Commercial Councillor's Office at the country level in Africa and the government body responsible for capacity-building and staff development. Opening up the whole process to applications from across individual countries would make the task of selection hugely more complex.

We have examined the fundamental question of whether China's aid explicitly reflects on its own development history, and on how its partners can learn from this experience. We have found that unlike its two Asian neighbours, South Korea and Japan, China does not refer publicly to its history of successful transformation, but takes a completely different line, of stressing how China and other developing countries can learn from each other.[11] There is an apparent contradiction that needs explanation here however. If mutual learning is indeed at the core of China's development assistance, why has so much effort gone into bringing African and

[11] It might appear that the 2011 China-DAC Study Group report contradicts this. Its title: 'Economic transformation and poverty reduction: How it happened in China, helping it happen in Africa' suggests learning from China's development experience. The China-DAC Study Group cannot be read as a Chinese position on this issue.

other developing world professionals to China, for the last ten and more years? Does this not suggest that learning is a one-way street, or in the words of the Director General of the Nigerian Institute of International Affairs: 'Is the relationship (between China and Africa) indeed strategic and mutually beneficial to both sides or is there noticeable lopsidedness?' (Eze, 2009: 24).

## *"China does not 'do' 'professional aid'"*[12]
We have often referred to China's aid to HRD, or to education and training in these chapters, and this may give the impression that there is an organisation responsible for this, just as there is in Britain, Sweden, Japan and South Korea. Also, it is frequently said that China's aid is delivered with enormous speed and efficiency; again this may give the impression of a highly efficient bureaucracy. It seems possible however that the efficiency and rapidity of China's aid activities is not dependent on a centralised aid bureaucracy, but rather on a somewhat fragmented set of responsibilities.

Thus, even in the case of education and training aid, as referred to briefly in Chapter 1, China's long-term scholarships to Africa are under the aegis of the China Scholarship Council (CSC) and at the level of the Chinese embassies in Africa, these are handled by the main political branch of the embassy. By contrast, the much larger number of short-term training awards are directly under the Ministry of Commerce, but recruitment for the hundreds of different training courses is devolved to the Economic and Commercial Councillor's office at the level of the individual African country. Chinese volunteers going to Africa are also handled by the Economic and Commercial Councillor's offices.

When it comes to building a small number of China-Africa schools in many of the African countries represented in the Forum on China-Africa Cooperation (FOCAC), doubtless the Ministry of Education in China and the Ministry of Commerce will liaise over distribution of the schools, but effectively the contract to build is handled by the Ministry of Commerce, as is the selection amongst a range of eligible Chinese contractors.

China also provides aid to construct the occasional tertiary level institution, such as the Ethio-China Polytechnic College in Addis Ababa. Here again the construction and contracting side will be handled exclusively through the Ministry of Commerce, but when there is a question of staffing and administering the institution for an initial period, the Ministry of Commerce will turn to the Ministry of Education, and that body in turn will look to whether there is an on-going university partnership between China and Africa which could take on the staffing challenge.

Despite this division of responsibilities, these various dimensions which we are loosely calling China's HRD support to Africa seem to work smoothly. It should perhaps be remembered that with several of the Western donors also there has been some fragmentation of responsibility

---

[12] The sub-title is taken from Yuan (2011b: 8).

for HRD support to developing countries. Thus in Germany, the bulk of the long-term scholarship support has been organized by German Academic Exchange Service (DAAD), whilst the bulk of short-term training is now supported by the German Agency for Development Cooperation (GIZ).[13] There are parallels in the UK, where even long-term scholarships have been associated with several different sponsoring bodies.

But when Yuan says that "China does not 'do' 'professional aid'", she means more than that they do not have a stand-alone, specialised development agency. She also argues that China differs substantially from the West in having a different approach to the financing of development initiatives, and to their evaluation.

Thus for all the HRD expenditures mentioned above, the responsibility for payments remains with the Chinese. For example, the 20,000 short-term training awards pledged at the FOCAC IV Conference in Sharm el Shaikh do not get transferred to the African Union, or to the individual recipient African countries. Here we have already referred to India's practice, where there has been a direct transfer of executive authority to the African Union, since the Indo-African summits of 2008 and 2011.

In the case of the China-Africa friendship schools also pledged in FOCAC IV or the hospitals pledged in FOCAC III, the funds are not transferred to the local Ministries of Health or Education, in what some Western donors would call sector budget support. Rather, in the words of the Chinese ambassador to Tanzania, the funds remain with the Chinese:

> For our aid projects, the advantage is, we can control the whole process, such as building the national sports stadium or the hospital or the schools. Tanzania does not have to control the money; so we can use the budget very efficiently. We say we devote 0.1 billion RMB, but the money is in the Chinese Ministry of Commerce. We have our own construction team and we give Tanzanians the finished product. Normally our speed is incredible for the Tanzanians. And on the other hand, compared with Western team [sic], we have less labour costs. (Liu, 11.08.08, quoted in Yuan, 2011b: 12)

This Chinese system of retaining full control of the financing for infrastructure and construction projects has been acknowledged as avoiding the 'leakage' of funds when such funds are transferred to the budget or to local contractors. Thus in a discussion of how this Chinese approach to aid financing manages to 'skirt corruption', it has begun to be argued that China's approach has some distinct advantages:

> But Beijing didn't just deliver the money and let Ugandan officials see the project through. It was built by Chinese workers in what aid watchdogs applaud as a model to help defeat the inefficiencies and cash-pocketing corruption associated with other systems of foreign aid delivery. (Muhumuza, 2012)

[13] See articles by Wagenfeld and by Jung in *NORRAG News No 45* (2011).

It is interesting to note that this approach which earlier might have been criticised as just another example of China's tied aid has been getting approval.[14] For instance, Sven Grimm, director of the Centre for Chinese Studies in Stellenbosch University, has commented specifically on this with a note that 'The China model is more effective. It's less prone to corruption' (ibid.).

It is noticeable that as some Western donors who have been involved in the so-called new aid modalities of general and sector budget support find it hard to show to their electorates what precise 'value for money'[15] can be attributed to their aid, there is a fresh recognition that China may be doing something right. The joint World Bank/China 2030 Report celebrates the fact that 'China's (aid) policies are in some respects beneficial to recipients', and that 'China's program of financial assistance has provided substantial benefits to developing countries, in some respects through mechanisms that are superior to the programmes of OECD countries (World Bank & China, 2012: 440, 442).

By financing directly, and delivering completed, turnkey projects, China of course manages to avoid the complications and transaction costs of monitoring and evaluation of the tranches of money going to recipient departments or ministries in Africa, under the usual processes of project or programme support. The whole arcane architecture of agreed 'targets' and 'triggers' for the release of aid funds (which are a new form of conditionality, and can be highly confrontational) is thus avoided by China.[16] More broadly, China, by its direct financing preferences, stays outside the world of the Paris Declaration with its targets for the 'use of country public financial management systems', 'use of country procurement systems' and its aim to 'strengthen capacity by avoiding parallel implementation structures' (OECD, 2005: 19).

Even though it was widely thought that China had finally entered the common donor framework of the aid effectiveness agenda through the 4th High Level Forum on Aid Effectiveness at Busan,[17] it should be remembered that the *Busan Partnership for Effective Development Cooperation*

[14] This is not to say that the very visibility and tied aid character of China's aid goes uncriticised in Africa. The spectacular $124 million 'gift to Africa' of the African Union (AU) headquarters by China has attracted some adverse commentary: 'it is an insult to the African Union and to every African that in 2012 a building as symbolic as the AU headquarters is designed, built and maintained by a foreign country – it does not matter which' (Ezeanya, 2012).

[15] For the rise of the preoccupation with 'value for money' in development aid, see *NORRAG News No 47* (April 2012). One of the more spectacular losses of aid money through budget support came to light in Kenya in 2009 where it was discovered that up to £80 million sterling of funds for universal primary education were lost through corruption: (http://www.uganda-correspondent.com/articles/2011/06/britain-asks-kenya-to-pay-back-80m-'stolen'-upe-money/)

[16] See King (2011d: 659) for an account of how these operate in Ghana in the Multi-donor Budget Support process.

[17] See for example the post by Nancy Birdsall of the Centre for Global Development on 5 December 2011, entitled: 'Aid alert: China finally joins the donor club', downloaded from: http://blogs.cgdev.org/globaldevelopment/2011/12/aid-alert-china-officially-joins-the-donor-club-2.php

crucially admitted that 'The nature, modalities and responsibilities that apply to South-South cooperation differ from those that apply to North-South cooperation' (4th HLF, 2011: 1). Moreover, despite the intention of the OECD organisers and of the host nation, South Korea, that Busan should bring the non-DAC donors such as China, India, Brazil, South Africa and some of the oil economies into the donor club, the 'Outcome Document' carefully admitted on its very first page that 'The principles, commitments and actions agreed in the outcome document in Busan shall be the reference for South-South partners *on a voluntary basis.* (1, emphasis added).

Before we leave this section on China's not doing 'professional aid', we need to return to the role of the Department of Aid to Foreign Countries (or Department of Foreign Aid). As mentioned in Chapter 1, there is virtually nothing on the English version of the Department's website, and one of the main items on the Chinese version of the site is merely a listing of the eight functions of the Department. There is not the usual statement of the Mission or Vision of China's foreign aid, as would be commonplace in JICA, KOICA, DFID etc. Nor is there a link to the 2011 White Paper on *China's Foreign Aid*, and no link to the historically significant list of Eight Principles of foreign aid, announced by Premier Zhou Enlai in 1964.

Apart from the limited links in the Chinese version of the Department's website, there has traditionally been a very great difficulty in accessing or interviewing personnel from the Department in Beijing. Even foreign scholars who have been working on China-Africa issues for years will admit that they have not a single contact with the Department. Similarly, there have been two doctoral theses written on aspects of China's aid in the last two years, which are known to the author. The first of these relates to China's educational aid to Tanzania, and it has been completed without any interview with the relevant department of Aid to Foreign Countries in MOFCOM, or with the Economic and Commercial Councillor's Office in Dar es Salaam.[18] A more general and theoretical doctorate on China's foreign aid will be available in 2013 and in the case of that too, there has been no interview done with the Department of Aid to Foreign Countries.[19] We recall however our earlier comment that personnel are possibly in short supply as are language skills if the demands for greater access were to be met.

It will of course be interesting to know if access is much easier for relevant scholars from China itself. And it will be valuable to know if the situation is changing rapidly in the period 2010–2013. This we shall turn to in a later section of this chapter.

[18] The title of this doctorate is 'China's educational "aid" to Africa: a different donor logic?' by Yuan (2011a).
[19] This doctoral thesis currently has the working title of: 'We Chinese: Understanding Chinese foreign policy through the making of diplomats' by Merriden Varrall.

*A different set of sectoral priorities?*
Apart from China's institutional fabric for aid being very different from stand-alone agencies, and its financing arrangements also being different from the agencies that transfer finance to recipient governments in various ways, there is also some considerable difference in terms of sectoral emphases.

In *China's African Policy* (2006), there are just four main sectors, but each of these covers a huge range. They are the Political Field; the Economic Field; Education, Science, Culture, Health and Social Aspects; and Peace and Security. There are no less than ten different dimensions of the Economic Field and a further ten dimensions for the human resources cooperation. In introducing the four main arenas of cooperation, the document states that its purpose is 'enhancing all-round cooperation between China and Africa'. And indeed 'cooperation' is the red thread that runs right through the short document, underlining an enormous diversity of areas for cooperation between the two actors.[20]

The different sectors are again picked out in the White Paper on *China's Foreign Aid*, and although this text is related to all the developing countries assisted by China, and not just Africa, it is possible to get something more of a sense of the scale of cooperation in respect of different sectors. In this document, there are no less than seven major sectors under discussion. They comprise: Agriculture; Industry; Economic infrastructure; Public facilities; Education; Medicine and public health; Clean energy. In this listing, there is more of a spin on what is the priority: it is this: 'improving recipient countries' industrial and agricultural productivity, laying a solid foundation for their economic and social development' (China, 2011a: 12). Interestingly, 'poverty' does appear in the White Paper, unlike *China's African Policy*, but once this is referring to China itself, once to global poverty reduction, and just once to this being a priority of China's aid, along with agriculture and rural development. It certainly still features much less than in many policy papers of Western donor agencies.

Although many of these seven sectors are said to be important priorities, in quantitative terms, it is worth noting that over the period to 2009 no less than 61% of China's concessional loans had gone to economic infrastructure, industry 16.1%, and energy and resources development 8.9%. China underlines the obvious point that 'Economic infrastructure is always an important part of China's foreign aid' (ibid.: 13). This central role for infrastructure in encouraging recipient countries to build up their 'self-development capacity' is not unique to China. Arguably, China's neighbour, Japan, to a greater extent than other bilateral agencies, has also regarded economic and social infrastructure 'as an indispensable condition for economic growth and sustained poverty reduction in developing countries' (JBIC, 2005: 6).

But the convergence is closer than two major Asian countries merely

[20] It will be recalled from an earlier chapter that 'cooperation' is mentioned no less than 78 times in just eleven pages in *China's African Policy*.

giving similar priority to infrastructure. In China's opening up from 1978, through the Japan-China Long Term Trade Agreement of 1978, a series of five five-year loans were agreed which over a period of 27 years provided US$28 billion to China through OECF/JBIC, covering all provinces and diversified sectors. According to Kitano, it is judged that the process had a positive impact on five dimensions in China: 'alleviating infrastructure bottlenecks, regional development, poverty alleviation, provision of advanced technologies, and transfer of institutional frameworks' (Kitano 2003: 467). Supported first by Japan and then other donors, China made an enormous investment in its own economic and social infrastructure development. Transferring this infrastructure priority from China's role as a recipient to a focal point of its own aid policy was a natural next step.

Although we mentioned earlier in this chapter that China does not follow Japan and South Korea in emphasising what other developing countries can learn from China's successful development experience, nevertheless when it comes to assessing the role of infrastructure-in-development, China makes an exception. Its Export-Import Bank claimed in 2006 that their activities enhanced 'development efforts by developing countries through transferring experiences and technology learned in the development of Chinese economy' (ExIm Bank, 2006).[21] Indeed, Brautigam (2009: 24) has argued that China's aid and economic engagement with the developing world has particularly drawn on Japan's early commercial involvement with China: 'Today in Africa, China is repeating many of the practices and the kind of deals it forged with Japan and the West in its own initial turn to the market.'

While learning from Japan proved influential in China's own aid policy in respect of infrastructure, we shall shortly note that there are new inter-agency engagements between China and Japan underway. But for other sectors, there continues to be more of a divergence between China and other donors.

In the case of Education, for example, China underlines the fact in its White Paper that it 'always attaches great importance to aid in education for other developing countries' (China, 2011a: 14). This is of course the case also for many other development agencies. But there the similarity ends. Several agencies support education in relationship to the two Millennium Development Goals in education (access to basic education and gender equity), but few make a stronger case for education investment than the UK's DFID:

> Education is fundamental to everything we do. It is the key to beating poverty and the greatest investment we can make for global prosperity and the future of our world. Education transforms countries and societies.[22]

---

[21] For a detailed account of the parallels between Japan and China, as well as the role of Japan in China's own development, see King 2007.

[22] http://www.dfid.gov.uk/What-we-do/Key-Issues/Education

This does not mean that DFID pays no attention to the role of economic growth. In fact it makes as large a claim for economic growth in relation to prosperity as has just been mentioned for education: 'Economic growth is the most important means of raising incomes and reducing poverty in the developing world.'[23] But the difference between China and the UK when it comes to supporting aid to education is that China sees this largely in terms of Chinese resources, Chinese experts, volunteers, and teachers, or exposure of students and trainees to Chinese universities. Illustrating the sheer magnitude of this ambition, former Premier Wen Jiabao promised at the UN in 2010 to bring no fewer than 80,000 trainees to China over the following five years to 2015. In other words, exposure to China is the key, but also the education level of those targeted for training in China is fundamentally different between China and UK Aid. China's HRD is aimed, in Wen's words at 'managerial and technical personnel in various professions', 'mid-career masters degree programmes', to build up 'human resources that are more valuable than gold' (Wen, 2010: 4).

DFID's targets by the same date (2015) are entirely located in the developing world, and there is no mention of exposure of trainees to the UK; furthermore, the great majority of those targeted by DFID (11 million) are at the basic education level:

By 2015 we will:
• support nine million children in primary school
• two million children in lower secondary school, at least half of which will be girls
• train more than 190,000 teachers and improve the quality of education and children's learning.[24]

China's emphasis on the role of its own experts, such as 3,000 medical experts, and 3,000 agricultural experts, promised by the former premier, along with the 10,000 Chinese teachers who had been sent abroad up to 2009, resonates with the key role that Japan also places upon its own long and short-term experts in translating technologies into action (King, 2004: 155–195).

It is sometimes suggested, as if in a historiography of aid, that what China is doing today with linking aid to the use of its own people, universities and firms, the more advanced countries were doing several decades ago (World Bank/China, 2012: 397). To an extent this may be true. A glance at what DFID's predecessor, the Overseas Development Administration (ODA), was doing in education some 20 years ago is reminiscent of China's current focus on training in China, and on the use of its own people overseas. The ODA was spending no less that £127 million sterling in 1990 on training 24,000 overseas students, at any one time, in the UK. But running through the whole account of what UK was doing in overseas educational

[23] http://www.dfid.gov.uk/What-we-do/Key-Issues/Economic- growth-and-the-private-sector/
[24] http://www.dfid.gov.uk/What-we-do/Key-Issues/Education/

aid was the underpinning role of the 'British resource' based in British universities, colleges and polytechnics (ODA, 1990:24, 18).

There is a problem, however, with this particular historiography of aid. Britain may have dramatically changed its aid orientation, slashed its training budget, and stopped using the 15–20 specialist departments in the UK for short-term training courses. But Japan has not, and amongst Western donors, Germany has not. Germany still supports annually an extraordinary number of long-term trainees (67,000), while the German Agency for Development Cooperation (GIZ) supports no less than 55, 000.[25]

Thus the idea that the very strong emphasis of Japan and China on the role of their own experts, on massive overseas training, and on people-to-people dimensions of educational aid, should be seen as a phase is not necessarily appropriate. These approaches have been central to both countries for several decades, and they show no indications of being changed.

## Aid data and transparency

This has been one of the areas where there have been some of the most critical comments made about the absence of data, and the difficulty of knowing what exactly was achieved. We have already discussed in different chapters some of the reasons why a country like China with many millions of very poor people would not publish a great deal of data on what it was providing free to countries in Africa. With China's very strong emphasis on bilateral relations, there are perhaps good reasons not to publish a great deal of information on what China was providing to one country versus the country next door.

Leaving these reasons aside for now, there have been some valuable explorations of the transparency of China's aid data. Of particular interest is Grimm et al.'s *Transparency of Chinese Aid* (2011), and of course sections of Brautigam's *The Dragon's Gift* (2009).[26] These are both very thoughtful about the challenges to greater transparency and the rationales behind them. However, at a time when the donor community is awash with discussions about evidence-based policy, impact evaluations, and, above all, 'value for money',[27] it should prove useful briefly to assess how much can be known about the human resources side of China's aid. We shall look accordingly at the data status of several of its main HRD modalities.

*1. Confucius Institutes (CIs)*
We have mentioned in Chapter 2 that there is a question-mark about the aid status of the CIs, as all CIs receive support from the CI headquarters in Beijing (Hanban) even if they are located in OECD country universities, in

---

[25]  See further *NORRAG News No 45* (2011).
[26]  See particularly, pp. 165 ff.
[27]  See the special issue of *NORRAG News* No. 47 for a wide-ranging review of 'value for money' in international education and training.

North America or in Europe. Nevertheless, there are multiple sources of information about individual CIs, located within their host universities. Most have their own web-site, or they have a semi-departmental status within the university's website.

Each CI is also represented on the main Confucius Institute headquarters' site. Thus the African CIs can be accessed, country by country, on the following site: http://english.hanban.org/node_10971.htm There is a good deal of difference in the extent to which the individual CIs have provided up to date information on the HQ site. But, following the Chinese fascination with institutional history, there is usually exact information on when the CI was inaugurated and by whom. Thus the CI in the University of Nairobi was launched by the Chinese and Kenyan Ministers of Education on 19 December 2005. The importance of the joint leadership of the CIs is illustrated by the names of the Chinese and the national directors. Considerable detail is available on courses, activities, cultural events, competitions, China Weeks, and so on.

Compared to the relative scarcity of information about projects and programmes about human resources on the site of the Department of Aid to Foreign countries, the Confucius Institute headquarters site is a rich source of information about every dimension of this world-wide programme: teachers, volunteers, resources, scholarships, publications, exchanges, media coverage and publications. Since March 2009, there have been published 22 issues of *Confucius Institute*, a glossy 100 page update on many different developments in the CI world. This publication, originally in Chinese and English, is now available in no less than seven other language editions.

Apart from the annual convention of Confucius Institutes that comes together in Beijing, there are also annual regional meetings, for example in Africa, which can raise valuable issues as well as controversies (Kotze, 2010). But what is clear from articles written by CI directors is that there is no single model for CIs across Africa, Asia or the world; rather 'CIs should be diverse and should function in a manner that is responsive and sensitive to local conditions' (Liu Yandong quoted in Vermaak, 2010).

In terms of our concerns about transparency and access to data, the CI system appears to be relatively accessible, and although there does not appear at the moment to be a monitoring and evaluation element publicised on the site, there is certainly a system of annual reporting which we have alluded to.

## 2. African scholars in China
Compared to the wealth of data about the spread of the Confucius Institutes, including in Africa, there is a good deal less publicly available information on the performance of the African dimension of China's scholarship programme. The annual reports of the China Scholarship Council (CSC) give some detail on breakdowns of scholars in China by source region, and they also show where Chinese students elected to go

abroad on China Scholarships. It can be seen that Africa, Asia and Latin America scarcely figure in the scholarship destinations of Chinese students. But Africa makes up a significant proportion of the total CSC students coming to China.

We have already referred in Chapter 3 to some of the few pieces of analyses carried out by academics on African scholarship students in China. One of the main contributions on this by Gillespie was based on fieldwork carried out in 1997, fifteen years ago. There was then the small report on *China-African Education Cooperation* (2005, in Chinese) which contained a whole section on African students in China.[28]

These ten pages are really the only accessible public evaluation of China's scholarship programme for Africa. They openly accept the 'dual purpose' of the African scholarship programme: 'promoting Sino-African educational cooperation and exchanges and African talents' development' (China, MOE, 2005: 18). In terms of evaluating African students' presence and satisfaction, there is a positive assessment of the two-way appreciation of Chinese and African cultures, an acknowledgement of the academic and social achievements of the majority of the African students. There is no mention of any of the racial difficulties discussed in Chapter 3. Finally, there is a positive assessment of the development impact for the students returning to Africa. Despite the inadequate statistics, 'effectiveness and impact of the Chinese government scholarship are increasingly apparent' (ibid.: 20). Several former African students are picked out and named for their subsequent careers in their home countries.

Possibly it was the absence of current analytical work on the growing scholarship programme that prompted Peking University's Centre for African Studies to propose to UNDP in 2011 a new study on the 'Evolution of the Chinese policy of funding African students and an evaluation of its effectiveness'. This would investigate selection processes, changes in policy over time, proportions of students returning home after studies, and, more challengingly, the 'developmental impact' on the sending countries of the scholarship programme. It will be recalled, from Chapter 3, that the major evaluation of Commonwealth scholars attempted this kind of impact assessment with some success. If this kind of careful evaluation of the China Scholarship Programme could be carried out, even for a small number of countries, it would make a considerable difference in our knowledge about one of the key components of China's HRD aid.

*3. MOFCOM's large scale short-term training programme*
We have already commented on the 80,000 trainees, world-wide, which former Premier Wen promised China was supporting between 2010 and 2015. The African component of that total is of course considerable. But what is known about how this massive programme is operating? The answer is that there are formal evaluations of each of the courses carried

---

[28] I am indebted to Zhang Zhongwen for the translation of this booklet.

out by the responsible institution in China. These will be used by the Ministry for its forward planning. Then at the level of the sending country, the Economic and Commercial Councillor's Office which is responsible for the scheme is at liberty to review the individual impact in liaison with the responsible host ministry. We do know that this has been carried by one Councillor's Office in one country (Kenya) for at least one year. The results were very interesting as we noted in Chapter 2.

As with the African scholars in China, the only piece of official analysis for the scheme was the *China-Africa Education Cooperation* (2005). At quite an early stage in the institutionalisation of the programme, and when the Ministry of Education had just identified fourteen university resource bases for providing the seminars, there is detailed information on the providing institutions, the participating countries, and even some detailed commentary on what took place.

The analysis is clear that there are at least two purposes. The first of these is conceptual: 'a more in-depth understanding of China's politics, economy, history and culture' (China, MOE, 2005: 14). The second is closer to cultural diplomacy: 'In order to let African guests learn more about China's long and splendid history and culture, the brilliant achievements of Chinese modernization, these contracted units also organize sightseeing' (ibid.:19). But the visitors were also shown the poor areas of China so that they 'had a more comprehensive understanding of China as a developing country' (ibid.).

There is one further level that emerges and is clearly an important part of the overall message. Even though at one level, the Chinese are the experts, and the Africans the recipients, this is not how it is written up. Rather the discourse emphasises mutual learning and south-south collaboration: 'This training has a very positive promoting role in helping the professionals of China and of African countries have a full exchange and communication, developing African research on local medicinal plants and enhancing Sino-African cooperation in developing medicinal plants' (ibid.: 21).

However, overall, there is little or no publicly available evaluation of this very large programme. Indeed, the formal link to the various seminars and training programmes of the Department of Aid to Foreign Countries even on the Chinese version of the Ministry of Commerce website reports these as unobtainable.[29] Nevertheless, other countries, such as India, with equally large short-term training programmes do not appear to carry out evaluations, presumably because of transaction costs and

---

[29] According to my key informant, Zhang Zhongwen, in the University of Edinburgh's Centre of African Studies, access to the site: http://yws.mofcom.gov.cn/aarticle/s/200405/20040500218044.html registers that 'an error occurred while processing this directive'. On the other hand there is some information about MOFCOM's training courses on the website of the Academy for International Business Officials (AIBO), but this is presented in the form of different speeches and does not contain a comprehensive listing of available courses: http://pxzx.mofcom.gov.cn/

complexity. But amongst OECD countries, Japan and Germany with very large short-term programmes have certainly conducted evaluations (Japan, MOFA, 2012).[30]

### 4. China-Africa Friendship Schools/ Rural Schools

At different FOCAC Conferences in 2006 and 2009, there have been pledges of providing 100 rural schools and 50 China-Africa Friendship Schools, respectively.[31] We shall note when we come to review FOCAC's role in respect of all these education pledges that they do have a mechanism for reviewing progress on the implementation of all the commitments. But there is no alternative way, outside that FOCAC process, for reviewing the achievement of the school-building pledge. It can be imagined that as most countries in Africa which are part of FOCAC will get at most two or three 3 schools out of the 150 committed to Africa, these will simply be selected in conjunction with the national ministry of education, and built by a chosen Chinese contractor in a location agreed between the Economic and Commercial Councillor's Office and the Ministry.

Currently we know very little about these schools apart from the fact that most of the 150 have been built. They are fundamentally turn-key gifts from China, a form of tied aid. At completion, there is no doubt of their aid status, as the Chinese and national flags both fly visibly. There is no place where they can be looked at as a stand-alone project, except as a part of the FOCAC pledges. To which we now turn.

### 5. FOCAC's education pledges and their evaluation status

In sharp contrast to the Department of Aid to Foreign Countries, the website of the Forum on China-Africa Cooperation is dynamic and attractive with the Great Wall of China on one side of the top of the site, and nine pictures of Africa, from the Sphinx, the Cape of Good Hope, to the terminus of TAZARA, constantly rotating on the other. But the information on the site is also regularly changing. The most recent items as of 30 March 2013, for example, are right up to the minute (www.focac.org/eng/). While the site is a very valuable source of historical activities, going back to the first Ministerial Conference of FOCAC of 10–12 October 2000, and its various documents, speeches and follow-up actions, however, as Grimm et al. (2011: 15) have noted 'There are no detailed reports on implementation of FOCAC pledges and where promised projects were implemented.'

The formal evaluation mechanism for all the various FOCAC pledges to Africa is the Chinese Follow-up Committee. This, as discussed by King (2009) in more detail, includes all the line ministries concerned with international development, as well as other key institutions – a total of 27

---

[30] There is also a very positive evaluation of Germany's short-term training, shortly to be made available.

[31] These should not be confused with the Project Hope schools. These are also mentioned on the FOCAC website: http://www.focac.org/eng/zxxx/t863105.htm, but they are a private charity supported by Chinese business.

organisations. The Follow-up Committee is thus entirely Chinese. Although there is no African Follow-up Committee for evaluating the FOCAC targets, there is the mechanism of the Senior Officials Meeting (SOM) which is made up of all the Beijing-based African ambassadors having diplomatic relations with China. This is specifically tasked to work on FOCAC planning and implementation and it has been meeting approximately once a year since the early 2000s. The first meeting since the 2009 Sharm el Shaikh FOCAC IV conference was held in Hangzhou on 26 and 27 October 2011; this 8th SOM reviewed progress on all fronts with the intention to meet and report on all the quantitative and qualitative goals by the time of the next FOCAC, which was scheduled for July 2012.[32]

Since FOCAC is essentially a bilateral mechanism, between China and individual African countries, under a Pan-African umbrella, it can be appreciated that individual African ambassadors do not have any way of knowing how FOCAC implementation as a whole has been progressing; at best they can know the FOCAC implications and achievements for their own country. By contrast, a long-standing issue amongst the African ambassador corps is how China can respond to regional, inter-country priorities, like inter-state highways, and so on, rather than just bilateral.[33] But so far, distribution and allocation of FOCAC pledges remains firmly bilateral.

There is similar lacuna at the African Union level. Unlike the Government of India, which followed its first Africa-India Forum in 2008 by giving the African Union the responsibility for distributing to different countries India's offer of new Africa-wide institutions,[34] China's FOCAC pledges of hospitals, schools and other resources continue to be decided bilaterally. China would argue that as soon as the African Union as a whole is in favour of that, they will go along with this decision (member of China Follow-up Committee to KK, July 2010). Intriguingly, on the African Union website, under Partnerships, there was a great deal of data, speeches, documents, and so on, under Africa-India; but under 'China Africa Cooperation Forum', despite 12 years of FOCAC, there was just a blank page with Africa-China at the top.[35] Now it is completely changed.

Summarising the role of FOCAC in relationship to aid data and transparency, we should emphasise that unlike some other China government websites, there is a great deal of information available on the FOCAC site. Most of the many items which China has committed through FOCAC to Africa can be found there. But they are found more in key speeches and in reports of meetings than in evaluations, reviews and analyses. Speeches and accounts of meetings are the modality which typifies the reporting of

---

[32] http://www.focac.org/eng/zt/som2011/
[33] The inter-regional, cross-border priorities have been particularly promoted by South Africa, both from Beijing and Pretoria.
[34] In the education sector, India is establishing an India-Africa Institute of Education, Planning and Administration (GOI, MEA, 2010).
[35] http://au.int/en/partnerships/africa_china. Bodomo makes the point that China-Africa is hugely more common than Africa-China (2009). For a useful commentary on FOCAC and its possible futures see, CCS China Monitor, 2012.

achievement. Thus it can be readily found, in speeches, that the China-Africa University 20+20 Cooperation Programme has been launched in June 2010; or that the China-Africa Joint Research and Exchange Programme 'is moving smoothly forward', and that all the other commitments have been implemented. As Jia Qinglin, senior political advisor, underlined prior to the opening ceremony of the new AU Headquarters for the 18th AU Summit: 'Since the inception of FOCAC in October 2000, the Chinese side has earnestly implemented all its cooperation commitments made at various ministerials and the Beijing Summit (of 2006).'[36]

Given China's reputation for delivering on time, or before time, it is easy for Jia to claim that 'These initiatives were warmly welcomed and positively appraised by African countries' (ibid.). What we have of course noted in this brief account of the sources covering China's human resources aid to Africa is that sources have been principally Chinese, and that a few of them, such as the website of the Department of Aid to Foreign Countries, have been very slight. Only the FOCAC and CI sites have been a rich source of information. Other regular sources of data on aid, such as AidData (AidData.org) simply draw a blank when it comes to reviewing the role of China as a donor in the many different fields where it operates.[37]

However, it is on the African side where there seems to be the greatest gap when it comes to FOCAC. Because of the structure of FOCAC, and the absence of an obvious African partner, then it is perhaps inevitable that all the information about achievements and implementation of China's pledges and commitments through FOCAC comes from FOCAC itself. In this respect, therefore, there is a parallel with OECD country development agencies: the great bulk of the best data on DFID, Sida, GIZ, or JICA comes from their own web-sites. There does seem however to be a particular problem when it comes to Africa's role in China-Africa analysis; far too little of the published work on China-Africa derives from Africa.[38]

---

[36] http://ng.china-embassy.org/eng/xw/t902991.htm. The scale of the achievements is captured in a couple of sentences: 'The aided agriculture demonstration centres, clean energy project, China-Africa friendship schools and other projects are progressing in an orderly manner. The human resources training work has been carried out in full swing. The forum on agricultural cooperation, forum on legal affairs, youth leaders forum, civil forum, science and technology cooperation forum, think tank forum, African culture in focus, China-Africa college cooperation program, China-Africa joint research and exchange program and other important events and programs have been launched successively, bringing China-Africa cooperation to a new height.' http://et.china-embassy.org/eng/zagx/t900715.ht

[37] In the Global Monitoring Report 2012, while there are papers on India and South Korea's aid to skills development, there is none for China. http://www.unesco.org/new/en/education/themes/leading-the-international-agenda/efareport/background-papers/2012/

[38] According to the Executive Secretary of CODESRIA, Ebrima Sall, only 7% of the current analysis of China-Africa in publications derives from the continent. http://ke.china-embassy.org/eng/zfgx/t882632.htm

## Distinctiveness; but the beginnings of convergence?

We have reviewed a number of the dimensions of China's distinctiveness as a donor, with specific reference to HRD. The issues of culture and tradition, its own experience of development, its financing, its professionalism as a donor, its priority aid sectors, and data transparency have all been examined, and these generally reinforce the view that China remains distinct as a donor. At the field level, too, in Africa, we have noted that China remains outside the multiplicity of donor working groups, with their sectoral specificities. In many ways, it is understandable, given what we have just analysed, that China remains outside the donor clubs.

In terms of its discourse and its emphasis on South-South Cooperation, it is entirely appropriate that when it comes to collaboration, the focus and the priorities should be to strengthen China-Africa mechanisms and modalities rather than China-Europe. Hence we have noted just how many different kinds of China-Africa fora have been inaugurated and encouraged, particularly since the FOCAC conference of November 2009 in Sharm el Shaikh.

Nevertheless, even though it is a lesser priority, there are distinct initiatives for greater collaboration between China and other agencies, both bilateral and multilateral. Indeed there is a whole short section of China's White Paper on foreign aid that is termed 'International cooperation in foreign aid' (China, 2011a: 16–17). Characteristically of China, however, the discourse about what is new is embedded in the claim that this collaboration has been going on for decades:

> China also has done its best to support and participate in aid programs initiated by organizations like the United Nations, and has actively conducted exchanges and explored practical cooperation with multilateral organizations and other countries in the field of development assistance with an open-minded attitude. (ibid.: 16)

Briefly, China reminds readers that it played a role 30 years ago, in 1981, in supporting the UNDP to implement the new concept of Technical Cooperation among Developing Countries; and that for fifteen years since 1996, China has supported the FAO's South-South Cooperation programme (ibid.; Brautigam, 2009: 65–66; 242). But as a country that is still prepared, modestly to say 'that China has a long way to go in providing foreign aid' (China, 2011a: 18), there are a series of markers of a new phase of more active inter-agency collaboration.

### 1. DFID and the China-Africa agenda
One of the collaborations that has developed over a period of six or seven years has been with Britain's DFID. Even when DFID was still providing development aid to China in a number of sectors, including in education

support to China's Western provinces, DFID Beijing had anticipated the end of its traditional donor relationship with China and was exploring a new emphasis on collaboration in approaches to African development. From as early as 2006, DFID Beijing was commissioning work on China's involvement with Africa.[39] First there was a valuable analysis of China's interest and activity in construction and infrastructure in four countries (CCS, 2006). This was followed by a high level symposium in Beijing, supported jointly by DFID Beijing and two departments of the Chinese Academy of Social Sciences, focused on China-Africa shared development. There was then an important review of *How China Delivers Development Assistance to Africa* (Davies et al., 2008). In 2009, a major event took place whose title underlines precisely the goal of China and the UK collaborating in relation to Africa: *Understanding China's Engagement with Africa & How the UK Can Build Relationships with China in Africa* (CCS, 2009). The purpose of the meeting was primarily how the lessons learnt by DFID Beijing about working with China could be shared with DFID's country offices in Africa, as well as the British embassies and high commissions in Africa. Even if the focus was on British staff in Africa learning more about engaging with China, it is interesting that the Ministry of Commerce was a participant through one of its Economic and Commercial Councillors, as well as large number of speakers from other major Chinese institutions concerned with development in Africa.

These several years of investment in DFID Beijing demonstrating the importance of understanding and engaging with China on Africa have clearly borne fruit. DFID is now one of the bilateral agencies with which MOFCOM has formally agreed to engage in global development work. This agreement in principle was reinforced by the then UK International Development Secretary's visit to Beijing on 28–29 November 2011. Andrew Mitchell's meetings with the Ministers of Commerce and of Foreign Affairs allowed him to confirm that a 'new era of collaboration between China and the UK was sealed by the visit' (DFID, 2011). The emphasis was that 'by sharing experience and expertise the UK and China could have a real impact on reducing poverty' (ibid.). From the DFID side, such an agreement with China would be an illustration of their new Global Development Partnership Programme with emerging powers.[40]

Whether this new spirit of cooperation was one of the factors that contributed to China's endorsing the Busan Outcomes Document the next day is a moot point, but whatever collaborative agreements are signed with DFID or other agencies, China may well see risks in fuller donor cooperation; it does not want to endanger its status as a developing country primarily involved in South-South relations; it does not yet want to get drawn into the requirements of the OECD donor club.

[39] See also DFID, 2006. The planning of DFID's engaging with China on Africa goes back to the middle of 2005.
[40] For a new possibility of trilateral cooperation with DFID, China and Africa, see Brautigam 'China, the UK and Africa: Trilateral Cooperation?' blog 20.11.12, www.chinaafricarealstory.com

## 2. Japan-China collaboration in development

Japan, and JICA in particular, have been actively exploring collaboration with Chinese institutions, including MOFCOM, in a similar way to DFID. There have been joint seminars with the China Eximbank in January 2009 and March 2010. With MOFCOM staff members there was a seminar on development assistance in October 2010. There was an important seminar in January 2011 for sharing experiences in agricultural development between Japan and China, in relation to Africa; it was hoped that this could actually lead to trilateral projects between China and Japan in Africa. Further seminars were held on health collaboration, as well as more generally on development. Japan participated in a workshop on international development cooperation and capacity development hosted by MOFCOM and the World Bank in August 2011.

Japan has also drawn South Korea into this new field of development collaboration, and a trilateral cooperation secretariat was set up in Seoul in September 2011, to promote cooperation across different sectors (Kitano, 2011). This could include cooperation in training, which all three countries regard as a key component of development. There are other fields of intellectual cooperation, where again all three countries share common priorities, whether in manufacturing, small enterprise development, or approach to national productivity.

Some of these quite frequent meetings discussed the possibility of joint projects for Sino-Japanese cooperation on aid to Africa, putting forward specific ideas and suggestions for aid work as a next phase. This is perhaps the litmus test of this new spirit of collaboration, whether it remains at the knowledge sharing stage, or translates into shared development activity. It is by no means an easy transition, as there are decades of separate institutional experience to be overcome. Even where all three countries are doing development work in the same country and in the same sector, it could well be that 'friendly competition' is as likely an outcome as joint development projects (Kitano, 2011).

## 3. Wider inter-agency collaborations with China

Apart from these two bilateral examples, there have been, in the last two years, a whole series of shared seminars, conferences and expert meetings with China, involving several UN multi-lateral agencies as well as the World Bank and the Asian Development Bank. Given that the focus of this book is education and training, it will be useful to illustrate something of this new openness by China to international cooperation from this education field.

The first example is of how a China-Africa project of South-South cooperation appears to be changing into a form of trilateral cooperation involving UNESCO headquarters. The particular project in question was no ordinary China-Africa project, but the partnership programme between twenty leading African and twenty leading Chinese universities was one of the several human resources pledges in the FOCAC Ministerial Conference of November 2009 in Sharm el Shaikh, (as mentioned in Chapter 2). There had been a formal competition organised by the Chinese Ministry of Education between December 2009 and January 2010 amongst Chinese universities keen to participate in the scheme (China MOE, 2011); and a launch meeting had duly been held in China in June 2010.[41] However, in the autumn of 2011, UNESCO announced a 'UNESCO-China-Africa University Leaders Meeting: Prospects for future collaboration'. The concept note in advance of this very high level meeting[42] which brought the majority of the twenty pairs of universities to Paris made no reference to the FOCAC origins of the partnership, nor of its short name, the 20+20 project, but presented the meeting as a new opportunity for trilateral cooperation:

> The UNESCO-China-Africa University Leaders Meeting aims to promote university partnerships between China and Africa and to establish an action plan for three-party collaboration between UNESCO, China and Africa. (UNESCO, 2011a)

An action plan was one of the expected outcomes of the meeting. It will be interesting to see what form such a trilateral project will take, and what role UNESCO will play in these originally two-way partnerships. It will not be a financing role,[43] but it will perhaps draw on UNESCO's mandate as a laboratory of ideas, clearing house, and catalyst for international cooperation to develop a convening and facilitating responsibility. Interestingly, at the FOCAC V Conference, one of the pledges was that China would provide US$2 million annually to support education development programmes in Africa, in particular higher education in Africa (FOCAC, 2012: 6.2.4.).

Examples of the new openness to collaborations also involve research projects that partner Chinese institutions with European and African counterparts in a trilateral arrangement. One illustration is a project that linked the Institute of African Studies of Zhejiang Normal University (China's largest African studies centre) with two research centres, one in Belgium and the other in Africa. This trilateral research cooperation was funded by the Belgian Ministry of Foreign Affairs, Foreign Trade and Development Cooperation, and it carried out research on both Chinese and Belgian aid projects in different sectors of the Congo (Pollet et al., 2011). This initiative provided a valuable opportunity to discuss trilateralism in development aid, as part of the final report (ibid.: 112ff.).[44] But the project itself was also an illustration of the challenges of genuinely joint activities mentioned earlier. In the event, the Chinese research team only looked at the Chinese aid projects, and the Belgian researchers only exam-

---

[41] See: 20+20: a new kind of 20/20 vision, *Chinafrica* October 2011.

[42] Most of the 40 universities were represented at the level of their President or Vice-Chancellor

[43] China paid most of the costs of the participants coming to Paris.

[44] This section of the report was entitled, 'Trilateral aid: a blessing or a curse?'

ined Belgian aid. The African researchers were in the fortunate position of looking at both.

### 4. New forms of trilateral or triangular cooperation

It should be noted that these few examples of openness by Chinese institutions, both government and university, to cooperation with new bilateral or multilateral partners in favour of Africa are all part of what is now called trilateral or triangular cooperation. There are many forms of this, but currently the commonest model is one DAC partner, one emerging donor, such as China or Brazil, and one developing country or region as the ultimate recipient. This North-South-South pattern contains an element of South-South cooperation within it therefore. This may suggest that although the Busan Outcome Document claims that South-South cooperation involves a different 'nature, modalities and responsibilities' than apply in North-South cooperation (HLF4, 2011: 1), triangular cooperation may benefit from elements of both.

Currently, it might appear that trilateral or triangular cooperation is of greater interest to the Northern DAC partner than to the other two partners, as it offers them a way of working with a major emerging economy, sharing their approaches, and possibly influencing the emerging donor's aid processes. Despite the evidence that China has been readier to reach out to bilateral and multilateral actors in the period 2010–2011, this may imply a greater interest in sharing experiences rather than actually pursuing joint development activities with these new partners in Africa. China might well be hesitant about being seen to be part of the DAC club through trilateral cooperation; it might also not wish its comparative advantage in very rapidly executed aid projects to be compromised by the very much greater transaction costs of triangular cooperation (Pollet et al., 2011: 117; Grimm, 2011; Langendorf and Muller, 2011: 16).[45] Nor might it want its sharply preferred approach to South-South cooperation to be weakened by being drawn into North-South-South cooperation.[46]

### 5. Reflections on opening up to other agencies

There are many more dimensions of this new-found openness than we have referred to here.[47] But because of the enormous interest in the DAC agencies in working with China, several of these initiatives are still under wraps, as DAC donors do not wish to embarrass China by publicly discussing proposed developments before they are firmly in place.

---

[45] Langendorf and Muller make the point that 'Trico [trilateral cooperation] requires intense communication. Three cultures and concepts of planning and collaborating need to be brought and kept together' (2011: 16).

[46] It is intriguing that the Busan Outcome Document always presents 'South-South and triangular cooperation' together, as if they are part of the same discourse.

[47] Others would include the University of Peking-UNDP proposal to evaluate the African scholarship programme to China which we have referred to at different points. And it is reported that 'Chinese aid specialists have held meetings with American aid specialists designed to study the U.S. aid programme' (see further Kurlantzick, 2009: 172).

But what is clear, as we mentioned at the beginning of this chapter, is that there is much more evidence of this new openness to be found amongst Chinese and other agencies in Beijing than there is at the country level in Africa. But even in the Beijing exchanges, the emphasis is basically on mutual learning and knowledge sharing. There is little or no joint development activity yet.[48] This is captured in the words of one seasoned agency analyst in the capital:

> I'd say the key point here is that China has now made a policy decision that engaging with and learning from others – and even just understanding better how other bilaterals and the international aid system works – is a good thing to do. That engaging, learning and understanding process is starting from a base of very little interaction prior to a year or so ago and is going to take several years. Anyone who claims to know what will come out of it at this stage is probably to be treated with skepticism! All we can say is that we will see China considering each of the practices of the traditional donors and deciding on a case by case basis whether it would be in China's interests (broadly defined) to incorporate them (as they are, or with Chinese characteristics) into their way of working. We have informal indications that some elements are already being considered, whereas others will likely simply not be feasible given the institutional set-up of Chinese aid. (Beijing-based agency analyst to KK, 31.1.2012)

## Concluding remarks

We started this chapter with an invitation to the author to comment on FOCAC past and FOCAC future. He was just one of many individuals and organisations who were doubtless asked for their views. These explorations are of course separate from the official interactions of participants at the 8th Senior Officials Meeting of FOCAC, bringing no less than 240 people together in Hangzhou in October 2011. 50 African countries and regional organisations were represented.[49] It would appear that China has been listening more intently this time to different views about one of its main aid modalities for supporting Africa than hitherto. It is not evident that the FOCAC V conference of July 2012 in Beijing differed substantially from those of 2009 and 2006 with their series of eight major pledges. Certainly, 'cooperation' appears several times on each page of the Action Plan, but there is no mention of trilateral or triangular cooperation.

In terms of whether China's approach towards aid has begun to

---

[48] There is some knowledge sharing at the level of the Chinese embassy in Africa. In the words of one embassy official in Africa: 'In the future, we hope to make joint programmes and projects with the World Bank, UNICEF and UNESCO. For the moment, our only cooperation with these agencies is at the level of exchange of information.' (I am indebted to Bjorn Nordtveit for this reference.)

[49] http://www.fmprc.gov.cn/eng/zxxx/t872814.htm

converge more with those of traditional DAC donors, there is little in what we have reviewed in this chapter that would indicate a significant change. The FOCAC mechanism remains firmly in place, and the whole series of China-Africa agreements on research, science and technology, exchange, and partnership, announced in FOCAC IV in Egypt, emphasise the continued, even increased importance of South-South cooperation. The same would be true of the outcome of the Busan high level forum; South-South cooperation is acknowledged for its distinctiveness from North-South much more than at Accra.

We should note in passing that although we have used 'convergence' in this chapter to imply China's aid policy moving towards those of the DAC donors, there is some discussion of quite the opposite trend, so-called traditional partners moving towards China. We had already referred to this awareness in the World Bank/China report of 2012 at the beginning of this chapter, but at a conference in Oxford University in March 2012, this other convergence was referred to by several speakers:

> The evidence suggests that China's approach to economic growth and development assistance is currently impacting development thinking and practices of traditional Western donors. In particular, one speaker illustrated to what extent China in Africa has created some pressures for the European Union to be more effective and expand its development cooperation beyond aid without compromising its own principles. Thus, it was suggested that traditional donors are changing and adapting their development paradigm more than the emerging donors. (Verhoeven and Urbina-Ferretjans, 2012)

However, the other markers of China's difference from traditional donors, including inaccessibility and transparency of aid data, remain in place. At the sectoral level too, the approach is different from most DAC donors, although there are obvious resonances with South Korea and Japan. Specifically in the education and human resources area, China's approach seems a world away from the Education for All (EFA) agenda, or the focus of the Global Monitoring Reports on the achievement of the EFA goals.

Indeed, the human resources approach of China is certainly not about the well-worn categories of primary, secondary, vocational and tertiary education that concern DAC donors. Ultimately, China's human resources perspective may need to be embedded in a wider debate about how it relates to, or even illustrates, China's soft power in Africa. To that we turn in our final chapter.

# 6

## China's Soft Power in Africa | Past, present & future

The different elements of China's human resources development with Africa have traditionally been embedded in the discourse of cooperation, mutual benefit and political equality, reinforced by the focus upon South-South cooperation. As we mentioned briefly in Chapter 1, the discussion of soft power seems to come out of a different universe – one of competition for cultural and public relations influence rather than of collaboration for development. Whether the rise in the use of the term soft power points to any evolution in China's aid policy, we shall need to examine, but also how the many different modalities of China's human resources cooperation may illustrate soft power.

However, one of the first things that is noticeable about the term soft power is that in some ways it is increasingly widely used in China, but in others, it is not used at all. For instance, in the White Paper on *China's Foreign Aid* (China, 2011a), soft power does not appear at all, and 'culture' and 'cultural' appear more in the sense of China's providing cultural utilities for other nations than in promoting its own culture overseas. The same is true for a document, *China 2030* (World Bank and DRC, 2012), which though it is principally concerned with China's domestic development does pay some significant attention to its 'development assistance' and 'foreign aid'. Given its subtitle, *Building a Modern, Harmonious and Creative High-income Society*, it might have seemed a natural location for some discussion of soft power, but there is none. A third illustration comes from China's White Paper of September 2011 on *Peaceful Development* (China, 2011a). There is no mention at all of soft power; but 'harmonious' and 'harmony' occur 24 times in 28 pages, and 'culture' and 'cultural' occur 17 times overall. The document is of crucial importance in terms of positioning China internationally. It is essentially about China's relations with the wider world, whether Europe, Asia, Africa or the Americas. Intriguingly, it does refer just once to China carrying its culture to the rest of the world, but this was the iconic event of six centuries ago with Zheng He; a single reference is the nearest the document gets to soft power. In this

172

chapter we shall note, however, that the idea that culture, technology, peace and friendship could constitute a kind of soft power with Chinese characteristics is an image that several commentators return to:

> The famous Ming Dynasty navigator, Zheng He, made seven voyages to the Western Seas, visiting over 30 countries and regions across Asia and Africa. He took along with him the cream of the Chinese culture and technology as well as a message of peace and friendship. (China, 2011b: 22)

We shall examine in this chapter the different accounts of how China's aid is seen as soft power. But we shall need to remember from Chapter 5 that the delivery of China's aid is extremely fragmented, and it can hardly be said that there is a single coherent story line about the rationale for assistance emerging from the Department of Aid to Foreign Countries.

## Confucius Institutes, the prime example of China's soft power?

In a number of Western sources, the Confucius Institutes (CIs) are viewed as a prime example of China's soft power initiative. They are frequently represented, wrongly, as parallel to the British Council, Goethe Institutes, Alliance Française and other comparators. In reality they are rather different. They are in most cases the result of the 'request mode'; in other words, they are a response to a request from a university level institution overseas to China for the establishment of an institute.[1] This is not at all the case with the other cultural promotion agencies. Equally, it is far from clear that Confucius Institutes are straightforwardly examples of China's foreign aid, since in all cases the host institution, whether in London, Edinburgh, Nairobi or Cape Town, has to provide accommodation and support to the visiting staff as well as to the Chinese Co-Director. Another distinguishing feature, referred to in earlier chapters, is that all Confucius Institutes outside China have a university partner on the Chinese Mainland. This suggests much more of a mutual learning and collaboration model than in the case of the European comparators just mentioned.

Despite this, the Confucius Institutes are frequently referred to as one of the prime examples of China's soft power, almost as if there were a single standard approach by China to spreading these kinds of institutions across the world. The reality would appear to be rather different. In a key speech about the mandate of the CIs in Beijing in 2009, the issue about whether China had a model of all CIs conforming to a common standard, or whether CIs should be able to respond to the local context and culture was decisively answered by a very senior Chinese official. It is reported

---

[1] The chief executive of the Confucius Institute Headquarters, Xu Lin, emphasised in July 2010 that she received between 40 and 60 requests daily from tertiary institutions across the world, to set up Confucius Institutes (Leong, 2010).

here by Marius Vermaak, the South African co-director of the Confucius Institute in Rhodes University:

> At the recent fourth Confucius Institute Conference in December 2009 in Beijing, State Councillor Liu Yandong gave a surprising keynote address. The gist of her message was that CIs should be diverse and should function in a manner that is responsive and sensitive to local conditions. I believe this was a very significant moment. The tension between two schools of thought regarding CIs, the "one size fits all" faction and the "let a thousand flowers blossom" faction, was resolved. The Hanban is clearly on a steep but successful learning curve concerning the constraints and opportunities offered by operating across the whole wide world. (Vermaak, 2010: 8)

The notion that the CIs are part of some centrally coordinated plan for the promotion of China's soft power was also powerfully deflated by the then Chinese ambassador for South Africa at a colloquium in the CI at the University of Rhodes in 2009:

> The ambassador to the People's Republic of China to South Africa, the Honourable Mr. Zhong Jianhua, was the guest of honour. During one of the discussions a postgraduate student from a country to the north challenged the diplomat: "Mr Ambassador, you need to tell us what China plans for us." Mr Zhong's response was: "You are asking the wrong question. You should not worry about what China wants to do to you, but what you want to do for yourself." The message was that Africans should stop thinking of themselves as passive victims – always on the receiving end, and begin thinking of themselves as active agents – at least sometimes creating their own future. (Vermaak, 2010: ibid.)

Despite these kinds of strong messages, there is a continuing tendency in some quarters to regard the establishment of a Confucius Institute in a university setting as a direct opportunity for Chinese propaganda to enter academia. Even in the case of an African university with a long liberal tradition like the University of Cape Town, the decision about the development of a Confucius Institute took a long time from the initial agreement in July 2007 to the formal launch in January 2010. Some of the delay was clearly linked to concerns about the potentially political role of the Confucius Institute. This however was taken care of at the very highest level of the University, and is now no longer an issue.

Elsewhere than Africa, there still appear to be examples of where the spread of interest in Confucius Institutes is interpreted politically. In the case of India, there have been reportedly sensitivities to the expansion of Confucius Institutes, and as of December 2012, there was only one Institute in the entire country, as compared to seventeen in South Korea, fourteen in Thailand, and fifteen in Japan.[2] However, at the secondary school

---

[2] The institutes have faced criticism in some quarters, with a number of universities declining to partner with Hanban. Most notably, India in 2009 rejected China's bid to establish language

level in India there would appear to have been a breakthrough with the signing of a Memorandum of Understanding (MOU) between Hanban and the Central Board of Secondary Education (CBSE) in August 2012. To respond to demand, the CBSE had decided to list Chinese in their foreign languages curriculum from April 2012, and offer the subject first in 500 schools and eventually in 11,500 (*Confucius Institute*, 2012: 19).

The more general concern about whether the Confucius Institutes worldwide could be presented as an exercise in soft power has been addressed head-on, on many occasions, by Xu Lin, the Director-General of Hanban and Chief Executive of the Confucius Institute Headquarters. For example in an interview in April 2010, she was reported in the following way:

> The CI has nothing to do with soft power. The Chinese culture is still a weak culture. So we go international in fact just to increase real face-to-face communication between Chinese and foreign cultures.

> I am against the term soft power. The CI has nothing to do with soft power. Indeed we go international in order actively to reflect and refresh our culture rather than export it.

> The purpose for CI to go international is to let more foreigners know more about China. The most important thing is that CIs provide a platform without any distance to increase face-to-face real communication between Chinese and foreign cultures.

> There is no ideological element in the CI; it is completely cultural. Therefore the CI can't be called a kind of Mao Zedong Institute; it has nothing to do with politics. (Interview *Global Times*, 9.1.2010 [original in Mandarin])[3]

It is, however, important to be clear what it is about the term soft power that the CI leadership wishes to distance itself from. Arguably, as can be seen from Xu Lin's comments above, it is specifically the link with politics and ideology that is firmly denied. Equally, the idea that there is a highly centralised planned outreach from Beijing across the world-wide network of Confucius Institutes with particular messages about China is frequently refuted. State Councillor, Liu Yandong, already quoted above, often returns to the theme of the individuality and specificity of each Confucius Institute in its own national context:

centres, calling a plot to spread soft power 'unacceptable', according to *The Telegraph* of Kolkata (Dawson, 2010). Interestingly, on the website of Hanban it mentions Jawaharlal Nehru University as having a CI, but according to a senior professor in JNU 'there is no Confucius Institute issue pending with the University and no likelihood of it in the near future', JNU professor to KK, 8 April 2012.

[3] I am grateful to Ma Yue, the Chinese Co-Director of the Confucius Institute in Rhodes University, for this reference. The text was kindly translated by Ying Danjun, Hong Kong Institute of Education http://www.hanyuwang.cn/index.php?o=article-show&artsid=4064%29%28http://cis.chinese.cn/article/2011–11/18/content_385665_4.htm

In line with different national situations, diversified cultural back-
grounds and multifaceted demands of Chinese language learning in
different countries, *Confucius Institutes are expected to adapt to the*
*local situations, mingle with the local particularities, and strive for their*
*own unique styles. They need to respect and embody cultural diversi-*
*ties....* (Liu, 2010: 4, emphasis in original)

This emphasis on there being no 'standard model', and on most CIs being
given 'a free hand to run their own centres' is the formal position of the CI
leadership. But Xu Lin would admit that the Confucius Institutes are more
than just language and cultures centres. Some of their rationale is similar
to centres established by Britain, Germany, France and Spain: China
wished to be better understood by the world through teaching its language
and culture. This was very different from wanting to influence others or
seeking supremacy over the rest of the world (Leong, 2010).

In the view of one Chinese consul general in Africa, the CI was merely a
tool to understand better China's 5000 years of civilisation. This was an heir-
loom and a heritage of mankind; so every people could share it (Consul
General to KK, 11 March 2010). Even if this is all true, the fact remains that
the Confucius Institute initiative, with its parallel of Confucius Classrooms
in secondary schools, has been quite simply the single largest language and
culture promotion that the world has ever seen, taking place in the short
period between the launch of the first Confucius Institute in Seoul in
November 2004 and the present. The sheer numbers appearing in the annual
reports of the Confucius Institute headquarters are dramatic. Even if Africa,
our continent of focus, has less than half of the more than 70 institutes that
can be found in the United States, it plays its share in contributing substantial numbers who are interested in acquiring Chinese for business or vocational purposes. But the overall programme at the end of 2010 claimed to
have reached some 360,000 registered students, if both Confucius Institutes
and Classrooms are included. The overall coverage of teaching and cultural
programmes was estimated at 5 million participants, double the record of
the previous year. But to put this figure into comparative perspective, it has
been estimated that more than 40 million foreigners were learning Chinese
in 2010 (Chen, 2010b). In other words, like the demand for Confucius Institutes and Classrooms themselves, the demand to learn Chinese is rising
dramatically, independent of the presence of Confucius Institutes and Classrooms. In many countries, including in Africa, as we saw in Chapter 4, the
presence of multiple Chinese businesses probably does more for interest in
Mandarin than a Confucius Institute. Thus when it comes to comparative
global cultural impact, Xu Lin would argue that 'the 70 Confucius Institutes
(in USA) put together cannot even beat the influence of one mega Hollywood
movie screened in China' (reported in Leong, 2010).[4]

---

[4] This remark was made in response to the US Ambassador in China, Jon Huntsman, telling Xu
Lin that the US government would want to set up US Information Service Centres in Chinese
cities as a countermeasure to the CIs in USA (Leong, 2010).

This theme of China's global cultural influence actually being very weak compared to the West is one we shall return to, but it is important to underline the point that is was the former Chinese President's concern with the relative *weakness* of Chinese culture *vis-à-vis* the West that led him to make his initial remarks about culture and soft power. His concerns, when he first used the term in relation to culture on 4 January 2006 and then again on 15 October 2007, were as much about the domestic environment —'to better guarantee the people's basic cultural rights and interests' as they were about international competitiveness (Hu, 2007).

Once the head of state had made the connection between culture and soft power, there was of course a new round of interest in the relationship. However, it was still not commonplace to resort to the discourse of soft power when discussing China's cultural development, whether domestically or internationally. Thus, when in 2009 the Minister of Culture, Cai Wu, produced a 40–page account in five languages of *China's Cultural Development in 30 Years of Reform and Opening Up*, there was very little use of the soft power language (Cai, 2009). Again, this was principally because his account was concerned with domestic cultural construction and development. Only on two brief occasions did he turn to reflect on the relative weakness of China's cultural soft power over against the forces of Westernisation within China. In comparison with its political and economic influence, China didn't carry much weight in the cultural sphere. Hence, there was a need 'to enhance culture as part of the soft power of our country' (ibid.: 111). Although it was argued that introducing Chinese culture to the world was a main way of enhancing China's global influence, and its 'national soft power', it was 'an extremely complicated issue': 'Which part of our culture should be introduced to the outside world and how?' (Ibid.)

It is worth noting that there is no mention of the role of Hanban or of the Confucius Institutes in his account, for the good reason that despite their role in relation to language and culture, the CIs do not fall under the remit of the Ministry of Culture at all. There is not therefore a single centralised authority charged with introducing Chinese culture to the wider world. Rather, it is through the Executive Council of the Confucius Institutes that the various line ministries and other bodies have been drawn into its international coordination, a little reminiscent of the way that the Chinese Follow-up Committee of FOCAC draws on a large range of similar ministries. Thus the Annual Report of CI Work for 2010 acknowledged the fruitful support, in a whole series of specific activities, of the Ministry of Education, Ministry of Finance, Ministry of Foreign Affairs, the National Development and Reform Commission, the Ministry of Commerce, the Ministry of Culture, the State Council Information Office and China Radio International, amongst several others (Xu, 2010b: 2). But just as FOCAC's Senior Officials Meeting accords a critical role to the corps of African ambassadors in China, so Hanban has no less than ten foreign

Council Members, drawn from the heads of the Boards of Directors of Confucius Institutes Overseas.[5]

Before concluding this brief account of the extraordinarily dramatic growth in the Confucius Institutes, we should note that, again like FOCAC, there is a critically important role given to the CI community coming together, for networking, in major regular meetings and conventions. Once a CI is operational with its link to a Chinese partner university formalised, it is not just left to pursue its objectives on its own; but it is regularly made aware of the regional dimension of CI developments (for instance through annual regional CI meetings in Africa, Europe etc), and annually also the two co-directors along with the president or vice-chancellor of the host university are invited to the national convention of CIs in Beijing. This conference is a unique opportunity for individual CIs to become aware of the range of best practice across the worldwide community of CIs. The diversity of this international experience is captured in the conference reference materials (e.g., CI Headquarters, 2010), to which the great majority of CIs contribute. This experience, and the funding to make it possible, builds a sense of belonging to a much wider international community – almost a movement – and not just a single language and culture initiative within a host university.

As to how this relates to soft power, the CIs are currently light years away from the impact of McDonalds or Hollywood blockbusters, to use Xu Lin's analogy. They have altogether a more modest ambition than global competition for influence with the West. That would be wishful thinking. Their goal is to encourage hundreds of thousands of people to see a China that is different from how it is often presented in the West. They are perhaps as much to do with undoing the damage of the West's soft power imaging of China as they are with promoting Chinese influence. In a thoughtful commentary on this process, Ma Yue, Chinese co-director of the Rhodes University CI in South Africa, has elaborated on this:

> Indeed, the value of CIs is indeed helping more and more people understand the language and culture of a nation that has always been distorted by western media. Just because of this, China feels the money spent is worthwhile. At least it brings many western people to see a real China when they begin to read for themselves rather than through western propaganda only; they start to see that China is just like their own country, a land that is filled with hope and also has problems of its own, but a country as normal as their own in many ways. They grasp at least that China is not a bad dragon puffing fearful fire, but a land where western people are treated so friendly and even above their own people sometimes so that the western people can easily make a living and make money from a land where lots of its own people are still in poverty. (Ma Yue to KK, 31.3.2012)

---

[5] http://english.hanban.org/node_7716.htm One of these Overseas Council Members has been the Vice-Chancellor of the University of Nairobi, for example.

If one characterisation of Confucius Institutes is that they are a modest but well-coordinated attempt in some 390 very different CI environments to expose thousands of ordinary people to another dimension and reality of China, then the process might be as much about undoing some of the damage of the West's soft power imaging of China as it is about China's soft power 'offensive'.[6]

But it seems that the experience of visiting China itself is an absolutely critical part of this understanding; hence we find the series of initiatives that bring CI students to China from across the world. These would include the regular China Bridge language competition, the summer camps, the conferences on the teaching and learning of Chinese exchanges, the CI scholarship programme, and the annual CI conference.

This emphasis on the direct experience of China, through visits, is what makes the CI similar to the large-scale programme of sending 30,000 African professionals to China for short-term training (through MOFCOM), or the CSC which has offered 6,000 scholarships annually to Africa between 2013–15. Even if only a fraction of those taking CI classes can actually gain this opportunity, there is a potential dissemination effect.

## Analytical perspectives on the Confucius Institutes

In concluding this account of how relevant the concept of China's soft power is to the mission of the Confucius Institutes, we should recall our initial comment that the CI are seen in some Western and Asian quarters as a prime example of China's soft power initiatives. We look briefly therefore at several rather different interpretations of China's culture, language and soft power, through Kurlantzick, Jacques, Yang, Rebol, Mosher, Breslin and Liu. All authors specifically mention Confucius Institutes in this regard, but in very different ways.

The first of these, Kurlantzick, though publishing just three years after the first CI had been founded in Seoul in 2004, had already identified Chinese language and culture as a key element in what he termed the 'tools of culture' in China's *Charm Offensive* (Kurlantzick, 2007). He drew on a relatively early reference to the promotion of Chinese culture as a way of building the country's soft power, just after former President Hu had first used the term, and argued that Chinese culture and language studies could become a 'major component of this public diplomacy' (ibid.: 67). Clearly the recently launched Confucius Institutes were identified as a vehicle for this. Like others, he regarded the CIs as 'reminiscent' of the British Council and Alliance Française, though their mode of operation, we have said already, was very different.

There is therefore really no attempt to discuss in any detail how this new institution would operate; indeed less than a page is allocated to the Confu-

[6] The term comes from Kurlantzick's 2007 title: *Charm Offensive: How China's Soft Power is Transforming the World.*

cius Institutes in the chapter on 'The Tools of Culture'. The focus of Beijing's language and culture diplomacy is more on the inward movement of foreign students and foreign scholars to China, but this process is presented in such coloured language that it is difficult to take it seriously.[7] Indeed, it is hard not to reach the conclusion, after reading the last chapter on 'Responding to the Charm Offensive' that the book is as much about the vital need to build up US soft power as describe China's. A line in the preface says it all: 'Perhaps most important, China's soft power could have a significant impact on American interests' (ibid.: xii). We return, however, to a more balanced account of China's soft power in Africa by Kurlantzick later in this chapter.

The second author, Jacques, has an even more sensational title than Kurlantzick: *When China Rules the World: The Rise of the Middle Kingdom and the End of the Western World* (2009), but is much more measured in terms of his assessment of the changing role of Chinese language, culture, universities and soft power. As far as language is concerned, he notes that the rise of China has led to increasing numbers of people worldwide deciding to learn Chinese. He estimates that some 30 million people in the world are now learning Chinese outside China, and that some 2,500 universities mount courses on it. The actual promotion of Chinese language and culture by the Chinese government is seen as secondary to this. Indeed, the establishment of the Confucius Institutes is treated very briefly, and again the parallel with European comparators is made (Jacques, 2009: 399). Their mode of operation is not detailed,[8] but there is no attempt to link them to any centralised soft power initiative of the Chinese government. The rise in the status of Chinese universities is properly noted, but there is no connection made between this new status and the Confucius Institute partnering with Chinese universities. Of course a key attraction of the CI process for many overseas applicants is precisely that it delivers a formally funded link with an appropriate Chinese university.

Jacques's treatment of 'Chinese culture as soft power' (ibid.: 403) is not presented as a separately crafted state policy, but almost a natural consequence of a country with very deep cultural heritage becoming dramatically powerful economically: 'Wealth and economic strength are preconditions for the exercise of soft power and cultural influence' (ibid.). Quite suddenly, a whole series of dimensions of China's cultural influence have gained world attention, whether sports, film, martial arts, Chinese medicine, or the Chinese art market. China's international media still lag behind the West, but very major investments have been made in Xinhua, the state news agency, and in international editions of the newspapers, and of TV. But the driver of China's soft power is the extraordinary

---

[7] 'Beijing also has tried to *lure* more foreign students to China'......'increasing spending to *lure* elite foreign scholars from the West to teach in China'...'make funds available to *entice* these Chinese-born scholars...to return' (Kurlantzick, 2007: 69; emphases added).

[8] The CIs are said 'often to be linked to local universities' rather than this being seen as *the* way they are organised overseas, distinguishing them from other European models (Jacques, 2009: 399).

change in the share of trade with China as a percentage of a country's total trade between 1992 and 2010. In many cases this increased tenfold in less than 20 years (Jacques, 2012a).

For Jacques, there are a series of much deeper defining characteristics of China's difference from other states. These help to position its culture, national identity and transformation much more effectively than any focus on its soft power.[9] In addition, what is intriguing about the second edition of his book (April, 2012b) is that it illustrates China's soft power, beyond the sphere of popular culture, in patterns of Chinese parenting and of education. He argues that expectations of high levels of achievement by parents and teachers characterise China and other Confucian-based societies in Asia.[10] What is interesting about these two examples of China's soft power is that along with language they are expected by Jacques to become influential in the West without their being promoted by China: 'There will be a growing clamour to learn Mandarin. And, as yet hardly recognized, we will find ourselves coming under the growing influence of Chinese soft power' (Jacques, 2012a: 29).

Our third author, Yang, is the only education specialist amongst the seven, and he has had a professional focus on higher education, especially in China. We had already quoted from his article: 'Soft power and higher education: an examination of the Confucius Institutes' in Chapter 1 as he had commented that the development of the CIs was 'arguably China's most systematically planned soft power policy' (Yang, 2010: 235). But the article actually goes further than this and claims that China's governance model and not just language and culture are being promoted by the CIs:

> The network of such institutes is a significant tool China has used to expand its international influence and promote its model of governance via the promotion of Chinese language and culture. (ibid.)

What is surprising in an article that makes this claim in the first paragraph of its introduction is that there does not seem to be any evidence in the article of the CIs being used to promote China's model of governance. This term is never used in the rest of the article.[11] Furthermore, a series of distinguished commentators connected to the CIs through being Director General of Hanban or being Vice-Chancellors of universities hosting CIs, such as Sheffield and Edinburgh, make it clear, at several points in the article, that there is no interference by the Chinese government in the operation of the CIs.[12]

[9]  See Chapter 12: The eight differences that define China (Jacques, 2009: 414–435).
[10]  As mentioned in Chapter 3, 'Teachers in China tend to believe that with due effort, a child should always be able to achieve the expected standard' (Cheng, 1990: 165).
[11]  The article draws on an earlier piece by Yang in 2007 which presented the institutes as an 'equivalent of a soft power offensive via the promotion of Chinese language and culture' (ibid. 25). Anticipating the later article, Yang worried that 'The more successful the institutes, the greater potential for them to be used as agents of Beijing's foreign policy in the future' (ibid).
[12]  In the words of one vice-chancellor: 'We have seen no evidence of the Chinese government using the university as a propaganda tool through CIs' (Yang, 2010: 238).

The last part of the article explores the interesting question of the extent to which the CIs constitute 'A new form of China's higher education internationalisation' (Ibid. 243). Again, like the claim about CIs and political propaganda at the beginning, there is a parallel claim about China's initiative in higher education going too far:

> Its use of international exchange and cooperation in higher education as an exercise of soft power is unprecedented, and has gone far beyond the comfort zone of traditional theories. (Yang, 2010: 243)

However, in what follows there is no attempt to explain how the CI university partnership illustrates such an unprecedented exercise of soft power. Nor is there any discussion of the very large number of Chinese higher education overseas partnerships that are not CI-related. For instance, the FOCAC commitment to partner twenty leading African tertiary institutions with universities in China in the 20+20 scheme is not mentioned.

There are therefore two mysteries outstanding about the article; both relate to the claim of inappropriate use by China of its soft power. Yet neither claim is substantiated.

Max Rebol, by contrast, situates the Confucius Institutes as straightforwardly falling into the area of cultural cooperation; indeed they are identified as 'the most obvious manifestation of cultural cooperation with Africa' (Rebol, 2011: 63). This is perceived to be important to China precisely because such cooperation with Africa is felt to be 'apolitical' and does not involve any interference in internal politics. Moreover, the promotion of culture becomes a naturally attractive vehicle of China's soft power: 'Chinese language also falls into this category and includes both the attractiveness of the language as such, and the direct benefit that the student expects out of acquiring the language' (ibid.).

With Mosher's March 2012 presentation to one of the subcommittees of the US House Committee on Foreign Affairs, it would be hard to believe that the same institution is being analysed as by Rebol. The very title, 'Confucius Institutes: Trojan horses with Chinese characteristics' suggests that the institutes are an extremely dangerous mechanism. This is exactly what the testimony suggests: 'what one of the chief purposes of the Confucius Institutes are [sic], namely, to subvert, coopt, and ultimately control Western academic discourse on matters pertaining to China' (Mosher, 2012: 2). The article seeks to establish this claim that the CIs are part of 'what is obviously an ideologically driven political power play' through a series of allegations many of which seem ill-founded. But the final message of the metaphor of the Trojan Horses is of course that the CIs are allegedly very different from what they seem. 'While ostensibly about promoting the Chinese language and culture, he (Paradise) says, they are "part of a broader soft power projection in which China is attempting to win hearts and minds for political purposes".' (Mosher, quoting Paradise, 2012: 5)

In reviewing briefly these first five highly diverse perspectives on

China's soft power through the CIs' promotion of language and culture, it can be seen that the entry of China into the world of cultural diplomacy has created ripples, even waves. This was an arena only occupied by the United States and by five or six European powers. No developing country had sought to promote their language hitherto. Even Japan as it rose to economic prowess had its historical reasons for not following the European and American examples.[13] But the sheer speed and scale with which China has achieved what it has through the CIs in under eight years were bound to create a reaction.

Nevertheless, the innovation in the modalities chosen for CI operation has deflected criticism. The fact that most universities hosting CIs have directly applied to be considered, and that all CIs are jointly led by host-university and Chinese co-directors has minimised concern about their being stand-alone Chinese cultural promotions. Indeed, depending on whether or not Mandarin was already in the university syllabus, they have in many cases been responsible for integrating a new degree subject into the existing curricular arrangements.

Beyond the explicit curriculum which itself differs a great deal, even within the African CIs (Mahmoud, 2010), there is what may be termed a Chinese account of soft power that is appreciably different from the idea of obtaining what one wants through cooption and attraction. One co-director of an African CI has put it like this:

> I agree that the Chinese do have a different definition for the term 'Soft Power' when they use it in the way of thinking China should also try to use soft power to 'win the trust, love and support from people in other parts of the world', rather than having in mind the original concept of the term soft power in its coinage. (Ma Yue to KK, 1 April 2012)

The above account is based on the understanding that in the mainstream Chinese view of soft power there is a lack of intention to convert other peoples to accepting Chinese values and way of life. Rather, the intention is to make others better appreciate Chinese values. In many cases, as mentioned earlier, this may be more a question of changing people's negative attitude towards China, as it remains the case that much of Western media is highly critical of China's role in Africa. Nor is it just the media. The Sub-committee on Africa, Global Health and Human Rights of the Committee on Foreign Affairs of the US House of Representatives was 'Assessing China's role and influence in Africa', in March 29 2012, and in full committee has been 'Investigating the Chinese threat', while in another sub-committee 'The price of public diplomacy with China' had been discussed.[14] Although there is acknowledgement of positive devel-

---

[13] Japan's negative experience of promoting the Greater East Asia Co-prosperity sphere from 1940 has meant that there has been a great reluctance formally or institutionally to encourage Japanese culture and language.

[14] See http://foreignaffairs.house.gov/hearing_notice.asp?id=1419; Mosher's testimony just discussed was presented in the last sub-committee.

opments in the assessment of China's role, there continues to be the argument that 'China's practices have in some cases undermined efforts to promote progressive business practices, democracy and good governance in Africa'.[15]

In this contested media and political environment, it should not be surprising that a more nuanced and balanced Western account of China's use of soft power is appreciated by those running the CIs. For example, Breslin's Chatham House paper on 'The soft notion of China's "soft power"' may better capture the complexity of the different meanings of soft power in China (Breslin, 2011). From a range of different dimensions, Breslin identifies 'national image promotion' as being the most appropriate characterisation of the CIs; it is something that many countries have undertaken, he claims, most for much longer than China.

For Breslin, the use of Confucius is that he has become a symbol for a set of values such as harmony that are also critical to the present. The name 'Confucius' also links to widespread interests in Chinese history and traditions in many parts of the world. Other names were considered during the gestation period of the CIs, but they did not have the same historical and international appeal.[16] But beyond this appeal to China's history, Breslin sees the past, symbolised by Confucius, as also critical in presenting current values, even if these differ from the West:

> ...it can be used to build a basis for understanding the way China is today: why it acts in the way that it does and how it will act in the future. It is a means of explaining 'difference' – a different understanding of the relationship between the individual and the state, a different understanding of how society is ordered and functions, and a different understanding of the nature and purpose of government – different from the dominant Anglo-European model of individualism and liberalism. (Breslin, 2011: 10)

The terms 'understanding' and 'explaining' are crucial to the role of the Confucius Institute as it integrates into more than three hundred and ninety very different university environments. We currently lack sufficient accounts of how those, from China and from the host countries, perceive their roles. But the few who have discussed their roles do not have the feeling of a politicised mission, as described in the Mosher testimony above. They see their 'mission' as basically educational, as they are primarily university academics: 'we promote academic related activities of teaching language and culture (both in a narrow and broad sense) that will facilitate students' understanding of the Chinese language and culture, so that they may understand China better and hopefully find a career that may utilize their knowledge acquired from us'. (Ma Yue to KK, 3.4.2012).

This light version of soft power has been captured very precisely by one of the Chinese co-directors of an African CI:

---

[15]  http://www.safpi.org/news/article/2012/assessing-chinas-role-and-influence-africa
[16]  Chinese co-director to KK 2 April 2012.

Definitely this is in line with the general goal of China in promoting understanding between the peoples. But what is lacking in our approach is the "soft power" of the original (Nye) definition: we have no intention to get people to do something we want them to do. We offer an educational service, but we have no intention to control or intention to gain anything from them. (Ma Yue to KK, 3 April 2012)

In concluding this discussion of language, culture and soft power issues as illustrated in the history and development of the Confucius Institutes, we have covered a wide range of different positions on the role of these institutions. Our own view is that they do offer what Breslin terms a soft version of China's soft power. It is inconceivable that they could have been accepted from Stanford to Chicago, London to Edinburgh, and Cape Town to Cairo if they were perceived to be 'agents of Beijing's foreign policy' or 'a soft power offensive' (Yang, 2007: 25).

The last word on their lack of a common centralised agenda set by Beijing goes to Liu Haifang, a scholar in Peking University, to whom we shall return. She makes precisely the same point that Vermaak, the South African co-director of Rhodes University, made at the beginning of this section: the CI phenomenon is an 'experimental and learning-by-doing approach rather than some initiative promoted through a well-established grand plan of cultural export':

> Until now, only the tablet tailored by Hanban bearing the inscription of the Confucius Institute has remained the same; everything else varies from one branch to another: there are no universal textbooks and teaching programmes, and the long-term goals and operation modes are very different (host universities or colleges can decide all these by themselves). ... The Confucius Institute appears to be the most open-minded institution China has ever had, due to this cooperative model as its distinctive characteristic (Liu, 2008: 31).

## China's scholarships and professional training as cultural diplomacy?

In contrast to the intensity of the debates around the Confucius Institutes, there has been virtually no discussion in the West about the potential impact or influence of China's large-scale, short-term training programme for African professionals or of the long-term scholarships for Africans. The numbers exposed to China from Africa over the triennium, 2009–2012, come to 20,000 for professionals and 5,500 for African scholars. The numbers registered for language courses across the whole of the 33 African CIs in any one year are unlikely to be any larger than the 25,500 offered education and training in China under these other two schemes. How are we to assess these in terms of cultural diplomacy or of soft power? Second, how are we to assess the worldwide impact of China's scholarships and training awards versus those from elsewhere? We shall start with an examination of the scholarship programme and then look briefly at the short-term training awards.

At the level of exposure to Mandarin alone, there can be little comparison between those taking courses in the CIs versus African scholarship holders who are required to have a full year of immersion in the language prior to commencing their degree courses. Their subsequent degree is also taken in Mandarin. The four, five or six years studying in Mandarin produces a significant community of Africans who are completely at home in the language.

In terms of scale alone, one of the world's most prestigious scholarships schemes has been the Commonwealth Scholarship and Fellowship Plan (CSFP). This scheme has supported some 27,000 individuals since it was initiated in 1959.[17] By contrast, China's White Paper on foreign aid would claim that it has supported no less than 70,629 students from 119 countries up to the end of 2009 (China, 2011a: 14).

When we turn to compare the rationales of the CSFP and the China Scholarship Council (CSC), the former emphasises 'the ideal of reciprocity and sharing' which has an interesting resonance with China's traditional focus on mutual benefit. One of the five principles of the Plan is that it should 'be based on mutual cooperation and the sharing of educational experience'.[18]

The China Scholarship Council rationales for studying in China are not of course specific to Africa, Asia or Europe, but apply to all regions like the CSFP. Intriguingly, the CSC also has five principles or rationales for studying in China.[19] Perhaps surprisingly, the top of the list is 'abundant job opportunities': that those who can speak Chinese and have first-hand experience of living in China are going to have a great advantage in terms of employment, in China. In terms of our concern with culture and soft power, it is interesting to note that access to diversified cultures is second in the list. Being a student in China and immersing oneself in local society 'will provide you with a new way of visualizing the world', very different from a textbook insight.

Like the Commonwealth Plan, another of the principles emphasises that China scholarships are deliberately aimed to 'strengthen mutual understanding and friendship'. But the two other reasons for studying in China are its relatively low cost which is presented in terms that would amaze many Western students.[20] Finally, 'vibrant campus life' is offered to

---

[17] http://www.csfp-online.org/in-touch.html

[18] The other four principles covered: additionality to other schemes, flexibility, Commonwealth-wide character, and recognition of highest levels of academic achievement (http://www.csfp-online.org/about.html)

[19] http://en.csc.edu.cn/laihua/newsdetailen.aspx?cid=63&id=1139

[20] 'You can afford a lifestyle you are unlikely to enjoy at home: get a housekeeper, travel every month, and enjoy frequent restaurant meals, massages, and nights on the town. Even wear tailor-made clothes!'

students, and the contrast with former conditions for students in China is made quite openly on the CSC home page: 'Compared with former generations of university students in mainland China, students nowadays enjoy great freedom and diversity of activities both within and outside their campuses'.

What is perhaps surprising in both the five CSC reasons for studying in China and the five CSFP rationales is that while they emphasise the importance of reciprocity and sharing, they do not refer to the creation of potentially influential leaders, or to the role of overseas scholarship as part of cultural diplomacy. By contrast, the UK's Foreign and Commonwealth Office (FCO) has explicitly defined its Chevening Scholarships, which have reached no less than 40,000 recipients since 1983, in terms of political, economic and social impact. These scholarships are

> for students with demonstrable potential to become future leaders, decision-makers and opinion formers. Chevening Scholarships are for talented people who have been identified as potential future leaders across a wide range of fields, including politics, business, the media, civil society, religion, and academia.[21]

The fact that the FCO explicitly mentions leadership in the scholarship objectives and the CSFP does not should not be taken to mean that there are no cultural diplomacy goals behind the latter. Governments may not wish openly to declare that this is one of their scholarship rationales. This becomes clear in the formal evaluation of the UK's contribution to the CSFP where it is acknowledged that for the Commonwealth Scholarship Commission 'since the late 1990s in particular, CSC policy has emphasized both development impact...and leadership, as well as international collaboration and partnerships' (CSCUK, 2009: v). The same would of course be the case with the China Scholarship Council: that the formally stated objectives on the website do not preclude there also being cultural diplomacy reasons for China's scholarship support.

There have been parallels of course in the United States where we have already alluded to the claim that several of the major American foundations were involved, especially in the Cold War days, in the opinion forming of scholarship recipients (Berman, 1983). Furthermore, understanding better this role of cultural diplomacy and international impact via scholarships is one of the reasons why Peking University proposed the analysis in 2012 of 'The evolution of the Chinese policy of funding African students and an evaluation of its effectiveness'. One of its outcomes would be an assessment of its influence and impact: 'Analysing the impacts that this type of development assistance has brought to both the sending countries and the hosting society as well as the bilateral relationship' (Li and Liu, 2012).

Even though China has not yet developed an explicit account of its scholarship policy beyond the more general discourse on its approach

[21] www.fco.gov.uk/en/about-us/what-we-do/scholarships/chevening/

being part of mutual trust, political equality and economic win-win coop-eration (Niu, 2009), there is already a critical Western account of China's aid in Africa which assumes that China does have a developed ideological interest in Africa. This critical account has been well analysed by Mawd-sley (2008) and Large (2006).[22]

It has also been argued that China's scholarship policy for Africa has at times been much more strategically connected to cultural and political diplomacy than any general aspiration to expose African students to China for the reasons mentioned on the China Scholarship Council website. Most specifically, a case has been made by Nordtveit that there was a direct connection between hard power and soft power in the aftermath of Tiananmen Square:

> The political events of 1989 thus provide the backdrop of the increasing cooperation between China and Africa in the 1990s, leading to the doubling of African students in China and the number of Chinese teachers in Africa. (Nordtveit, 2011a: 101)

It is certainly the case that the total number of African scholarship students in China did double during the 1990s (from 2,245 to 5,569), but the statistics make it clear that the annual numbers of African scholars in fact fell during 1989 and remained lower than 1987 and 1988 right through till 1996. It was only in the last four years of the 1990s that the annual numbers of scholarship students quadrupled (China, MOE, 2005: 15–16). So there was certainly no rapid offer of increased scholarships in 1989 or the following five years.

China may not use the discourse of soft power to discuss the influence of its scholarships to Africa, but there is no doubt that it takes delight in the positions that its alumni have taken up in Africa on their return: 'The effectiveness and impact of the Chinese government scholarship are increasingly apparent' (ibid.: 20). There follows an account of the precise numbers of students in leadership positions politically in Africa, as well as those in economic, trade and cultural relations with China. The ulti-mate goal of cultural diplomacy (or soft power) is that the scholarship experience makes China attractive over the longer term. This is one of the claims of the Ministry of Education: 'Although they have their own home countries, many African students still think of China as their "second home"' (ibid.: 21).

Before concluding this review of scholarships and training awards in terms of their impact and influence, we need to examine the professional training programme which has brought no less than 45,000 short-term trainees to China from Africa over the period covered by the last three FOCAC commitments (2003, 2006 and 2009). Compared to the long-term

---

[22] Large (2006: 4) quotes Hevi who had sized up this Western approach to China in Africa from as early as 1967: 'With an holier-than-thou air, Western countries have arrogated to themselves the sacred duty of protecting Africa from the encroachments of the East's ideological invasion… everybody assumes that Africans do now know what is right for them.'

scholarship holders over the same period, the numbers of professional trainees is four times larger than the 11,500 African scholars who have been supported over these three triennia. However, there is a big difference between coming to China for a degree course of four to five years, including language training, and coming for three weeks to three months on one of the several hundred specialised courses.

Most notably, in terms of language acquisition, very little beyond essentials can be picked up on the shorter three-week courses compared to the degree training of scholarship holders. But this may not mean that there is little impact. Those African professionals selected to participate in the different training courses are given rather special treatment; they are hosted in good hotels as opposed to student dormitories, and they are escorted to a wide range of relevant experiences depending on the focus of the seminar. Again, depending on where their seminar is located, they are even taken for a day to Yiwu, the largest market of Chinese consumer goods in the world, for shopping prior to departure.

For African middle and high-level civil servants, university professors or presidents, whose exposure to China in Africa may have been hitherto almost minimal (apart from seeing a Chinese construction project, restaurant or a China mall), the three weeks or months can be an eye-opener. Depending on the subject focus, they see some of the best that China can offer, whether in roads, railways, rice cultivation or rural development. They are lectured to in English, French or Arabic according to the countries they come from in Africa. They may also be shown some of the poorer provinces in China, to remind them that China is also a developing country, and, as we mentioned in Chapter 2, they are not preached at about what should be improved in Africa.

Surprisingly, for such a massive operation of knowledge sharing between China and Africa, there is almost no information about the hundreds of seminars on the website of the Department of Foreign Aid, as we noted in Chapter 5. Further, there is no publicly available feedback, though each seminar is evaluated at the level of the host institution in China. In the anonymous feedback form which we helped to arrange for the almost 200 short term trainees of 2010 who went to China from Kenya, there was an extraordinarily high level of positive comment, as may be recalled from Chapter 2. If this level of satisfaction is commonplace across the 45,000 African professionals then this is surely a powerful source of cultural diplomacy or soft power. Here is a reminder of their flavour:

> The training courses offered were of absolute importance in terms of understanding China by an outsider and appreciating the challenges that this country has encountered and how it has overcome them. Top of the list of challenges is population control, food security and management of its water resources.

> In all these there are important lessons to be learned. Perhaps what will be immortalized in my mind for me is the resilience of the Chinese

people and sheer hard work evident in their appreciation and embracing technological advancements to their advantage.
Everywhere we went we felt honored and accepted. (Kenyan feedback form 2010)

To be honest, China for a long time was depicted as closed country where other citizens of the world could not visit. Now that I have been able to visit and learn from there, I am now convinced beyond any reasonable doubt that there is a lot Kenya and I personally can learn from this Great Country of yours. I was particularly moved by visiting Chinese rich historical sites. Keep it up. This was a quick way of appreciating your culture. (Kenyan feedback form 2010)

It is worth noting that several participants had arrived, as one of these above, with a very different view of China than they came away with. Whether the extremely labour-intensive process of arranging this kind of training for 45,000 African professionals is regarded by the Chinese, as knowledge sharing, South-South solidarity, cultural diplomacy or soft power, it would appear to be, at minimum, a highly successful public relations activity.

The question of whether the massive scheme is an African priority or a Chinese, or both is important to determining whether it is a response to African demands as FOCAC would argue, or something that Chinese policy makers have decided upon as an aid priority. Intriguingly, the penultimate draft of what would become the Beijing Declaration and Action Plan of 2006 was originally somewhat short of quantifiable targets. The draft of mid-October talked merely of aiming 'to train more African professionals over the next three years' and of planning to 'gradually increase the number of scholarships for African students in China which now stands at 1,200 per year'. These gradualist intentions were suddenly quantified two weeks later at the summit into 15,000 professionals and 4,000 scholarships. The same thing had happened to China's aid intentions overall. The penultimate draft had talked of the intention to 'gradually increase such assistance in keeping with the growth of the economy' while the final version had decided to 'double the size of its assistance to African countries'.[23]

What the factors were which produced the quantifiable targets we shall perhaps never know for certain. But the summit in Beijing had no less than 40 heads of state from Africa present which may have increased the pressure for target numbers; equally the Gleneagles G8 meeting of the previous year had promised to double aid to Africa. Thus, African states had a target model available from 2005, even if most G8 members failed to deliver on their promise in Scotland.

Before concluding this section on China's scholarships and training awards, it may be useful to position them in relation to a few other

---

[23] See King 2006b for a detailed account of the target process at the FOCAC Summit of November 2006.

national scholarship schemes. One of the first issues to be underlined is that the motives or rationales for the provision of scholarships do not remain the same over time. Hence the periodisation of scholarship support is important. Thus the Netherlands scholarship programme used to be principally for the development benefit of the developing countries, but that has changed dramatically and is now much more oriented to the economic benefit of the Netherlands itself.[24] There have been similar changes even within the fifty years of the Commonwealth Scholarships. As far as UK, the largest contributor to these is concerned, these used to focus primarily on the intellectual value to the recipient. Later on, considerations of development impact and leadership potential of the recipients were added, partly influenced by the changes in funding. It is also the case that the current focus in Japan for aid to have 'a Japanese face' has affected their scholarships and training awards. A 2012 evaluation of JICA's training and dialogue programme commented: 'The Scheme has also contributed to increased exposure to international issues within Japan, and has nurtured significant "pro-Japan" groups of people in the recipient countries' (Japan, MOFA, 2012: 2).

Likewise, in Germany which has in the German Academic Exchange Service (DAAD) the largest funding body of its kind in the world, there has been a shift from individual scholarship support in the earlier years[25] to structural support for higher education overseas and development cooperation (DAAD, 2011: 8). Among its five goals now are 'promoting the international dimension and appeal of German universities' and 'strengthening German Studies and the German language in foreign universities' (ibid.: 16).

In general, the growing concern, particularly in Western aid agencies with value for money (VFM), has begun to raise new concerns about the precise quantitative value of different aid modalities, including scholarship support.[26] Even within the Chinese Ministry of Commerce, there has been discussion about the costs and the value for money of the thousands of professionals coming from Africa for the 2–3 week courses.[27]

As far as China's scholarship programme is concerned, there has been, in the view of some commentators, a parallel change in its motives and

[24] 'In the olden days Netherlands Fellowship Programme awards were given for purely developmental reasons. It should benefit developing countries, and nothing else. Over the last 10 years the thinking of DGIS in The Netherlands has changed. Alumni became to be recognized as 'ambassadors' of the Netherlands and the network of alumni as a useful instrument to strengthen economic and political relationships. Funding of activities of alumni associations in partner countries was initiated. More recently fellowships are also seen as a strategy to attract brains with beneficial effects on the quality of education and research in the Netherlands and for the Dutch economy.' Ad Boeren, NUFFIC to KK, 18 April 2012.

[25] See the comment at the front of the 2010 Annual Report by Nobel prize winner, Wangari Maathai: 'The DAAD significantly changed my life because it gave me the opportunity to learn what I needed for my academic career' (DAAD, 2011: Frontispage).

[26] For a wide ranging analysis of overseas scholarships and awards, see *NORRAG News 45* (2011); and on Value for Money in International Education and Training, see NN 47 (2012).

[27] MOFCOM representative to KK, October 2008, Beijing.

rationales, reflecting the different political periods China has experienced over 60 years. Thus Nordtveit (2011) sees a first 'period of political alignments (1950 to 1989)'; then a period in which China perceived 'Africa as a source of political support (1989–2000)'; and finally a period of an 'increasing economic relationship (2000 – present)'. By contrast, He (2006) does not see any change over the 60 years in the general strategy and policy guiding bilateral cooperation in education and training; there is only a change in the different forms and focuses of education support. Interestingly, she does perceive the general China-Africa policy to have had three distinct phases: 1) 'rich ideology and reinforcement of political benefits'; 2) 'Weakening ideology and valuing economic benefits'; 3) 'Sino-African relationship after the end of the cold war: attaching importance to both political and economic benefits' (He, 2005). However, Li and Liu (2012) would argue that 'Little is known about the rationales behind the African scholarships programme, and whether or how these have changed over time' (Ibid.: 1). In addition, Li would claim that there is no single rationale operating in the scholarship programme today, but a mutual benefit approach between China and Africa.[28] This is almost certainly the case with the large-scale short-term training awards.

In this review of three key elements of China's support to African human resource development, there has been one modality, scholarships, which has been in place since the first four Egyptian students came to China to study art, philosophy and agriculture in 1956. The second oldest programme of offering professional seminars in China was started in the field of education in 1998 with a vocational education workshop (He, 2006), and in 1996 for African diplomats. Finally, the promotion of and response to demands for Confucius Institutes in Africa only goes back to 2004, with the first African CI in the University of Nairobi in 2005.

All of these can in some sense be regarded as part of China's development cooperation, though they are supported through different agencies, and all can be considered elements of China's international cultural and education promotion. It is time to review whether as elements of China's international cooperation, they can be considered forms of soft power, and indeed whether aid itself can be so considered.

## China's Aid, Education and Soft Power in Africa

We need to enter several caveats in discussing China's position in respect of these. We already know that there have been decades of Chinese hesitation about the 'aid' word, even though the English translation of the 2011 White Paper on foreign aid uses it in the title. The very use of the word suggests a parallel activity to Western aid agencies, whereas China has been at pains to point out that their engagement with Africa is funda-

---

[28]  Li Anshan to KK, 17 April 2012.

mentally different from a traditional aid relationship. The discourse of mutual benefit and 'win-win' cooperation amongst equals sits more easily with most policy makers. There are similar problems with soft power, even if it has been used by many Chinese policy makers and academics, including Hu Jintao's use of the term since 2006.

For senior academics such as Li Anshan of Peking University's Centre for African Studies the term cannot be fully disentangled from its development in the USA. In fact, Nye's first account of it comes just after the fall of the Berlin Wall, symbolising the end of the Soviet Union's hard power (Nye, 1990). But for Li, its adoption in the USA is linked to the decline and loss of legitimacy of American military, hard power in a number of interventions in recent years. If soft power is a post-Cold War US strategy for its international relations, China would 'undoubtedly be in danger of falling into the control of the western discourse if we unthinkingly borrow this concept which has a specific background and special meaning' (Li, 2012). An additional problem with the term is that in a situation where Beijing has projected its foreign policy as a peaceful rise towards the construction of a harmonious world, soft power gives a different message: 'If we use the concept of "soft power", it is against China's international strategy and will scare off those developing countries who would like to make friends with China' (ibid.).

This comment may recall our concern, in Chapter 1, that soft power and South-South cooperation come out of different universes, and are in some sense in conflict with each other. Soft power, in some hands, is suggestive of an international relations competition in which there are winners and losers, while China's perspective on South-South cooperation is of a situation where both China and Africa are winners. Regardless of these concerns, we must acknowledge that in the era of the knowledge economy, and with the recognition of the role of knowledge-for-development from 1998,[29] it should not be surprising that soft power has been adopted as a catch-all term for covering a whole range of institutional strategies. The term, soft skills, has similarly emerged to capture a set of different capacities in the field of education and training.[30]

In the present case, however, we should examine the extent to which the terminology and the concept of soft power play a useful role in analysing China's aid, and in particular the human resource development dimension of that cooperation. Clearly, as we shall see, the different aid strategies were all in place long before soft power arrived on the scene. Historically, the particularity of China's approach to relations with and assistance to other developing countries had been set by Zhou Enlai in the 1950s with the Five Principles of Peaceful Coexistence of 1954. What is

[29] For the spread of knowledge for development through the agency world, see King and McGrath, 2004.The *World Development Report* focused on Knowledge for development in 1998.
[30] Soft skills are often used to cover negotiating skills, team skills, problem-solving, literacy and numeracy as well as behavioural skills such as perseverance and self-confidence as compared to harder technical and vocational skills (King and Palmer, 2008).

striking about these is the uniquely central role of the term 'mutual'. It speaks of a different world than that of donors and recipients, or of competition for influence (or soft power):

Mutual respect for sovereignty and territorial integrity
Mutual non-aggression
Non-interference in each other's internal affairs
Equality and mutual benefit
Peaceful coexistence

These, and the Eight Principles of Foreign Aid set out by Zhou Enlai a decade later on his trip to Africa,[31] arguably derive from China's own bitter experience of foreign aid, dependence and occupation, and remain today a remarkable agenda for how China intends to relate to other developing countries, including those in Africa. Again in the Eight Principles there is a strong emphasis on the same issue of 'equality and mutual benefit'. At the same time, the expressed purpose is not to win friends and influence them to rely on China. Quite the opposite: 'the purpose of the Chinese Government is not to make recipient countries dependent on China but to help them embark step by step on the road of self-reliance' (China, 2000). This seems very far from Nye's initial conceptualisation of soft power as promoting values and norms in order to get others to want what you want (Nye, 1990). But we shall see later in this chapter that the very difference of this Chinese aid approach from changing Western approaches is considered by some as part of its soft power.

We remarked earlier about the crucially important role of China's own equipment, technology, technical assistance and experts in the delivery of Chinese aid. These can of course all be described as tied aid, but the prescribed values and norms of China's experts are a world away from the all-too-common, high expenses, expert-counterpart culture of so many development projects in Africa. By contrast, Chinese experts in developing countries 'will have the same standard of living as the experts of the recipient country' (China, 2000) according to Zhou Enlai in 1964, and in most cases they still do.

Of course, it is widely acknowledged that aid principles are frequently very different from the practice of aid. So it is possible that the tens of thousands of Chinese technicians in Africa by the early 1980s[32] were actively promoting Chinese values and norms, regardless of the principles of encouraging self-reliance. Interestingly, however, Brautigam went to Africa for the first time in 1983, and reported that 'In interview after interview, people told me that the Chinese working in their countries spent almost no effort trying to convince them to adopt their model' (Brautigam, 2009: 38).

This is not to say that Chinese experts, like many Japanese experts, did

[31] For a full statement of the Eight Principles, see Appendix 1.
[32] Snow has claimed, as we saw earlier, that there were 150,000 Chinese technicians in Africa by the early 1980s (Snow, 1988: 147).

not offer plentiful examples of very hard work, in the rice paddies of Africa rather than in the offices of the African ministry (ibid.: 39). This is also what many of our African students, in Chapter 3, had reported in their years of studying in China, and what African entrepreneurs said, such as the man in Lesotho's comment on the Chinese traders in his country: 'He noted that locals had a lot to learn from the Chinese in terms of skills, hard work and business know-how' (McNamee, 2012: 34).

It is surely debatable whether the Chinese culture of hard work constitutes soft power unless it is being powerfully promoted for willing adoption. In fact, both Snow and Brautigam have chapters in their respective books with the word missionary: 'The Chinese as Missionary' and 'Missionaries and Maoists', but Snow is probably correct in claiming that there was not a Chinese civilizing mission or a Chinese gospel for Africa, for Chinese volunteers and experts: '...there is little evidence to suggest that they felt the personal calling which prompted occasional Europeans like Livingstone and Schweitzer to give their lives to the peoples of this strange continent' (Snow, 1988: 168). Even if hard work was the norm of Chinese experts and volunteers, doctors and teachers, it does not appear to have been actively sold or promoted for Africa.

## Connecting soft power to China's development aid for Africa

Although we can already see that there are several conceptual problems with connecting soft power to China's aid discourse, there have been a number of academics and policy analysts who have examined the relationship. We shall review a number of these to determine what perspective they seek to take and whether there are any insights into the specific place of human resource development within aid policy. We shall analyse He (2009; 2010; 2012), Varrall (2012), Large (2008), Fijalkowski (2011), and Sheng (2010), all of whom have commented on China's soft power in some measure.

However, we shall start with a few remarks from the architect of soft power himself, Joseph Nye, in January 2012 on 'Why China is weak in soft power' (Nye, 2012). His remarks came just a few days after former Chinese President, Hu Jintao, commented as follows: 'We must clearly see that international hostile forces are intensifying the strategic plot of Westernizing and dividing China, and ideological and cultural fields are the focal areas of their long-term infiltration', he wrote, adding that 'the international culture of the West is strong while we are weak' (Hu, 4 January 2012, quoted in Nye, 2012). Nye's analysis is a confirmation and an explanation of former President Hu's comments about China's international culture (and soft power) being comparatively weak.

Nye is concerned with a larger canvas than our interest in China's aid, but it is relevant to note that after claiming that China is spending billions of dollars on a 'charm offensive', his first example is drawn from China's aid projects: 'The Chinese style emphasizes high-profile gestures, such as rebuilding the Cambodian Parliament or Mozambique's Foreign Affairs Ministry' (Nye, 2012). It is surprising perhaps that he did not illustrate this with the $US 200 million gift by China of the African Union Conference Hall, and African Union Commission building, which were opened in January 2012.

He further illustrates the charm offensive in the Beijing Olympics and the 70 million visitors who came to the Shanghai Expo. What he does not mention, however, is that the extraordinary Africa Pavilion at the Expo which housed the great majority of African nations was itself a Chinese aid project. He returns to the aid theme almost immediately after mention of the Olympics and Shanghai, clearly recognising them as a key illustration of soft power. He claims that 'Chinese aid programmes to Africa and Latin America are not limited by the institutional or human rights concerns that constrain Western aid' (ibid.). In other words, he is arguing that in soft power terms China's aid has a competitive advantage over Western aid as there are less conditionalities and hence greater attractiveness. But like many Western commentators on China's aid, he sees it as a threat to the West's allegedly higher aid standards.

Continuing directly with his theme of soft power as cultural attraction, he notes that not only does China have an attractive traditional culture, 'but that it has created several hundred Confucius Institutes around the world to teach its language and culture' (ibid.). Moreover, in human resource terms, he underlines the fact that almost a quarter of a million foreign students have been attracted to China in 2010, compared to just 36,000 in 2000.

Despite these examples and others such as the expansion of China Radio International and the Xinhua News Agency internationally, Nye rates these soft power initiatives as having a limited return because international cultural narratives are compromised if they are inconsistent with China's domestic realities. Restrictions, censorship, and arrests of individual artists and lawyers within China, he argues, effectively torpedo China's global soft power campaign.

Interestingly, as mentioned above, this discussion about the domestic realities of Chinese soft power is a direct response to Hu Jintao's essay, in the journal, *Seeking Truth*, on the competition between Western cultural products and Chinese specifically within China (Wong, 2012). Though the article appears to be mostly concerned with the measures to be taken to secure and bolster Chinese culture domestically against the inroads of Hollywood and international media, it is very much set in the tradition of soft power as direct competition both at home and abroad: 'The overall strength of Chinese culture and its international influence is not commensurate with China's international status' (Hu quoted in Wong, 2012).

Since the official recognition of the role of culture as soft power by the then Chinese President in January 2006 and its reinforcement in 2007 at the 17th CCP Congress, studious attention has been given to the place of China in international cultural influence. There is even a soft power research group at Peking University. While China's development assistance is not given an explicit role in these discussions about cultural diplomacy and international cultural impact, it is noteworthy that the Confucius Institutes do feature centrally. In an article in *People's Daily* on 'How to improve China's soft power', the Confucius Institutes are picked out as a prime positive example:

> China has been striving to build the Chinese cultural value system and increase its influence in the world, and has achieved remarkable results. For example, the country has established 282 Confucius Institutes and 241 Confucius Classrooms worldwide, a total of 523 located in 87 countries and regions within five years from 2004 to 2009, making Confucius Institutes the bridgehead for teaching Chinese abroad, carrying out exchanges and cooperation in domestic and overseas education, cultural fields, and others. He [a researcher at Communication University of China] believes that Confucius Institutes have greatly promoted the globalization of Chinese culture, and have increased the popularity and reputation of China. (*People's Daily* Online, 12 March 2010)

Before turning to review a number of Western commentators, including Chinese based in the West, on their analysis of China's soft power and its possible connection with China's aid, it is important to start with one of China's leading Africanists, He Wenping, who is based at the Institute of West Asian and African Studies (IWAAS) under the Chinese Academy of Social Sciences. Her articles on 'Building China's soft power in Africa' (He, 2010), her treatment of 'Soft power construction' within her chapter on 'China's African Policy' (He, 2009), and her 2012 think-piece on 'More soft power needed in Africa' all touch on the role of aid as soft power. Indeed, she has suggested that 'Africa is perhaps the most important testing ground for the promotion of Chinese soft power' (He, 2009: 115).

Crucially for our own theme, she identifies human resource development (HRD) through aid as central to this promotion: 'These efforts have come in mainly two forms: bringing Africans to China and sending Chinese to Africa – exchanges which strive to share China's experience in national development' (ibid.). These two-way efforts in human resource training are seen as soft power. Even though she was writing a few months before the human resource dimension of China's aid would be dramatically expanded in the FOCAC IV meeting in Egypt in November 2009, she identifies professional seminars in China and dispatch of experts to Africa as soft power construction. So too, she claims, are the other modalities of human resource development discussed in this chapter and in this book – the 'robust' promotion of Chinese language instruction overseas through the CIs, and the scholarships for African students to go to China.

Beyond culture and language, mediated by HRD through aid, soft power may also encompass some of the appeal of China's development experience, and some of the traditional features of China's identity formed of consensus approaches, peaceful coexistence and respect for diversity. 'Africa will be an important frontier where China will test and perhaps cultivate that identity along with its new-found soft power' (ibid.: 117). The challenge, she perceives, in a world where China is too often thought of as being 'strong and fearful' is to present it as 'strong and cordial'. Soft power might thus come close to Chairman Mao's vision of China becoming a 'big power that is amiable' (ibid.).

Sharing China's own experience of development and its approach to development elsewhere, He argues, is especially salient in Africa, given the consistency of China's policy towards Africa over half a century. The Five Principles for relating to Africa and Asia, and the Eight Principles of Zhou Enlai mean that, for her, China's aid is a key illustration of soft power. Unlike the West which has continually reinvented its aid priorities in the search for a 'recipe' that works (Brautigam, 2009: 11),[33] He Wenping sees China as avoiding tying aid to democracy or human rights conditions. She summarises Zhou Enlai's Eight Principles to conclude that 'The African people have come to recognize China as being completely different from the Western nations that once colonized them' (He, 2010: 64).

With the emergence of the Forum on China-Africa Cooperation (FOCAC) in 2000, and its aid and investment programme covering both economic and human development, He Wenping comes close to characterising FOCAC as representing both hard and soft power potential,[34] the former successful, and the latter still with a long way to go. Despite the positive side of its two-way human resource exchanges, she sees the persistence of negative perceptions and misconceptions about China at home and abroad. For this reason, the visibility of notions like 'harmonious world' and 'peaceful rise' is vitally important, and she includes in this soft power agenda even the idea itself of South-South cooperation between developing countries (ibid.: 66).

For He, a further dimension of soft power is the role of civil society, academia and think tanks. Despite her criticism of Western aid's conditions in Africa, she acknowledges that multi-party democracy has actually encouraged NGOs and other civil society actors in Africa. By contrast with the increasing visibility and voice of African and international NGOs, 'Chinese NGOs are nowhere to be seen, thus making China lose out on one of soft power's key instruments' (Lu quoted in He, 2010: 66).

Indeed, He Wenping sees this weakness as going beyond the absence of NGOs and including 'Chinese scholars' low level of exposure on the inter-

---

[33] The constant search for 'what works' in Western aid can also be construed as 'development fads' (Ellerman, 2012); see also the 'what works clearinghouse' in McGrath (2012).

[34] The eight pledges of the FOCAC III and FOCAC IV conferences of 2006 and 2009 include both hard power (economic) and soft power (HRD) commitments.

national stage' (ibid.). This is surely one reason why the development of African studies centres in China became one of the key dimensions of China-Africa cooperation in education (China, 2003). But the lack of sufficient Chinese scholarly expertise on Africa is just one of many wider channels of soft power dialogue that need to be developed between China and Africa, in business, academia and society more generally. This, she feels, will be a 'long and arduous process' compared with the speed with which what she calls hard power has been put in place, both in China and in Africa.

In a revealing comment which nearly parallels Nye's view of China's weakness in soft power, He Wenping emphasises that success in soft power in Africa is inseparable from success domestically in China in freeing up soft power:

> The development of soft power is not only a diplomatic affair, but is also closely related to internal factors such as the degree of free thought, an intellectually diverse academic atmosphere and a focus on the development of individuals within the society (not a 'great power, little people' mentality). (He, 2010: 68)

In He's February 2012 think-piece on 'More soft power needed in Africa', her ideas have developed a stage further, and she makes a neat parallel between China's aid in Africa focused on hard (power) projects, while Western countries, including the US, have concentrated on soft (power) projects, 'such as the construction of civil society in Africa, capacity-building for African leaders and academic researches that involve African intellectuals' (He, 2012a). Even though, as we noted above, FOCAC has supported bilateral cooperation in HRD in Africa, and a new joint research and exchange project, these soft power elements are much smaller than the investment in 'hard projects'.

She makes a very powerful point about the presence of some 2000 Chinese companies in Africa and some one million Chinese nationals, and yet 'Chinese professors rarely make appearances to teach in African universities and China's voice is hardly heard in the African media' (He, 2012a). Her message is clear. China is doing a good job on hard power through aid and trade in Africa, but aid-as-soft-power, and especially through HRD, still has a long way to go to challenge the West.

We turn now to a number of other commentators on soft power who also touch upon its connections to China's aid. Despite the provocative title of her work, 'Debunking the myth of China's soft power' Varrall does seek to tease out the extent to which China's aid policy and practice in three different periods over 60 years might illustrate soft power. While it appears that soft power can be detected, even if it was unintentional, at certain points in China's changing aid experience, Varrall's overall conclusion is that the use of development 'assistance for soft power gains has actually been very limited'; and she ends with the very strong assertion that 'any claim that the Chinese leadership is using foreign assistance as a strategic tool for international soft power gains is overstated, and this myth should not be perpetuated' (Varrall, 2012: 156). She claims that it is particularly non-Chinese who tend to assert that when China gives aid, it does so as a means of achieving soft power benefits. As we have just seen, this assumption is close to He Wenping's discussions of soft power.

Large, our second commentator on soft power, is not directly writing about it at all, but providing a detailed guide to the growing literature on China-Africa relations up to 2008. In passing, however, he makes a crucially important historical and comparative point about the reappearance of themes from the earlier literature of the Cold War period in the present day China-Africa relations. In particular, he contrasts the Western (and Soviet) reaction to Zhou Enlai's dramatic safari in 1963–4 with the emergence of 'China Threat' analysis in recent years, and also the older language about China's 'indoctrination' and 'propaganda' with the newer language critical of 'soft power' (Large, 2008: 49). In doing so for the latter, he will have reminded the reader of this chapter of how readily some analysts used soft power and propaganda interchangeably when discussing the China threat of the Confucius Institutes.

Our third commentary on soft power comes from Fijalkowski (2011), who is valuable to our discussion since he claims that in Africa 'the primary evident tool of Chinese soft power is development assistance' (ibid.: 230). At the same time, however, he suggests that all the instruments of a nation's international communication such as diplomacy, cultural, scientific and educational centres are the instruments of soft power. He makes no mention of Confucius Institutes but they would be clearly included as one of the instruments, as a cultural and educational centre. As far as China's aid policy and practice are concerned, he seeks to present as soft power the traditional Chinese discourse about equality and mutual benefit being at the core of its partnership with Africa. He also sees what he calls the '"win-win" cooperation mantra' as an instrument of soft power. Presumably, it illustrates soft power as it aims for both sides to be winners.

This is an intriguing position which at a certain point comes close to He Wenping's, just discussed. We have presented soft power as being part of a communication strategy where there are winners and losers, and we have assumed therefore that China's strategy of South-South cooperation is not appropriately termed soft power. The manipulative assumptions behind the soft power idea of 'getting others to want what you want' (Nye, 1990) seem rather distant from South-South cooperation. For Fijalkowski, however, the win-win strategy is attractive to the African elites who run most of the continent. But as these elites, he argues, have disenfranchised the majority of their citizens, 'the reach of any notional Chinese soft power in Africa appears very limited indeed' (Fijalkowski, 2011: 231). Fijalkowski does not discuss at all how the wider communication strategies of China work out in Africa, including in education and culture. But, like He Wenping, he leaves us with a challenge to consider whether if the current win-win strategy of China is close to soft power, then presumably so are the Five Principles of peaceful coexistence, and the Eight Principles of Zhou Enlai. The very distinctiveness of this aid tradition can perhaps make it an instrument of soft power.

Our next commentary comes from a Chinese academic in the USA, Sheng, who looks at China as a rising power from the perspective of soft power. He not only traces China's soft power back to Zhou Enlai in Africa in the 1960s, as we have seen with He and Fijalkowski, but he also identifies soft power as 'comprehensively utilised' by ancient Chinese rulers for two millennia. He may not discuss Confucius Institutes, but he claims that Confucius' golden rule of 'do unto others what you would have them do unto you' is easily identified as a soft power idea (Sheng, 2010: 262).

China's aid is not a central part of his analysis but he does regard China as 'very sophisticated in using its international aid to establish a favourable national image in those developing countries' [of Africa and Latin America] (ibid.: 268–9). Like Nye's comments on China's aid, he identifies it as providing 'iconic infrastructure projects, from new parliament buildings and conference centres, to football stadiums and school buildings' (ibid.: 269). He does not follow He Wenping in identifying these as hard power, but puts them in the same category as the generous distribution of government scholarships or the broadcasts of China Radio International.

Despite acknowledging China's dramatic head start in soft power historically, he ends up suggesting that other countries should encourage China to join the club – or as he puts it – 'integrate itself into the existing international political and economic systems'. His final suggestion is that 'United States and China's neighbors in particular should engage China and use their own abundance of soft power to encourage China's willingness to begin real political reform, respect human rights, implement responsible foreign policies, and so forth' (ibid.: 272).

We have already met our next author, Kurlantzick, through his comments on the Confucius Institutes and critical comments on training in China. In this later chapter from 2009, he examines specifically China's soft power in Africa, while his book had looked at China's 'charm offensive' world-wide. Here in a section on 'China's tools of soft power' he pays particular attention to its aid, as he judges that 'In Africa, development assistance may be the most important tool' (Kurlantzick, 2009: 171).

Unlike He Wenping, he does not distinguish soft and hard aid projects, but acknowledges that much of China's development assistance goes to infrastructure, although it is recognising the need to build its appeal through 'people-to-people contacts'. Under this rubric he places the youth volunteer scheme launched in 2006 for Africa, as well as rural schools and clinics, although he makes no mention of the limited reach of these projects.[35]

---

[35] The FOCAC III summit in Beijing committed China to providing 100 rural schools to Africa over three years, 2007–9; 300 youth volunteers, and 30 anti-malaria clinics in the same period (FOCAC, 2006).

However, he does note the important significance of China's 'training programmes for African opinion leaders' which are a component of the large-scale, short-term training initiative of the Ministry of Commerce which we have been analysing throughout this book. He estimates that China's training programme is probably a larger component of its aid than that of other countries in the region such as Japan. This is not the case; Japan takes its parallel short-term training programme very seriously indeed, and it is at least as large if not larger than China's.

It is equally not so that the bulk of China's massive short-term training programme is for 'opinion leaders'. Granted that there have been courses for African diplomats right back to 1996, and courses also for African media,[36] but the great majority of those coming on China's several hundred different training courses are from many specialised sectors, ministries and universities in Africa.

Kurlantzick is correct, however, in pointing to the crucially important role of China's language programme in Africa via the Confucius Institutes and Confucius Classrooms (ibid.: 173). Equally, these programmes remain comparatively small across the continent as the Confucius Institute (CIs) initiative is demand-driven, and many African universities have not had the resources to offer counterpart funding. There are just 33 CIs across the whole of Africa and five Confucius Classrooms in secondary schools. Thus less than half of the 54 countries in Africa have a CI. When it is noted that several countries such as Egypt, Kenya, Nigeria and South Africa have more than one CI, it can be seen that perhaps only 26 countries in the whole of Africa have a CI at all. So the preoccupation which we analysed earlier in this chapter with the impact of soft power and the influence of the CIs in Africa may be seriously overstated.

However, Kurlantzick believes that the combined impact of the training and visitor programmes, along with technical assistance, amounts to a soft power presentation to African leaders of the Chinese development experience, the so-called Beijing Consensus or model of development. Although development aid was thought to be the most important tool of soft power, this Chinese model of development, he suggests, may be the 'most compelling aspect of China's soft power to African elites' (ibid.: 173). It combines high growth with a degree of state intervention rather than the neoliberal assumptions of the Washington Consensus. While arguing this 'model' could be a powerful instrument of soft power, Kurlantzick admits that China is very far from actually promoting this; rather, each nation is encouraged to follow its own development path.

Returning to our aid focus, however, Kurlantzick fears that China's tradition of not coordinating with other donors may undermine these donors' support for better governance in Africa. His view, then, that

---

[36] See Keita for an overly-critical account of China's role in Africa's free press problem: www.nytimes.com/2012/04/16/opinion/africas-free-press-problem.html?_r=2
See also Brautigam's (2012a) response to Keita: 'Africa's free press problem: is China causing it?' http://www.chinaafricarealstory.com/2012/04/africas-free-press-problem-is-china.html

China's aid could actually contribute to environmental problems, poor labour standards and endemic corruption 'since China does not coordinate with other donors to make sure aid money was spent wisely and in accordance with international standards' seems far-fetched (ibid.: 177). Indeed, we noted in Chapter 5 that China's preference for direct aid actually minimised the corruption 'associated with other systems of aid delivery' (Muhumuza, 2012).

In conclusion, Kurlantzick is a commentator who, in his 2009 study, takes China's aid very seriously, and especially its aid to training and language promotion, as a principal instrument of soft power. He may even risk exaggerating its impact as he does not follow He Wenping in noting that 'hard' aid projects are much more common than 'soft' in Beijing's armoury. Where he shares some of the same ground as He is in recognising that China will have to work its soft power charms much more with the 'African Street – NGOs, media, unions and other important actors outside of typical leadership circles' (ibid.: 180).

A last commentary on China's soft power comes from the scholar, Liu Haifang, who is now in Peking University, where she has focused on cultural history professionally, and whose perspective therefore is cultural soft power.[37] She prefers the term 'cultural diplomacy' to soft power in the two articles (2008 and 2011) which we review here. The first of these is 'China-Africa relations through the prism of culture: The dynamics of China's cultural diplomacy with Africa'. Historically, the use of cultural diplomacy goes back earlier than the acknowledgement of soft power by the then Chinese President in 2006; indeed, he argued for cultural diplomacy as a priority as early as 2004 (Liu, 2008: 11).

Liu's key contribution lies in linking culture to cultural cooperation and exchange with Africa, and with the intellectual cooperation between China and Africa in its various stages. She provides a great deal of detail on the range of universities in China that are now part of the African training 'industry'. She knows that training covers a huge range: 'from trade, computers, agriculture, medical botany, distance learning, vocational education, nursery education, economic management, and military administration to journalism, culture and tourism and even low-interest loan provision' (ibid.: 29). In soft power terms, she certainly sees training as 'gaining hearts, exhibiting Chinese businesses, and disseminating China's experience of development' (ibid.: 30).

For Liu, it is not Chinese Cultural Centres under the Ministry of Culture that are currently leading on cultural cooperation, but Hanban, under the Ministry of Education. Yet with only three cultural centres in Africa (in Egypt, Benin and Mauritius) and 33 CIs, the continent can hardly be seen as illustrating some grand plan of soft power penetration, as we noted some analysts fear. If Africa is so vital to China in tactical terms, Liu hints, then perhaps fully aided CIs will be needed in some key but poorer

---

[37] Liu was mentioned earlier in this chapter for her strong views on the diversity of Confucius Institutes.

African countries, since the cooperative demand-driven model does not work when national resources are so thin on the ground (ibid.: 34).[38]

Even if cultural and language outreach works well, and the inviting in to China of African professionals contributes to China's image building, Liu sees that cultural diplomacy cannot rely on the Chinese government agencies alone. Increasingly, as we saw in Chapter 4, China's soft power will be associated with the role of Chinese companies in Africa. It is they who are creating the desire to learn Chinese, for vocational reasons. Through corporate social responsibility, they will be encouraging training schools, scholarships and the arts more generally (Liu, 2011: 153).

## Positioning China's aid and soft power in Africa

This chapter opened with a question mark over China's policies on aid and on soft power in Africa. It seemed possible to argue that the recent fascination with soft power, both by Chinese and Western commentators, came out of a different universe than its traditional discourse about cooperation. Now, at the end of the chapter, we are less sure. So many of our commentaries have identified aid and especially human resource cooperation as prime tools of soft power that we may need to reconsider this alleged difference.

However, difference has been at the heart of this book;[39] so it is hard to conclude it by admitting that China is engaged in the same soft power promotion and competition as the rest of the world, even if its former President has spoken out about the cultural offensive of the West in China. Therefore, in this final section, we shall take a number of the themes we have touched throughout the book, to revisit them through the prisms of diversity and soft power, but also with an eye on the future.

First, there is the debate about language in Africa, and we have noted the concern in some quarters about the new role of Confucius Institutes in promoting Chinese. But the Confucius Institutes in Africa are encouraging Chinese in a language situation which is massively skewed in favour of English, French, Portuguese and Arabic. In almost no country in Africa are the universities or even the secondary schools teaching through some of the major local languages of the country, as they are in India, not to mention the small countries of Europe. There is a unique determination in Africa to cling on to what Julius Nyerere once called the gold standard of English, or elsewhere the other 'metropolitan' languages. Higher education, and often parliament and the courts, are

---

[38] If the spread of CIs world-wide, with its dependence on local resources, generally illustrates the saying 'to go to the sea in a borrowed ferryboat', then 'Africa is still lacking the kind of ferryboat to be borrowed' (ibid.).

[39] It is relevant to note that 'delivering difference' is seen by Alden and Large (2011) as a way of describing the distinctiveness of China's engagement with Africa. See also Large (2006: 3) for a discussion of the differences in China's official development discourse.

conducted in languages that the mass of ordinary citizens do not understand.

This situation will not be altered easily, even if, as is likely, many more countries in Africa have universities which will ask for Confucius Institutes. Despite the huge prejudice in favour of Africa's four international languages, Mandarin is however making a mark, and is doing so as successfully now as German or Spanish. Critical to that success is the CI link to visiting and experiencing China, but in the case of all the four European languages in Africa, the presence of scholarships to study abroad reinforces the study of the language in Africa. The same is true of Chinese. Without the link to scholarship options in China, the Confucius Institute could be an isolated initiative.

The second issue is that the teaching of Mandarin at African universities has an advantage over all the other European languages where they are not already the medium of instruction in higher education: that is the presence of over a million Chinese-speaking immigrants, distributed across Africa. They create a demand-driven mechanism for Mandarin learning that is very powerful, since all but the very smallest micro-entrepreneurs from China are associated with job opportunities. It is a dimension of China's soft power that has not been brought to light in current studies.

A third dimension is related to the second. Chinese enterprise in Africa is not only encouraging language learning but providing services, skills and even development. The Chinese belief in investment, trade, and technology as levers for development (as we quoted from Brautigam at the end of Chapter 4) are being applied across Africa, in a culture of immensely hard work. Indo-African skills and technology transfer did something similar in three or four countries of Africa, or parts of countries (such as Durban in South Africa) in the early 20th century. Indian migrants have done something similar in many towns and villages of the UK, especially since the expulsion of Indians from Uganda in the early 1970s. Many more Africans are probably acquiring skills through Chinese enterprise in Africa than through China's scholarships and short-term training programmes. This dimension of HRD might also be called soft power – Africans want the language skills which the Chinese prefer them to have – but the jury is still out on what kind of skills and technology transfer process this might be. Will it only make Africans entrepreneurs where enterprise is already in the African culture, as with parts of Eastern Nigeria and Central Kenya? Africans may have 'a lot to learn from the Chinese in terms of skills, hard work and business know-how' as was mentioned by McNamee (2012) earlier in this chapter, but if these 'soft skills' are to become another element in China's soft power, African governments will need to provide an enabling environment.

The fourth angle relates to the future of HRD in the next FOCAC VI Conference of 2015 in Africa. What will happen to scholarship and training targets? The 'numbers game' puts China under great pressure to continue to increase the long- and short-term training awards, almost as if the mere numbers correspond to 'development'.[40] Last time, at FOCAC V in Beijing in July 2012, the HRD numbers significantly increased and there were additional categories such as China Research Centres in African universities. Will the new leadership in China since November 2012 make any difference to the FOCAC process, and might China be influenced in its preparations for FOCAC VI by the wide-ranging global preoccupation with the post-2015 development agenda, to be finalised in September of that same year?

Even though, as we mentioned in Chapter 5, MOFCOM had for the first time taken advice on the FOCAC targets and process, in preparation for FOCAC V, will it not retain or even increase what He Wenping termed the soft HRD side of the FOCAC commitments? Surely, China would not cut back these soft targets before even carrying out the kind of review which JICA did of its short-term training, or Peking University has undertaken for the scholarships to Africa.

A fifth perspective on China's aid might be on whether it should join the donor club, as Sheng suggested above, and support the EFA goals and education MDGs. Currently, China's support for African HRD is fundamentally different from the education projects and programmes of DAC donors, as we saw in Chapter 5. It would be highly unlikely that, at the very point when most aid agencies are preoccupied with thinking about the new aid architecture post-2015, China should align with the EFA and MDG processes. China did host UNESCO's Third International Congress on Technical and Vocational Training in Shanghai in May 2012 (UNESCO, 2012a), and that may have been a factor in a new priority for skills development for the next FOCAC V triennium, 2013–2015.[41] But as far as the debate about the post-2015 architecture is concerned, China has not so far sought to engage with this at the global level, since it already has its own cooperation and investment architecture in place for Africa; so implementing the pledges of the FOCAC V triennium, 2013–2015, is likely to be more relevant to Chinese planners than blue-sky thinking about the post-2015 landscape.

A sixth facet of the soft power face of China's HRD is the sheer attraction of studying in China. Nye in this chapter pointed to the numbers having risen from 36,000 in 2000 to almost a quarter of a million a decade later. This does not take into account Obama's pledge to send 100,000 US students over the five years from 2010, and the French pledge of 10,000 over the same period (King, 2010f, 3). It was expected by the Ministry of Education that the foreign student numbers would reach 500,000 by 2020.[42] Like the dramatic rise in the number of Confucius Institutes and

[40] For a sharp critique of the gospel that ODA numbers and percentages somehow translate into 'development', see Leroy (2012).
[41] See 'China will provide assistance for Africa's vocational skills training facilities, train professionals and technical personnel for African countries, and, in particular, help African young people and women enhance their job skills' (China, 2012: 5.2.3).
[42] *China Daily*, 24.11.2010: 3. This future estimate compares to 690,000 foreign students in the USA as of 2009/10; see Belyavina, 2011: 67.

Classrooms in just eight years, so this rise in foreign student numbers is quite unprecedented. (As we noted for the Ghanaians at the end of Chapter 3, the great majority of the students attracted by China are now self-funded.) Arguably, students electing to go to China of their own accord are a more persuasive indicator of soft power than those encouraged by scholarships.

A seventh aspect of China's HRD as soft power must be the 45,000 professionals from Africa who have been invited to go on short courses in China over the last nine years. At least that same number will have come from Asia, and Latin America. Unlike the quarter of a million currently studying in China, most of whom have elected to study there, the professional trainees are all fully covered financially by China. Like their large comparator cohorts going to Germany and Japan, these thousands of professionals going to several hundred different training courses are almost certainly not going to see their numbers cut. This is a potent vehicle of China's soft power, even if it has not been formally evaluated yet.

Eighth, and lastly, we return to the question of whether soft power derives from a different discourse than China's discourse about aid and cooperation with Africa. We have already acknowledged He Wenping's point that China's aid is made up of both soft power and hard power projects, with the balance currently towards hard power infrastructure projects. But even within the soft power HRD projects and initiatives we might make a distinction between what we might call 'soft soft power' – or what Ma Yue called earlier in this chapter the use of soft power 'to win the trust, love and support from people in other parts of the world', and hard soft power, when there is a powerful public relations or propaganda dimension of promotion, and especially when this is political propaganda.

It was this latter soft power from which Xu Lin, Director General of Hanban, wanted to distance herself when she said that 'The CI has nothing to do with soft power.' Perhaps it was also this dimension that Li Anshan had in mind in discouraging the use of the term. In contrast, we can arguably claim that the traditional Chinese discourse about 'friendship' in the discussion of cooperation with other developing countries falls within the soft, soft power ambit. As we noted in Chapter 1, terms such as 'friendship', 'mutuality', and 'equality' occur all the time in *China's African Policy* and in *China's Foreign Aid*. They do not occur at all in the White Papers of other agencies such as DFID. So there is a conceptual difference here, and it is doubtless a difference that China's partners have remarked upon and appreciated. 'Soft soft power' may not be the most elegant way to describe it. We may have to resort to that old favourite, soft power 'with Chinese characteristics' if we want to retain this terminology in relation to China's aid and cooperation with other developing countries.

# CONCLUSION

This safari to Africa with China and from Africa to China has been one of our main preoccupations for these last six years. In this final very short section, we raise just a few of the larger questions that will need more attention if we are to understand China's reach into Africa, both centrally directed and more or less completely uncontrolled.

We have discussed versions of soft power that are competitive, about winners and losers, about Hollywood versus Confucius. But there is a Chinese policy view about the world situation that recognises, in Zhou Enlai's terms, that we are all in the same boat. Greece is not Europe's problem; it is everyone's. In the words of the Chinese ambassador in South Africa: 'Interdependency amongst countries is so deep and necessary. All countries are in the same boat. You suffer; we suffer' (Ambassador to KK, 15.10.12).

This takes us beyond the special relationships of South-South cooperation into global cooperation. It is a timely reminder, after six chapters of FOCAC and China-Africa cooperation, that China is engaged with Latin America, the Middle East, Europe, North America, and Asia-Pacific, including with many small states. Our preoccupation with FOCAC should not blind us to SACF, the Sino-Arab Cooperation Forum, which has been in existence for eight years, or to the China-Latin America and Caribbean Cooperation Forum, which was being proposed in 2012, as well as the China-Central Asia Cooperation Forum. These are just a few reminders that although China has been involved with the African continent for 60 years, it has also become very active almost everywhere else. It is also worth remembering that global agreements as much as continental or regional can be obstacles or otherwise. Equally, cultural practices are difficult to break – so China works in Africa as it works at home – at full tilt. In the words of one of our key correspondents, 'The Chinese, like the leopard and his spots, find it difficult to change from how they operate at home. They don't find it easy when in Rome to do as the Romans do' (Nigerian alumnus/businessman to KK, 17.12.12).

We have not looked at China-in-Africa via the oil, mining or resources lenses, vitally important though these are. Rather our lens has been human resources, with several different prisms, from African students and trainees in China, to Confucius Institutes and enterprise-based training. We have talked to hundreds of Chinese and Africans, both in China and in Africa. However, we are acutely conscious of how much more research needs to be done, if we are really to understand whether there is a threat to the Kenyan informal (*jua kali*) sector from Chinese traders, what is the adoption of Chinese technology and business practice by other African traders and entrepreneurs; what is the vocational impact of learning Chinese through a CI or a CC in any of 890 different institutions; or the intellectual and institutional advantage of being part of the 20+20 partnership. These are just a handful of the research challenges that are left at the end of this six-year safari. There are many more, and we have sought to hint at them throughout this journey.

Tens of thousands of the African actors in the China-African drama are in what may be called the formal sector; they have received short- or long-term training awards; they are enrolled in Confucius Institutes or Confucius Classroom classes across the continent; or they are receiving graduate telecom engineering education from a Chinese multinational. But much larger numbers are less formal, serving up-front in the Chinese Malls, across Africa, sometimes on behalf of Chinese owners who do not yet speak English or French, while others are working in Chinese factories in Africa, from Ethiopia to Nigeria, or are partnering with Chinese in mining from Zimbabwe to Ghana and Sierra Leone.

The jury is almost completely out on the large-scale impact of training in China for these thousands of African alumni even if the accounts from our individual African student interviews seem rather positive. Similarly, for the tens or even hundreds of thousands in Chinese companies, we know very little. Individual cultures of learning in different African societies are part of the answer, but is there firm government support to negotiate and capture new technologies associated with the Chinese, as there is by China in the case of foreign direct investment in China? Or are the Africans basically 'minding the shop' for Chinese entrepreneurs, or are there already hundreds of African 'graduates' from Chinese companies, setting up on their own? Are the 'China alumni and alumnae', the majority of them now privately funded, competing at a disadvantage with those returning from USA, UK and France?

Arguably, there is a need for many more in depth studies of the China-Africa tapestry unfolding across the continent, as we said in the preface. It is now forty years exactly since I started work on the *African Artisan* in Kenya, and twenty since the research began in 1992 for *Jua Kali Kenya*. What would any new fieldwork, two decades later, in 2012–3, reveal about the Chinese *jua kali* setting up across Kenya, and their Kenyan 'graduates' and competitors?

Or in universities such as Nairobi, Kampala or Dar es Salaam, where many of us Africanists started our careers in colleges that were partnered with the University of London, what will it mean by 2015 that there has been a Confucius Institute partnership between Nairobi University and Tianjin Normal for ten years? What will the 20+20 partnerships with major Chinese universities have brought to the Universities of Pretoria, Cairo, and Lagos by the time they too have been in place for ten years?[1] Will the Centre for Chinese Studies in Stellenbosch still be the only such centre on the continent in 2015, or will the ambition of FOCAC V mean that African universities are supported in establishing China research centres? That China is actively responding to the establishing of knowledge networks with, and research bases in, African universities could be viewed as a good thing and part of the mission of universities. Like African studies, Chinese studies have sometimes struggled to find a space within many universities. But are Shinn and Eisenman right in suggesting that it is 'unlikely that Chinese culture will have a strong influence on Africans' (Shinn and Eisenman, 2012: 369)?

What of the institutions built and initially staffed in part by China, such as the Ethio-China Polytechnic College in Addis Ababa, the Science and Technology University in Malawi, the agricultural demonstration centres, or the hospitals? Will there be a continuing presence of Chinese staff and expertise in 2015, and will the issue of sustainability have been handled any differently from Western institution building in Africa?

The bulk of China's HRD modalities impacting on Africa have been implemented almost without any policy blueprint, beyond a few lines in an *African Policy* (2006) or a paragraph in a FOCAC action plan between 2000 and 2012. It can be assumed that the new leadership in China will maintain the Pan-African FOCAC umbrella, and that in 2015, in some location in Africa, fifteen years of cooperation with Africa will be celebrated but without generating a great deal of policy paper.

In September that same year, the already massive preoccupation with the post-2015 millennium development agenda will have been settled, along with any parallel Education for All (EFA) Goals. By April 2013, the resetting of the MDGs and EFA Goals had already generated an enormous number of policy papers, briefings, blogs, panels, and meetings. Thus far, the great bulk of this has been catalysed by institutions based in the North, whether development agencies, think tanks or international NGOs. China and India have been minimally engaged in this process so far.

Whether any new global agenda will manage to be universal and not be focused primarily on the developing economies remains to be seen. Possibly one reason that India and China have been so little involved is that the debate has been so far too closely related to the traditional actors in development aid. The MDGs only received a single passing mention in *China's African Policy*. But it will be important to follow whether this

---

[1] New research on the 20+20 partnership led by Li Jun (Chinese University of Hong Kong), Kenneth King and Bjorn Nordtveit will start in May 2013.

global post-2015 agenda plays any significant role in the development of the next FOCAC VI agenda over these next three years.

We have remarked on the 'targetisation' of FOCAC especially over the last ten years since FOCAC II, and especially in relation to the iconic HRD numbers for the current triennium. These targets and goals are part of a rather different discourse than that of friendship, equality, mutual benefit and common good which has been a red thread running through this account. 'China-Africa traditional friendship', and 'mutual benefit', which run through the latest FOCAC action plan are a tall order, not least when the great bulk of the one million or so Chinese migrants, traders, settlers, teachers, businessmen and volunteers are not centrally directed and do not need to report to the Chinese embassies in Africa.

Yet it may just be the case that if this ethical African agenda, including of FOCAC, is not just 'symbolism and spin' (Taylor, 2012: 38), but translates into genuine cooperation and learning from and about each other over the longer term, then China and Africa may indeed turn out to be in a special relationship. At the moment, we do not know enough to be sure, but historically, like most incomers, the Chinese where they have settled have got on peacefully with life. China towns have added to the culture of those cities in which they exist. Hence the continuing appeal of Zheng He, in the official Chinese discourse, for having visited Africa, all those centuries back, without taking land or slaves.

Twenty five years ago in 1988, just before Tiananmen and long before FOCAC's foundation, Philip Snow, on the last page of his book on *China's Encounter with Africa*, asked some penetrating questions about the future of China's engagement with Africa, just as we saw he did in our analysis of Chinese business in Africa. These questions are much more fundamental than assessments of aid effectiveness or value for money, whether in North-South or South-South cooperation. They resonate with Zhou Enlai's principles of engagement. Ultimately, they may suggest that soft power is about friendship, commitment, the sharing of talent, and 'people-to-people and cultural exchanges between China and Africa' (FOCAC, 2012: 6.4.3):

> But would these [Chinese] benefactors be able to build on the slow growth of human understanding? Would they be able to grasp, what Africans took for granted, that personal contact mattered, that good works were valuable but not enough? Could they adapt to their surroundings? Could they make friends? If they failed, the chances were that the Chinese impact would be, once again, ephemeral. Like Zheng He's ships they would sail away into the sunrise, stately, inviolate and leaving no more than a memory to suggest they had ever been. But perhaps a few might learn...to walk and talk with Africans and to make a second home in African lands. In that case there was a hope that the talent and drive of the Chinese people would leave a more lasting mark on the continent's future. (Snow, 1988: 212)

A preliminary reaction by Snow in December 2012 to his own questions of 25 years ago is as follows:

> My impression from what I read is that substantial numbers of Chinese may now have established for the first time a potentially lasting presence in parts of the continent in the sense that they have adapted to the local environment and wish to remain. Whether this potential is realised, however, still depends on the underlying human relationship, or lack of it, and of this we don't yet have a clear picture. I would want to see, for example, a lot more evidence that Chinese firms were hiring and training local employees rather than relying solely on compatriots to operate their projects and run their shops. (Snow to KK, 16.12.12)

Our own sense of the success and of the challenges of China-Africa cooperation in education and training would be that Chinese destinations for further study or professional training by Africans are no longer being debated; they are becoming accepted across Africa. Similarly, there is in many parts of Africa no question about the value of learning Chinese whether in a primary school, as in Kisumu, Kenya or in schools around Stellenbosch, South Africa, or in a Confucius Classroom or a Confucius Institute in Addis Ababa; this too is becoming increasingly obvious and accepted. However, as to working in one of the many thousands of Chinese companies in Africa, the issue would not so much be whether one would be merely employed but whether, as an African employee with determination, there was a chance, over time, to acquire and develop Chinese technology. This crucial technological adaptation would depend as much on a culture of learning as on anything else. We return full circle to whether the many different African societies and communities in question have such a culture of learning and capability, supported by strong government technology policies. If so, the 'talent and drive of the Chinese people' will surely fall on fertile ground.

On the other side of the equation, one of our key Nigerian alumni from a Chinese university, now a collaborator with Chinese business in Nigeria, would argue that though the situation of China-Africa learning in business is slowly improving, it will not progress rapidly until:

> ...the Chinese make more conscious efforts to adapt to the local environment and trust the ability of the citizens of their host countries to be engaged in management and operational positions in their companies. ... Collaboration with the Chinese is really difficult; this is the unfortunate truth. I would say the success I had with them has had many ups and downs but with understanding, commitment and integrity we have been able to win the confidence of the Chinese. I hope we can have more of this (Nigerian alumnus-businessman to KK, 17.12.12).

While in Accra on January 15th 1964, Premier Zhou put forward the following Eight Principles for China's aid to foreign countries. These principles for aid or development cooperation have stood the test of time very well:

1. The Chinese Government always bases itself on the principle of equality and mutual benefit in providing aid to other countries. It never regards such aid as a kind of unilateral alms but as something mutual.
2. In providing aid to other countries, the Chinese Government strictly respects the sovereignty of the recipient countries, and never attaches any conditions or asks for any privileges.
3. China provides economic aid in the form of interest-free or low-interest loans and extends the time limit for repayment when necessary so as to lighten the burden of the recipient countries as far as possible.
4. In providing aid to other countries, the purpose of the Chinese Government is not to make the recipient countries dependent on China but to help them embark step by step on the road of self-reliance and independent economic development.
5. The Chinese Government tries its best to help the recipient countries build projects which require less investment while yielding quicker results, so that the recipient governments may increase their income and accumulate capital.
6. The Chinese Government provides the best-quality equipment and material of its own manufacture at international market prices. If the equipment and material provided by the Chinese Government are not up to the agreed specifications and quality, the Chinese Government undertakes to replace them.
7. In providing any technical assistance, the Chinese Government will see to it that the personnel of the recipient country fully master such technique.
8. The experts dispatched by China to help in construction in the recip-

ient countries will have the same standard of living as the experts of the recipient country. The Chinese experts are not allowed to make any special demands or enjoy any special amenities.

# BIBLIOGRAPHY

Accra Agenda for Action (AAA), 2008. *Accra Agenda for Action*. Third High Level Forum on Aid Effectiveness, 4 September 2008, Accra.

Adamson, B, Nixon, J. and Su, F. (Eds), 2012. *The Reorientation of Higher Education: Challenging the East-West Dichotomy*. Comparative Education Research Centre, Hong Kong University/Springer, Hong Kong.

Ajakaiye, O. 2006. China and Africa: opportunities and challenges. Presentation at African Union Task Force on strategic partnership between Africa and the emerging economies of the South, September 2006, Addis Ababa.

Ajakaiye, O., Kaplinsky, R., Morris, M. and N'Zue, F. 2009. Seizing opportunities and confronting the challenges of China-Africa investment relations: insights from AERC scoping studies. Policy paper No. 2. AERC, Nairobi.

Alden, C. 2007. *China in Africa*. Zed Books, London.

Alden, C. and Large, D. 2011. China's exceptionalism and the challenges of delivering difference in Africa. *Journal of Contemporary China*, 20 (68), 21–38.

Atomre, E., Odigie, J., Eustace, J. and Onemolease, W. 2009. Chinese investments in Nigeria. In: Baah, A. Y. and Jauch, H. (Eds), *Chinese Investments in Africa. A Labour Perspective*. African Labour Research Network, Accra and Windhoek.

Baah, A. Y. and Jauch, H. (Eds), 2009. *Chinese Investments in Africa. A Labour Perspective*. African Labour Research Network, Accra and Windhoek.

Barr, M. 2011.*Who's Afraid of China? The Challenge of Chinese Soft Power*. Zed Books, London.

Begum, H. 2010. China: from recipient to donor. What have we learned? *NORRAG News 44*, 111–113. Accessed at www.norrag.org

Belyavina, R. 2011. The United States as a destination for international students. *NORRAG News,* 45, Special Issue on the Geopolitics of Scholarships and Awards, 67–8. Accessed at www.norrag.org

Berman, E. 1983. *The Influence of Carnegie, Ford and Rockefeller Foundations on American Foreign Policy: The Ideology of Philanthropy*. State University of New York, Albany.

Bird, D. 1998. *Never the Same Again: A History of VSO*. Lutterworth, Cambridge.

Birdsall, N. 2011. Aid alert: China finally joins the donor club. Accessed at: http://blogs.cgdev.org/globaldevelopment/2011/12/aid-alert-china-officially-joins-the-donor-club-2.php

Bodomo, A. 2009. Africa-China relations: Strengthening symmetry with soft power. *Pambazuka News*, 440, 2 July 2009. Accessed at *http://pambazuka.org/en/category/africa_china/57385*

Bodomo, A. 2012. *Africans in China: A Sociocultural Study and Its Implications for Africa-China Relations*. Cambria Press, Amherst, New York

Brautigam, D. 2008. 'Flying geese' or 'hidden dragon'? Chinese business and African industrial development. In: Alden, C., Large, D. and Soares de Oliviera, R. (Eds), *China Returns to Africa: A Rising Power and a Continent Embrace*. Hurst and Company, London.

Brautigam, D. 2009. *The Dragon's Gift: The Real Story of China in Africa*. Oxford University Press, Oxford.

Brautigam, D. 2011a. Aid 'with Chinese characteristics'; Chinese foreign aid and development finance meet the OECD-DAC aid regime. *Journal of International Development*, 23, 752–764. DOI: 10.1002/jid.1798

Brautigam, D. 2011b. Ethiopia's partnership with China: China sees Ethiopia as a land of opportunities, but the African country remains in charge of any deals. Poverty Matters Blog, *The Guardian*, posted 30 December 2011.

Brautigam, D. 2012a. Africa's free press problem: is China causing it? http://www.chinaafricarealstory.com/2012/04/africas-free-press-problem-is-china.html

Brautigam, D. 2012b. China's health aid in Africa: Same old problems, 25 April 2012: http://www.chinaafricarealstory.com/2012/04/chinas-health-aid-in-africa-same-old.html

Breslin, S. 2011. The soft notion of China's 'soft power', Asia Programme Paper: ASP PP 2011/03, Chatham House, London.

Cai, W. 2009. *China's Cultural Development in 30 Years of Reform and Opening Up*. Ministry of Culture (also in Mandarin, French, Spanish, and Russian), Beijing.

Carayannis, T. and Olin, N. 2012. *Preliminary Mapping of China-Africa Knowledge Networks*, Social Science Research Council, New York.

Cardenal, J.P. and Araújo, H. (2013) *China's Silent Army: The Pioneers, Traders, Fixers and Workers Who Are Remaking the World in Beijing's Image*, Allen Lane, Penguin Press, London.

Centre for Chinese Studies, 2006. *China's Interest and Activity in Africa's Construction and Infrastructure Sectors*, Stellenbosch University, Stellenbosch.

Centre for Chinese Studies (CCS), 2009. *Understanding China's Engagement with Africa & How the UK Can Build Relationships with China in Africa*, 23–25 June 2009, conference report, Centre for Chinese Studies, University of Stellenbosch.

Centre for Chinese Studies (CCS), 2012. Quo Vadis FOCAC? Special Edition, *China Monitor*, University of Stellenbosch, Stellenbosch.

Chan, S. 2008. Ten caveats and one sunrise in our contemplation of China and Africa. In: Alden, C., Large, D. and Soares de Oliviera, R. (Eds), *China Returns to Africa: A Rising Power and a Continent Embrace*. Hurst and Company, London.

Chen, J. 2010a. Class act promotes global 'soft power'. *China Daily* 11 November 2010 (Hong Kong edition), 1.

Chen, J. 2010b. 40 million foreigners learning Chinese. *China Daily*, 13 December 2010.

Cheng, K-M. 1990. The culture of schooling in East Asia. In: Entwistle, N. (Ed.), *Handbook of Educational Ideas and Practices*. Routledge, London.

Cheru, F. and Obi, C. (Eds), 2010. *The Rise of China and India in Africa*. Zed Books, London.

China, People's Republic of, 2000a. Premier Zhou Enlai's Three Tours of Asian and African Countries. 2000/11/17, Ministry of Foreign Affairs, accessed 2 July 2011 at http://www.fmprc.gov.cn/eng/ziliao/3602/3604/t18001.htm

China, People's Republic of, 2000b. 'Beijing Declaration', China-Africa Forum on Cooperation, 12 October 2000, Beijing, accessed at: www3.itu.int/MISSIONS/China/chinaafricaforum/forum008.htm

China, Ministry of Education, 2003. *China-Africa Education Cooperation*, Department of International Cooperation and Exchanges, Ministry of Education, Beijing.

China, People's Republic of, Ministry of Education (MOE). 2009. Notice of the application for 'China-African 20+20 universities of higher education cooperation', International Exchange and Cooperation MOE, Beijing.

China, Ministry of Foreign Affairs, 2005a. 'Beijing Declaration', Sino-African Education Minister Forum, 27 November 2005, Beijing, accessed at: www.fmprc. gov.cn/zflt/eng/zt/zfjybzlt/t223750.htm

China, Ministry of Education (MOE) 2005. *China-Africa Education Cooperation,* Peking University Press, Beijing (in Chinese).

China, People's Republic of, 2006. *China's African Policy,* 12 January 2006, accessed at: gov.cn/misc/2006–01/12/content_156490.htm

China, People's Republic of, 2009. *Brief Introduction of China's Aid to Foreign Countries.* Ministry of Commerce, Beijing.

China, People's Republic of, 2011a. *China's Foreign Aid.* Information Office of the State Council, Beijing. Accessed at: http://www.scio.gov.cn/zxbd/wz/201104/t896900

China, People's Republic of, State Council, 2011b. *China's Peaceful Development.* Information Office of the State Council, Beijing.

China, People's Republic of, 2012. *The Fifth Ministerial Conference of the Forum on China-Africa Cooperation Beijing Action Plan (2013–2015)* 23 July 2012, Beijing. Accessed at http://www.focac.org/eng/zxxx/t954620.htm

*Chinafrica,* 2011.20+20: A New Kind of 20/20 Vision. vol. 3, October 2011.

Churchman, M. 2011. Confucius Institutes and controlling Chinese languages. *China Heritage Quarterly,* No. 26, June, Australian National University. Accessed at : http://www.chinaheritagequarterly.org/articles.php?searchterm=026_confucius.inc&issue=026

Commonwealth Scholarship Commission in the UK (CSCUK) 2009. *Evaluating Commonwealth Scholarships in the UK: Assessing Impact in Key Priority Areas.* Commonwealth Scholarship Commission, London.

Confucius Institute (CI) Headquarters, 2010. *The 5th Confucius Institute Conference Reference Materials.* CI Headquarters, Beijing.[1]

*Confucius Institute,* volume 22, September 2012.

Corkin, L. 2008. China's strategic infrastructural investments in Africa. In: Guerrero, D. and Manji, F. (Eds), *China's New Role in Africa and the South: A Search for a New perspective,* Fahamu, Oxford.

Corkin, L. 2011.Chinese Construction Companies in Angola: A Local Linkages Perspective. Making the Most of Commodities Programme, Paper No. 2. Centre for Social Science Research, University of Cape Town, Cape Town. Accessed at: http://www.cssr.uct.ac.za/publications/incidental-paper/2011/750

Cyranowski, D. 2010. China boosts African research links. *Nature,* 464, 25 March 2010.

DAAD (The German Academic Exchange Service), 2011. *Annual Report 2010.* DAAD, Bonn.

Davies, M. with Edinger, H., Tay, N. and Naidu, S. 2008. *How China Delivers Development Assistance to Africa.* Centre for Chinese Studies, University of Stellenbosch, Stellenbosch.

Dawson, K. C. 2010. Confucius Institutes enhance China's international image. *China Daily* 23 April 2010. Accessed at http://www.chinadaily.com.cn/china/2010–04/23/content_9766116.htm

DFID. 2006. *China: Country Assistance Plan.* DFID, London.

DFID Ethiopia. 2011. *DFID Ethiopia. Operational Plan 2011–2015.* DFID, Addis Ababa.

DFID (Department For International Development),1997. *Eliminating World Poverty: A Challenge for the 21st Century.* White Paper on International Development. Cmd 3789, HMSO, London.

---

[1] As the materials run to almost 4000 pages, they are contained on a CD.

DFID (Department For International Development), 2000a. *Eliminating World Poverty: Making Globalization Work for the Poor.* White Paper on International Development. Cm. 5006. HMSO, London.

DFID (Department For International Development), 2000b. *The Challenge of Universal Primary Education. Strategies for Achieving the International Development Targets.* (Target Strategy Papers), DFID, London.

DFID (Department For International Development), 2006a. *Eliminating World Poverty: Making Governance Work for the Poor.* White Paper on International Development. HMSO, London.

DFID (Department For International Development), 2006b. *The Importance of Secondary, Vocational and Higher Education in Development.* Briefing Paper. DFID, London.

DFID (Department For International Development), 2007. *Technical and Vocational Skills Development. A Practice Paper.* DFID, London.

DFID (Department For International Development), 2009. *Eliminating World Poverty: Building Our Common Future.* Cmd. 7656, HMSO, London.

DFID (Department For International Development), 2010. *Learning for All: DFID's Education Strategy 2010–2015,* DFID, London.

DFID. 2011. UK International Development Secretary visits Beijing. 29 November 2011, press release. http://www.dfid.gov.uk/Documents/publications1/press-releases/UK%20International%20Development%20Secretary%20visits%20Beijing.pdf

Dikötter, F. 1992. *The Discourse on Race in Modern China.* Hurst, London

Dowden, R. 2008. *Africa. Altered States, Ordinary Miracles.* Portobello Books, London.

Ellerman, D. 2012. Do we need an Institute for the Study of Development Fads? *NORRAG News* 47, 30–31. Accessed at www.norrag.org

Export-Import Bank (China). 2006. *Infrastructure Development in Africa Supported by the Export-Import Bank of China.* 3rd Annual Meeting of the Infrastructure Consortium for Africa, 17 January 2007, Berlin.

Eze, O. C. 2009. Dealing with the Issues: Confronting Reality. In *ChinAfrica,* October 2009.

Ezeanya, C. 2012. Tragedy of the new AU headquarters. 26.1.2012, *Pambazuka News,* issue 567. Accessed at http://pambazuka.org/en/category/features/79400

Ferdjani, H. 2012. *African Students in China: An Exploration of Their Increasing Numbers and Their Motivations in Beijing.* Centre for Chinese Studies, September 2012, University of Stellenbosch.

Fijalkowski, L. 2011. China's 'soft power' in Africa. *Journal of Contemporary African Studies,* 29. 223–231.

Forum on China-Africa Cooperation (FOCAC), 2006a. *Beijing Action Plan (2007–2009)* Draft of October 2006, FOCAC, Beijing.

FOCAC (Forum on China-Africa Cooperation). 2006b. *Forum on China-Africa Cooperation. Action Plan (2007–2009),* 16 November 2006, FOCAC, Ministry of Foreign Affairs, Beijing. Accessed at: www.fmprc.gov.cn/zflt/eng/ltda/dscbzjhy/DOC32009/t280369.htm

FOCAC (Forum on China-Africa Cooperation), 2009. *Forum on China-Africa Cooperation Sharm El Shaikh Action Plan (2010–2012),* 12 November 2009, FOCAC, Ministry of Foreign Affairs, Beijing. Accessed at: http://www.focac.org/eng/dsjbzjhy/hywj/t626387.htm

FOCAC (Forum on China-Africa Cooperation) 2012. *Fifth Ministerial Conference of the Forum on China-Africa Cooperation Beijing Action Plan (2013–2015).* Ministry of Foreign Affairs, Beijing. Accessed at: www.focac.org/eng/ltda/dwjbzjjhys/

Fourth High Level Forum of Aid Effectiveness (HLF4). 2011. *Busan Partnership for Effective Development Cooperation.* 29 November -1 December 2011, Busan.

Francis, M. and Francis. N. 2011. *When China Met Africa.* Documentary film,

Speak-it films, Zeta Productions, London.
Fransman, M. and King, K. 1984. *Technological Capability in the Third World*. Macmillan Press, Basingstoke.
Fredriksen, B. 2010. Education aid effectiveness: The need to rethink the allocation of education aid to increase its impact. Editorial. *Journal of International Cooperation in Education*, 13: 2. October 1–9.
Gadzala, A. 2009. Survival of the fittest? Kenya's jua kali and Chinese businesses. *Journal of Eastern African Studies*, 3: 2, 202–220.
Garside, J. 2012. China's electronics giant moves out of the shadows to challenge west's big names. *The Observer*, Business, 23 March 2012, 45.
Gaye, A. 2008. China in Africa: After the gun and the bible....A West African perspective. In: Alden, C., Large, D. and Soares de Oliviera, R. (Eds), *China Returns to Africa: A Rising Power and a Continent Embrace*. Hurst and Company, London.
Gillespie, S. 2001. *South-South Transfer: A Study of Sino-African Exchanges*. Routledge, New York.
Gillespie. S. 2009. African students in China: past and present. In: Chisholm, L. & Steiner-Khamsi, G. (Eds), *South-South Cooperation in Education and Development*. Teachers College and HSRC Press, New York and Cape Town, 210–225.
GOI (Government of India). 2008. *India Africa Forum Summit, 8–9 April 2008*. Ministry of External Affairs, New Delhi. Also http://itec.mea.gov.in
Government of India (GOI), Ministry of External Affairs, 2010. Visit of African Union Delegation, March 10–13, 2010, New Delhi.
Gontin, M. 2009. China's cultural interest in Sino-African cultural exchanges, *Pambazuka News*, 31 January 2009, No.417. *http://pambazuka.org/en/category/africa_china/53759*
Grimm, S. 2011. Engaging with China in Africa – Trilateral cooperation as an option? Policy brief no 9, February 2011, EDC 2020, EADI, Bonn.
Grimm, S. with Rank, R., McDonald, M. and Schickerling, E. 2011. *Transparency of Chinese Aid: An Analysis of the Published Information on Chinese External Financial Flows*. Centre for Chinese Studies, University of Stellenbosch, Stellenbosch.
Grover, I. 2011. India a non-DAC partner in capacity building and training of human resources, in: Rethinking Development in an Age of Scarcity and Uncertainty. In: EADI/DSA Conference 19–22 September 2011, University of York.
Gu, J. 2009. China's private enterprises in Africa and the implications for African development. *European Journal of Development Research*, 21, 570–587. doi:10.1057/ejdr.2009.21
Gu. J. 2012. New developments in the internationalization of higher education in China and implications for China-Africa cooperation in higher education, International Forum on Higher Education Exchange and Cooperation, 10–11 September 2012, Zhejiang Normal University, Jinhua.
Guerrero, D. and Manji, F. (Eds), 2008. *China's New Role in Africa and the South: A Search for a New Perspective*. Fahamu, Oxford.
Guliwe, T. 2009. An introduction to Chinese-African relations. In: Baah, A. Y. and Jauch, H. (Eds), *Chinese Investments in Africa. A Labour Perspective*. African Labour Research Network, Accra and Windhoek.
Haglund, D. 2009. In it for the long term? Governance and learning among Chinese investors in Zambia's copper sector. *The China Quarterly* 199, 627–646.
Harneit-Sievers, A., Marks, S. and Naidu, S. (Eds), 2010. *Chinese and African Perspectives on China in Africa*. Pambazuka Press, Fahamu, Oxford.
Haugen, H. 2012. Nigerians in China: A second state of immobility. *International Migration*, 50 (2), 65–80.
Haugen, H. [2013]. China's recruitment of African university students: policy efficacy and unintended outcomes. *Globalisation, Societies and Education* (in press).

He, W. 2005. 'All weather friend': The evolution of China's African policy. In: Conference on Afro-Chinese Relations: Past, Present and Future, 23–25 November 2005, Johannesburg.

He, W. 2006. Educational exchange and cooperation between China and Africa. In: 3rd Roundtable Discussion on African Studies, organised by African Studies Group, University of Hong Kong, 25 May 2006, Hong Kong.

He, W. 2009. China's African Policy: driving forces, features and global impact. In: Liu, H. and Yang, J. (Eds), *Fifty years of Sino-African Cooperation: Background, Progress and Significance. Chinese Perspectives on Sino-African Relations.* Yunnan University Press, Yunnan. (An earlier version of this paper appeared as 'The balancing act of China's Africa policy' in *China Security*, 3: 3 Summer 2007, 23–40).

He, W. 2010. Overturning the wall: Building China's soft power in Africa, *China Security*, 6, no. 1. 63–69. Accessed at: www.chinasecurity.us/index.php?option=com_csissues&view=section&layout=blog&id=20&Itemid=8&lang=en

He, W. 2011. 'From "aid effectiveness" to "development effectiveness"? What China's experiences can contribute to the discourse evolution', Workshop on China-Africa Relations, University of Hong Kong, 6–7 May 2011.

He, W. 2012a. More soft power needed in Africa. 27 February 2012, *China Daily*.

He, W. 2012b Morsi visit opens a new chapter, *China Daily*, 31 August 2012. Accessed at http://www.chinadaily.com.cn/opinion/2012–08/31/content_15722766.htm

Henock, K., Olukoshi, A.O. and Wohlgemuth, L. (Eds), 1997. *A New Partnership for African Development. Issues and Parameters.* Nordic Africa Institute, Uppsala.

Hevi, E. J. 1963. *An African Student in China.* Praeger, London.

Holm, J. D. and Malete, D. 2010. Nine problems that hinder partnerships in Africa, *The Chronicle of Higher Education*, 13 June 2010. Accessed at http://chronicle.com/article/Nine-Problems-That-Hinder-P/65892/

Hu, J. 2006, Full Text: address by Hu Jintao at the opening ceremony of the Beijing Summit of the Forum on China-Africa Cooperation, 4 November 2006, downloaded from http://english.focacsummit.org/2006–11/04/content_4978.htm

Hu. J. 2007. Hu Jintao calls for enhancing 'soft power' of Chinese culture. Special report, CPC 17th National Congress, 15 October 2007. Accessed at http://news.xinhuanet.com/english/2007–10/15/content_6883748.htm

Human Rights Watch (HRW), 2011. *"You'll Be Fired If You Refuse": Labour Abuses in Zambia's Chinese State-Owned Copper Mines.* Human Rights Watch, New York.

Iarossi, G. 2009. *An Assessment of the Investment Climate in Kenya.* World Bank, Washington.

ITEC (Indian Technical and Economic Cooperation), 2011. *Civilian Training Programme, Indian Technical & Economic Cooperation (ITEC) and Special Commonwealth Assistance for Africa Programme (SCAAP),* Ministry of External Affairs, New Delhi. Accessed at:t http://itec.mea.gov.in/

Institute of African Studies (IAS), 2010. *African Museum.* Zhejiang Normal University, Jinhua.

Jacques, M. 2009. *When China Rules the World: The Rise of the Middle Kingdom and the End of the Western World*, Allen Lane, London.

Jacques, M. 2012a. Why do we continue to ignore China's rise? Arrogance. *The Observer*, 25 March 2012, 28–29.

Jacques, M. 2012b. *When China Rules the World: The Rise of the Middle Kingdom and the End of the Western World.* 2nd edition, Penguin, London.

Jansen, J. 2005. Targeting education: the politics of performance and the prospects of Education for All. *International Journal of Educational Development*, 25, 368–380.

Japan Bank for International Cooperation (JBIC). 2005. *Basic Strategy of Japan's ODA Loan: Medium Term Strategy for Overseas Economic Cooperation Operations.* 1 April 2005 – 31 March 2008, JBIC, Tokyo.

Japan, Ministry of Foreign Affairs. 2003. *Japan's Official Development Assistance Charter.* Ministry of Foreign Affairs, Tokyo.
Japan, Ministry of Foreign Affairs, 2010a. *Enhancing Enlightened National Interest: Living in Harmony with the World, and Promoting Peace and Prosperity.* Final Report, Ministry of Foreign Affairs, Tokyo.
Japan, Ministry of Foreign Affairs. 2010b. *Japan's Official Development Assistance White Paper 2010. Japan's International Cooperation.* Ministry of Foreign Affairs. Tokyo.
Japan, Ministry of Foreign Affairs (MOFA), 2012. *Evaluation of Training and Dialogue Programmes.* Global Link Management, for MOFA, Tokyo.
Jian, J. 2009. Confucianism is a vital string in China's bow. 9 October 2009, *Asia Times* on line.
Japan International Cooperation Agency (JICA), 2004. *The History of Japan's Educational Development: What Implications Can Be drawn for Developing Countries Today?* Institute for International Cooperation, JICA, Tokyo.
Japan International Cooperation Agency (JICA), 2010. *JICA's Operation In Education Sector: Present and Future.* JICA, Tokyo.
Japan International Cooperation Agency (JICA), 2011. Sino-Japan's Aid to Africa Experience-Exchanging Meeting Held in Department of International Cooperation Chinese Academy of Agricultural Sciences (DICCAAS) [translated from Japanese].
Jin, L. 2010. Aid to Africa: What Can the EU and China Learn from Each Other? South African Institute of International Affairs (SAIIA), Occasional Paper No 56, University of Witwatersrand, Johannesburg.
Johanson, R. and Adams, A.V. 2004. *Skills Development in Sub-Saharan Africa.* World Bank, Washington.
Jones, T. J. 1922. *Education in Africa.* Phelps-Stokes Fund, New York.
Jones, T. J. 1924. *Education in East Africa.* Phelps-Stokes Fund, New York.
Jung, I. 2011. Human capacity building: professionals learning for a sustainable future. *NORRAG News 45,* 41–43. Special Issue on the Geopolitics of Overseas Scholarships and Awards. Old and New Providers, East & West, North & South. Accessed at www.norrag.org
Keita M. 2012. Africa's free press problem. 15 April 2012. *New York Times.* Accessed at www.nytimes.com/2012/04/16/opinion/africas-free-press-problem. html?_r=2
Kim, S. 2011. Bridging troubled worlds? An analysis of the ethical case for South Korean aid. *Journal of International Development,* 23, 802–822.
King, K. 1971. *Pan-Africanism and Education. A Study of Race, Philanthropy and Education in the Southern States of America and East Africa.* Clarendon Press, Oxford.
King, K. 1977. *The African Artisan.* Heinemann Educational Books, London.
King, K. 1985. North-South Academic Collaboration in Higher Education: Academic links between Britain and the Developing World. Occasional Paper No. 8, Centre of African Studies, University of Edinburgh, Edinburgh.
King, K. 1991. *Aid and Education in the Developing World. The Role of the Donor Agencies in Educational Analysis.* Longman, Harlow.
King, K. 1995. *Jua Kali Kenya. Change and Development in an Informal Economy 1970–1995.* James Currey, London.
King, K. 2006a. China and Africa: new approaches to aid, trade and international cooperation. In: Annual General Meeting of the Comparative Education Research Centre (CERC), 26 March 2006, University of Hong Kong. Accessed at http://www.hku.hk/cerc/KK-Article.htm
King, K. 2006b. Aid within the wider China-Africa partnership: a view from the Beijing Summit. In: China-Africa Links Workshop, 11–12 November 2006, Hong Kong University of Science and Technology, Hong Kong. Accessed at http://www.hku.hk/cerc/KK-Article.htm

King, K. 2006c. The Beijing China-Africa Summit of 2006: the new implementation implications of aid to education. In: Symposium of China-Africa Shared Development, 18–19 December 2006, sponsored by the Institute of West Asian and African Studies and the Department for International Development, Beijing. Downloadable at http://www.hku.hk/cerc/KK-Article.htm

King, K. 2007a. China's ambitious training aid for Africa: implications for the Mainland and for Hong Kong, In: Keynote presentation at Comparative Education Research Centre, April 2007, University of Hong Kong. Accessed at http://www.hku.hk/cerc/KK-Article.htm

King, K. 2007b. African Studies in the UK and Europe: Lessons for China and the UK? In: Presentation at the Foundation of the Institute of African Studies, Zhejiang Normal University, 1 September 2007. Accessed at http://www.hku.hk/cerc/KK-Article.htm

King. K. 2007c. Commitment to learning: China's treasure within. In: Living Knowledge Seminar, March 2007, Jinguan Community Learning Centre, Gansu Province.

King, K. 2007d. China's aid to Africa: A view from China and Japan. In: Lead paper to the JICA Seminar on China's Aid to Africa – the Beijing Summit and its Follow-up, 29 January 2007, Japan International Cooperation Agency (JICA), Tokyo. Accessed at http://www.hku.hk/cerc/KK-Article.htm

King, K. 2009a. China's education cooperation with Africa. Meeting the FOCAC targets? In: Africa Day Workshop African Studies Programme, HKU, 25 May 2009, University of Hong Kong, Hong Kong.

King, K. 2009b. Higher education and international cooperation: the role of international collaboration in the developing world. In: Stephens, D. (Ed.), *Higher Education and International Capacity Building: Twenty-five years of Higher Education Links*, Symposium Books, Bristol.

King, K. 2010a. New donors, new paradigms, *NORRAG News 44*, 8–12. Accessed at www.norrag.org

King, K. 2010b. China's cooperation with Africa, and especially South Africa, in education and training. A special relationship and a different approach to aid? *Journal of International Cooperation in Education*, 13 (2), 73–88.

King, K. 2010c. China–Africa human resource development: Partnership or one-way? *Pambazuka News,* 23rd September 2010, Issue 497. http://pambazuka.org/en/category/comment/67178.

King, K. 2010d. China's cooperation with education and training in Kenya: A different model? *International Journal of Educational Development*, 30, 488–496.

King, K. 2010e. Representing Africa to China and the world: The African Pavilion at the Shanghai Expo 2010, *Pambazuka News* 9 September 2010, Issue 495. *2010–09–09*, Issue 495 http://pambazuka.org/en/category/comment/66795

King, K. 2010f. Trends in the Internationalisation of China's Mainland Universities – What Implications for Hong Kong? In: 8th Salon of Continuing Education & Lifelong Learning, 25 November 2010, HKU Space, Hong Kong.

King, K. 2011a. China's cooperation with Ethiopia. With a focus on human resources, *OSSREA Bulletin,* VIII, 1, 88–113. Accessed at: http://www.ossrea.net/images/stories/ossrea/bulletin-feb-2011.pdf

King, K. 2011b. Skills development and lifelong learning. Challenges for poverty reduction, sustainable growth and employability. In: International Symposium on Lifelong Learning 12–13 January 2011, Hong Kong Institute for Education, Hong Kong. Accessed at www.ied.edu.hk/isll/Keynote_present.html

King, K. 2011c. Eight proposals for a strengthened focus on technical and vocational education and training (TVET) in the Education for All (EFA) agenda. Background paper for EFA GMR 2012; 2012/ED/EFA/MRT/PI/06, UNESCO, Paris. Accessed at www.unesco.org/new/fileadmin/MULTIMEDIA/HQ/ED/pdf/gmr2012–ED-EFA-MRT-PI-06.pdf

King, K. 2011d. The new aid architecture in Ghana: influencing policy and practice? *European Journal of Development Research*, 23. 648–667.

King, K. 2012a. The geopolitics and meanings of India's massive skills ambitions. *International Journal of Educational Development*, 32 (5), 665–673. http://dt. doi.org/10.1016/j.ijedudev.2012.02.001.

King, K. 2012b. Sino-African relations and the internationalization of China's universities. In: Adamson, B, Nixon, J. and Su. F. (Eds), 2012. *The Reorientation of Higher Education: Challenging the East-West Dichotomy*. Comparative Education Research Centre, University of Hong Kong/Springer, Hong Kong, 134–147.

King, K. 2012c. South-South Cooperation in the internationalisation of African higher education. Keynote at 6th Annual UKZN Teaching and Learning Conference, 25–27 September 2012, Howard Campus, Durban.

King, K. and McGrath, S. 2004. *Knowledge for Development? Comparing British, Japanese, Swedish and World Bank Aid*. Zed Books, London.

King. K. and Palmer, R. 2008. *Skills for Work, Growth and Poverty Reduction: Challenges and Opportunities in the Global Analysis and Monitoring of Skills*. British Council, and UK National Commission for UNESCO, London.

King, K. and Palmer, R. 2011. *New Trends in International Cooperation: Background Paper for the World Report on Technical and Vocational Education Training (TVET)*, UNESCO, Paris.

King, K. and Palmer, R, 2012. Education and skills in the post-2015 global landscape: History, context lobbies and visions. Background paper for NORRAG workshop on Education and Skills in Post-2015 MDGs and EFA: Actors, Agenda and Architecture, 12 September 2012, IHEID, Geneva.

King, K. and Rose, P. (Eds), 2005. Special Issue – International and National Targets for Education: Help or Hindrance in *International Journal of Educational Development*, 25, 4.

Kitano, N. 2004. Japanese contribution in supporting China's reforms: a study based on ODA loans, in *China Report* (New Delhi) 40: 4, 461–488.

Kitano, N. 2011. Korea and China: Enhancing Development Aid. Memorandum, JICA, Tokyo.

Knorringa, P. 2009. Responsible production in Africa: The rise of China as a threat or an opportunity. In: Van Dijk, M.P. (Ed.), *The New Presence of China in Africa*. Amsterdam University Press, Amsterdam.

Kotze, R. 2010. Notes from the recent Confucius Institutes Africa Regional Conference. Special Issue of *China Monitor*, No 47. 'Let a Thousand Flowers Blossom': Confucius Institutes in Africa. Centre for Chinese Studies, University of Stellenbosch, Stellenbosch.

Kotze, R. 2012. Promoting the integration of Confucius Institutes into local university and community. Presentation at Africa Regional Conference of CIs, 11–13 September 2012, University of Stellenbosch.

Kragelund, P. 2011. Back to BASICs? The rejuvenation of non-traditional donors' cooperation with Africa. *Development and Change*, 42, 2, 585–607.

Kurlantzick, J. 2007. *Charm Offensive: How China's Soft Power Is Transforming the World*. Yale University Press, New Haven.

Kurlantzick, J. 2009. China's soft power in Africa. In: Li, M. (Ed.), 2009. *Soft Power: China's Emerging Strategy in International Politics*. Lexington Books, Plymouth.

Langendorf, J. and Muller, U. 2011. Triangular cooperation: a promising new mode of development cooperation in DAC- and non-DAC donors. In: Rethinking Development in an Age of Scarcity and Uncertainty. EADI/DSA Conference, 19–22 September 2011, University of York.

Large, D. 2006. The 'new' politics of development in Africa: A warning example in China. In: Seminar on 'A Chinese Scramble?' The Politics of Contemporary China-Africa Relations, 12–13 July 2006, Sidney Sussex College, University of Cambridge.

Large, D. 2008. Beyond 'Dragon in the bush': the study of China-Africa relations. *African Affairs*, 107/426. 45–61.

Leong, W. K. 2010. Confucius Institutes: Cultural centres 'not about power', *Straits Times,* 12 July 2010, A21.

Leroy, M. 2012. The aid industry is threatening partner countries with its ROD – Results Obsession Disorder. *NORRAG News* 47, 55–56. Accessed at www.norrag.org

Li, A. 2007. China and Africa. Policy and challenges. *China Security,* 3, 3, 69–93.

Li, A. 2011. Chinese medical cooperation with Africa: With special emphasis on medical teams and anti-malaria campaign. Discussion Paper No. 52, Nordic Africa Institute, Uppsala.

Li, A. 2012. Letter to readers, *Peking African Tele-Info,* No 86. 10 April 2012 (in Chinese).

Li, A. and Liu, H. 2012. The evolution of the Chinese policy of funding African students and an evaluation of its effectiveness. Research proposal, UNDP, Beijing.

Li, A. and Liu, H. 2013. The evolution of the Chinese policy of funding African students and an evaluation of its effectiveness. Draft report. Centre for African Studies, Peking University, Beijing.

Li, J. 2012. World-class higher education and the emerging Chinese model of the university. *Prospects.* 42, 319–339.

Li, M. 2008. China debates soft power. *Chinese Journal of International Politics.* 2, 287–308.

Li, M. (Ed.), 2009. *Soft Power: China's Emerging Strategy in International politics.* Lexington Books, Plymouth.

Li, W., Huang J., Wang, K., Mao, X., and Chen, F. 2010. Education assistance to Africa: We can do more and better, *Transition Studies Review*, vol. 17. No. 2. 280–296.

Livingstone, D. 1858. *Missionary Travels and Researches in South Africa Including a Sketch of Sixteen Years' Residence in the Interior of Africa.* Harper & Brothers, New York.

Liu, H. 2008. China-Africa relations through the prism of culture: The dynamics of China's cultural diplomacy with Africa. *China Aktuell, The Journal of Current Chinese Affairs*, 2008/3, 9–43.

Liu, H. 2009. The status and trend of Chinese companies in Africa. In: Liu, H. and Yang, J. (Eds), *Fifty years of Sino-African Cooperation: Background, Progress and Significance. Chinese Perspectives on Sino-African Relations.* Yunnan University Press, Yunnan.

Liu, H. 2011. From equal exchange to learning from each other: Whither the China-Africa cultural and intellectual cooperation? In: de Sousa, I.C., Diakite, A. D., and Iwaloye, O.O. (Eds), *Africa: New Types of Exchange, Cultural Identity and Emerging Relations in a Globalised World.* St. Joseph Academic Press, Macao.

Liu, H. and Yang, J. (Eds), *Fifty Years of Sino-African Cooperation: Background, Progress and Significance. Chinese Perspectives on Sino-African Relations.* Yunnan University Press, Yunnan.

Liu, Y. 2010. Working together towards the sustainable development of Confucius Institutes. Keynote speech at the 5th Confucius Conference, 10 December 2010, Beijing.

McGrath, S. 2012. The unbearable lightness of evidence-based VET practice. *NORRAG News* 47, 16–18. Accessed at www.norrag.org

McNamee, T. 2012. Africa in their words: A study of Chinese traders in South Africa, Lesotho, Botswana, Zambia and Angola. Discussion Paper 2012/03, Brenthurst Foundation, Johannesburg.

Mahmoud, R. 2010. How to promote Chinese language teaching through cultural activities? *Confucius Institute*, No 6, November 2010.

Manji, F. and Marks, S. (Eds), 1997. *African Perspectives on China in Africa.*

Fahamu, Oxford.

Marris, P. and Somerset, H.C.A. 1971. *African Businessmen: A Study of Entrepreneurship and Development in Kenya.* Routledge and Kegan Paul, London.

Mawdsley, E. 2008. Fu Manchu versus Dr. Livingstone in the dark continent? Representing China, Africa and the West in British broadsheet newspapers. *Political Geography* 27, 509–529.

Mawdsley, E. 2011. The changing geographies of foreign aid and development cooperation: contributions from gift theory. *Transactions of the Institute of British Geographers,* NS 2011, The Royal Geographical Society, London.

Mawdsley, E. 2012. *From Recipients to Donors: Emerging Powers and the Changing Development Landscape.* Zed Books, London.

Melber, H. 2013. Europe and China in Africa: Common Interests and/or Different Approaches. Asia Paper. Institute for Security and Development Policy. Stockholm.

Michel, S. and Beuret, M. 2010. *China Safari: On the Trail of Beijing's Expansion in Africa.* Nation Books, New York.

Monson, J. 2008. Liberating labour. In: Alden, C., Large, D. and Soares de Oliviera, R. (Eds), *China Returns to Africa: A Rising Power and a Continent Embrace.* Hurst and Company, London.

Monson, J. 2009. *Africa's Freedom Railway: How a Chinese Development Project Changed Lives and Livelihoods in Tanzania,* Indiana University Press, Bloomington.

Mosher, S. 2012. Confucius Institutes: Trojan horses with Chinese characteristics. Testimony presented to the Subcommittee on Oversight and Investigations, House Committee on Foreign Affairs, 28 March 2012, Washington.

Moyo, D. 2012.*Winner Takes All. China's Race for Resources and What It Means for Us.* Allen Lane, London.

Muhumuza, R. 2012. China Skirting Corruption in Direct Aid. Associated Press, 9 February 2012.

Mwanawina, I. 2008. China-Africa economic relations: The case of Zambia. AERC Scoping Study, AERC, Nairobi.

Niu, C. 2009. China and Africa: a new paradigm in educational cooperation. In: Liu, H. and Yang, J. (Eds), *Fifty Years of Sino-African Cooperation: Background, Progress and Significance. Chinese Perspectives on Sino-African Relations,* Yunnan University Press. Kunming.

Nordtveit, B. 2010. China and Egypt: The continuation of a long friendship. *NORRAG News,* 44, 60–63. Accessed at www.norrag.org

Nordtveit, B. 2011a. An emerging donor in education and development: a case study of China in Cameroon. *International Journal of Educational Development,* 31, 2, 99–108.

Nordtveit, B. 2011b. Politics, *guanxi,* and the search for objectivity: the intricacies of conducting research in Chinese contexts. *Comparative Education,* 47, 3, 367–380.

*NORRAG News 41, 2008.* Special issue on the Politics of Partnership: Peril or Promise? Accessed at www.norrag.org

*NORRAG News 44, 2010.* A Brave New World of 'Emerging', 'Non-DAC' Donors and Their Differences from Traditional Donors. Accessed at www.norrag.org

*NORRAG News 45, 2011.* Special Issue on the Geopolitics of Overseas Scholarships and Awards. Old and New Providers, East & West, North & South. Accessed at www.norrag.org

*NORRAG News. 47.* Special Issue on Value for Money in International Education and Training: A New World of Results, Impacts and Outcomes? Accessed at www.norrag.org

Nye, J. 1990. *Bound to Lead: The Changing Nature of American Power,* Basic Books, New York.

Nye, J. 2012. Why China is weak in soft power. 12 January 2012, *New York Times,*

New York. Accessed at www.nytimes.com/2012/01/18/opinion/why-china-is-weak-on-soft-power.html

OECD/DAC, 2005. *The Paris Declaration on Aid Effectiveness*, OECD/DAC, Paris.

OECD/DAC. 2011. *Busan Partnership for Effective Development Cooperation*, Fourth High Level Forum on Aid Effectiveness, 29 November -1 December 2011, Busan, South Korea.

OECD DAC. China-DAC Study Group. 2011. *Economic Transformation and Poverty Reduction: How It Happened in China, Helping It Happen in Africa*. China-DAC Study Group, OECD, Paris and IPRCC, Beijing.

ODA (Overseas Development Administration). 1990. I*nto the Nineties: An Education Policy for British Aid*. ODA, London.

Ogunkola, E. O., Bankole, A. S., and Adewuyi, A. 2008. China-Nigeria economic relations. AERC Scoping Study, AERC, Nairobi.

Park, Y. J. 2008. *A Matter of Honour: Being Chinese in South Africa*. Jacana Media, Auckland Park. S. Africa.

Park, Y. J. 2009. Chinese migration to Africa. SAIIA Occasional Paper, No. 24, Johannesburg.

*People's Daily* Online, 2011. How to improve China's soft power. 11 March 2010. Accessed at http://english.peopledaily.com.cn/90001/90776/90785/6916487.html

Pollet, I., Huyse, H., Li, P., Shomba, S. and Zhang, X. 2011. *Neither Comfort, Nor Conflict: The Co-Habitation of Chinese and Belgian Aid in the D.R.Congo*. HIVA, Catholic University of Leuven.

Pong, T. 2011. Hong Kong aspires to attract the 'best and the brightest' PhDs. In *NORRAG News* 45, 93–4. Accessed at www.norrag.org

Ramo, J. 2004. *The Beijing Consensus*. The Foreign Policy Centre, London.

Rebol, M. 2011. Pragmatism and non-interference: Explaining China's soft power in Africa. Doctoral dissertation, Department of International Relations and Public Affairs, Fudan University, Shanghai.

Rist, G. 1997. *The History of Development*. Zed Books, London.

Rotberg, R. (Ed.) 2008. *China into Africa: Trade, Aid and Influence*. Brookings/World Peace Foundation, Cambridge, MA.

Sautman, B. 1994. Anti-Black racism in post-Mao China. *The China Quarterly*, 138, 413–437.

Sautman, B. and Yan, H. 2006. East Mountain tiger, West Mountain tiger: China, the West and 'colonialism' in Africa. University of Maryland Series on Contemporary Asian Studies, Baltimore.

Sautman, B. and Yan. Y. 2008. Friends and interests: China's distinctive links with Africa. In: Guerrero, D. and Manji, F. (Eds), *China's New Role in Africa and the South: A Search for a New Perspective*. Fahamu, Oxford.

Sautman, B. and Yan, H. 2009. African perspectives on China-Africa links, *The China Quarterly*, 199, 749–51.

Sautman, B. and Yan, H. 2011. Barking up the wrong tree: Human Rights Watch and copper mining in Zambia. *Pambazuka News* No. 563, 14 December 2011. http://pambazuka.org/en/category/features/78660

Sautman, B. and Yan, H. (forthcoming). African students in Tianjin universities: a comparative study of attitudes to China, work in progress, HKUST, Hong Kong.

Sawamura, N. 2002. Local spirit, global knowledge: a Japanese approach to knowledge development in international cooperation. *Compare*, 32, 3, 339–348.

Sheng, D. 2010. Analysing rising power from the perspective of soft power: A new look at China's rise to the status quo power. *Journal of Contemporary China*, 19 (64), 255–272.

Shinn, D. and Eisenman, J. 2012. *China and Africa: A Century of Engagement*. University of Pennsylvania Press, Philadelphia.

Snow, P. 1988. *The Star Raft. China's Encounter with Africa*. Weidenfeld and Nicolson, London.

Snow, P. 2008. Foreword, in Alden, C., Large, D. and Soares de Oliviera, R. (Eds), 2008. *China Returns to Africa: A Rising Power and a Continent Embrace.* Hurst and Company, London.
Sweden, Ministry for Foreign Affairs, 1998. *Africa on the Move. Revitalising Swedish Policy Towards Africa for the 21st Century.* Ministry for Foreign Affairs, Stockholm.
Tan, S. 1989. *Best Chinese Idioms.* Hai Feng Publishing Co., Hong Kong.
Tang, X. 2010. Bulldozer or locomotive? The impact of Chinese enterprises on local employment in Angola and DRC. *Journal of Asian and African Studies,* 45 (3) 350–368, DOI: 10.1177/0021909610364777
Taylor, I. 2009. *China's New Role in Africa.* Lynne Rienner, London.
Taylor, I. 2011. *The Forum on China-Africa Cooperation (FOCAC).* Routledge, Abingdon.
Taylor, I. 2012. From Santa Claus to serious business: Where should FOCAC go next? In: Special Edition: Quo Vadis FOCAC? *The China Monitor.* Centre for Chinese Studies, University of Stellenbosch, Stellenbosch.
Taylor, L. 2007. 'Give a man a fish' ... and foreign aid. Policy Note, Schwarz Centre for Economic Policy Analysis, New School, New York.
Tumushabe, A. 2012. Chinese company arms teachers with phones in bid to improve teaching. *Daily Monitor,* March 12, 2012, 30.
UNESCO, 2010. *Education for All Global Monitoring Report 2010. Reaching the Marginalized.* EFA GMR, at UNESCO, Paris.
UNESCO. 2011a. UNESCO-China-Africa University Leaders Meeting: Prospects for future collaboration. Concept Note, UNESCO, Paris.
UNESCO. 2011b. UNESCO-China-Africa University Leaders Meeting: Prospects for future collaboration. Programme, 24–25 October 2011, UNESCO, Paris.
UNESCO, 2012a. *Transforming Technical and Vocational Education and Training: Building skills for work and life. Main Working Document,* Third International Congress on Technical and Vocational Training, 14–16 May 2012, Shanghai.
UNESCO. 2012b. *Youth and Skills: Putting Education to Work. EFA Global Monitoring Report 2012.* UNESCO, Paris.
Van Dijk, M.P. (Ed) 2009. *The New Presence of China in Africa.* Amsterdam University Press, Amsterdam.
Varrall, M. 2012. Debunking the myth of China's soft power: Changes in China's use of foreign assistance from 1949 till the present. In: Lai, H. and Lu, Y. (Eds), *China's Soft Power and International Relations.* Routledge, London.
Varrall, M. 2012 (forthcoming). We Chinese: Understanding Chinese foreign policy through the making of diplomats. Unpublished doctoral dissertation, Macquarie University and Free University of Amsterdam.
Verhoeven, H. and Urbina-Ferretjans, M. 2012. China as a Development Aid Actor: Rethinking Development Assistance and its Implications for Africa and the West. OUCAN Aid Symposium Report, 14 March, 2012, St. Antony's College, University of Oxford.
Vermaak, M. 2010. What should Confucius Institutes do? Special Issue of *China Monitor,* No 47. 'Let a Thousand Flowers Blossom': Confucius Institutes in Africa. Centre for Chinese Studies, University of Stellenbosch, Stellenbosch.
Wagenfeld, F. 2011. The German Academic Exchange Service (DAAD) at a glance. In *NORRAG News* 45, Special Issue on the Geopolitics of Overseas Scholarships and Awards. Accessed at: www.norrag.org
Wen, J. 2009 'Building the new type of China-Africa strategic partnership', 4th Ministerial (FOCAC) Conference, 8 November, Sharm el Sheikh. See also: http://www.focac.org/eng/dsjbzjhy/hywj/t626387.htm
Wen, J. 2010. Towards the attainment of the Millennium Development Goals. Address to the UN High-level Meeting on the Millennium Development Goals, 22 September 2010. Accessed at http://www.un.org/en/mdg/summit2010/debate/CN_en.pdf

Wong, E. 2012. China's president lashes out at Western culture. *New York Times* (Asia Pacific), 3 January 2012; accessed at http://www.nytimes.com/2012/01/04/world/asia/chinas-president-pushes-back-against-western-culture.html

World Bank, 1998. *World Development Report 1998/9: Knowledge for Development.* World Bank, Washington.

World Bank, 2004. *Investment Climate Survey. Kenya: Enhancing the Competitiveness of Kenya's Manufacturing: The Role of Investment Climate.* World Bank, Washington.

World Bank and China, the People's Republic, Development Research Centre (DRC) of the State Council. 2012. *China 2030: Building a Modern, Harmonious and Creative High-Income Society.* World Bank, Washington.

Wu, Y. 2012. The rise of China's state-led media dynasty in Africa. Occasional Paper no 117, South African Institute of International Affairs, University of the Witwatersrand, Johannesburg.

Wyatt, D. J. 2010. *The Blacks of Premodern China: Encounters with Asia.* University of Pennsylvania Press, Philadelphia.

Xu, L. 2010. Plenary address to 5th Convention of Confucius Institutes, 11–12 December 2010, China National Convention Centre, Beijing.

Xu, L. 2010b. Annual Report on the 2010 Work and 2011 Plan. The Confucius Institute headquarters, presented at 4th Assembly of the CI Council, 9 December 2010.

Yan, H. and Sautman. B. 2012. Chasing ghosts: Rumours and representations of the export of Chinese convict labour to developing countries. *The China Quarterly*, 210, 398–418.

Yang, R. 2007. China's soft power project in higher education. *International Higher Education.* No. 46, winter 2007, 24–25.

Yang, R. 2010. Soft power and higher education: an examination of China's Confucius Institutes, *Globalisation, Societies and Education*, 8: 2, 235–245.

Yin, B. 2012. Chinese donations: Tale of frustration that lies behind health aid to Africa. Accessed at http://www.ft.com/cms/s/0/67e9f95a-87a9–11e1–ade2–00144feab49a.html#axzz1uB86fBRC

Yuan, T. 2011a. China's educational 'aid' to Africa: A different donor logic? Unpublished doctoral dissertation, Graduate school of Education, University of Bristol.

Yuan, T. 2011b. China's aid modalities of human resource development in Africa and an exploration in Tanzania: differences and recognitions. In: Rethinking Development in an Age of Scarcity and Uncertainty, EADI/DSA Conference, 19–22 September 2011, University of York.

Zhe, R. 2010. Confucius Institute: China's soft power? In: Policy Commentary, June 2010, Sigur Centre for Asian Studies, George Washington University, Washington DC.

Zimmermann, F. and Smith, K. 2011. More actors, more money, more ideas for international development cooperation. *Journal of International Development*, 23, 722–738.

# INDEX